THE
ETHICUREAN
COOKBOOK

1 3 5 7 9 10 8 6 4 2

Published in 2013 by Ebury Press, an imprint of Ebury Publishing

A Random House Group Company

The Random House Group Limited Reg. No. 954009

Addresses for companies within the Random House Group can be found at www.randomhouse.co.uk

A CIP catalogue record for this book is available from the British Library

The Random House Group Limited supports the Forest Stewardship Council® (FSC®), the leading international forest-certification organisation. Our books carrying the FSC label are printed on FSC®-certified paper. FSC is the only forest-certification scheme supported by the leading environmental organisations, including Greenpeace. Our paper procurement policy can be found at www.randomhouse.co.uk/environment

To buy books by your favourite authors and register for offers visit www.randomhouse.co.uk

Photography by Jason Ingram

Design by Two Associates
Front cover engraving by Andrew Davidson

Copy editor: Jane Middleton

Props styling by Jaine Bevan

The authors and publishers would like to thank Le Creuset and Goodfellow & Goodfellow Ltd for supplying equipment used for the photography.

Printed and bound in Italy by Graphicom S.r.l.

ISBN 9780091949921

THE
ETHICUREAN
COOKBOOK

RECIPES, FOODS AND SPIRITUOUS
LIQUORS, FROM OUR BOUNTEOUS
WALLED GARDEN
IN THE SEVERAL SEASONS
OF THE YEAR

EBURY
PRESS

Cook's Notes

All vegetables are peeled unless otherwise specified.

All eggs are medium, free-range.

Butter is unsalted, unless otherwise specified.

Above, left to right: Jack, Matthew, Ocho, Paúla and Iain

CONTENTS

ethicurean *adj.* the pursuit of fine-tasting food while being mindful of the effect of one's food production and consumption on the environment

The Ethicurean sits below an overgrown Georgian estate, sometime haunt of Wordsworth and Coleridge. Its gardens are a labyrinth of roses, pergolas and chipped statues. The restaurant and kitchen are housed in two of the original glasshouses within Barley Wood Walled Garden, built for Henry Herbert Wills of the Imperial Tobacco Company in 1901. This was the year in which Queen Victoria took her final breath. Our Walled Garden is filled with neat rows of cabbages and espaliers of greengages and apricots. Hundred-year-old vines have bullied their way through a small brick hole in one of the glasshouses. Cambered red-brick paths frame a patchwork garden of cannellini beans, marching Tom Thumb and a quilted statis. The garden is cut in half by a yew-lined corridor; in spring lavender grows at just the right height to tear off small handfuls as we walk up from the lower orchard. In summer the purple mass gives way to campanula, day lilies and hundreds of aster. Mark, the gardener, brings us trugs of vegetables each morning and the starched white flash of a chef's tunic can be seen around the herb borders just before lunch.

British seasonality, ethical sourcing of ingredients and attention to the local environment are the foundations of our business. We are four friends: Jack Adair-Bevan, Paúla Zarate and Matthew and Iain Pennington. Between us we have overlapping areas of expertise that range from the practical and organisational knowledge needed to run a business, to the science of cooking and the wild food that grows outside the walls of our restaurant. We are self-taught and want to offer an approach to British food that is neither exclusive nor isolating; and one that is fundamentally about sharing knowledge and passion.

Sustainability has become a buzz word in recent years, and all anybody can ever do is work towards a more sustainable way of life – we Ethicureans are doing our best. We took over the restaurant in 2010: over five days we completed a refit with the help of our family and friends, knocking down walls, redecorating, and pausing only to take a decent lunch and supper on the long tables overlooking the Wrington Vale. On the sixth day we opened for business and began a full apple season, picking, pulping and juicing. We started researching the seventy varieties of apple that we now had to look after in our two orchards.

Food and the narrative surrounding it is in a constant state of evolution: it is political, artistic and completely delicious. The Mendips in Somerset, the home of The Ethicurean, is a place on the verge of something incredible. Artisans from across the country are moving their production here. Community farms, orchards and collaborations are popping up across the county. We are watching day by day as our friends, customers and suppliers are re-establishing and strengthening their rural communities and taking control of their food production. We are seeing and enjoying the rediscovery of old techniques and adaptations for the future.

From our opening day, we changed our menu on a daily basis according to what was available; we continue to celebrate every single day of the British season. In this book we have recorded not only recipes, but our relationships with our producers, our land, our lives and our history – all of which are intricately connected with the food we eat.

We rarely leave this beautiful walled garden; it is an absolute paradise.

WINTER

THERE are a couple of special requirements for the Walled Garden in winter – first, a lighter to defrost the padlocks and secondly a good torch for evening trips around the garden, unless there is a full moon. Frosts in the Wrington Vale are spectacular. The air hoar that decorates the trees creates a landscape that is more akin to Siberia than Somerset. In an early-morning drifting fog, the view from the glasshouse is divine. During our first year at Barley Wood, we had heavy snow and several hoar frosts, and the pathway through the centre of the garden lay under a good three inches of snow. Jack clipped on his skis and, armed with two bamboo canes pinched from Mark's beans, managed to ski right through it. Morning trips to the compost heap at the bottom orchard, the reserve of the luckiest in summer, become a task to be avoided by all of us.

By early December we try to finish pressing the last of the season's apples, as working in the icy cider barn is harsh. Elena, Paûla's mum, and Phil, Jack's dad, run the apple business. Both are used to warmer climates – Mexico and the Gulf respectively. You'll find them in the barn, clothed in multiple layers, debating which varieties of apples to blend. Their fridges at home are bursting with labelled specimens: Tydeman's Late Orange sits next to Reverend James. The season's last pressings require juggling the final few trugs of sweet varieties with the later cookers, such as the infamous Bramley and the cloud-textured Blenheim Orange.

The cold weather acts as a gentle prod towards more full-bodied, buttery food and drink. By December, calorific caution is thrown aside as we march towards the inevitable feast, and by Christmas we are trotting full-bellied towards absolute gluttony. Partridges are synonymous with this time of year: we all know the song. These plump birds virtually fly out of the kitchen, roasted and glazed with a coat of hawthorn jelly with its wild-fruit tartness.

Winter is a chance to deploy all of those chutneys, jams, pickles, jellies, liqueurs, infused gins, beers, ciders and wines that have been squirrelled away during seasonal gluts. It's a time for experiments, sweet concoctions such as membrillo-infused vodka and vanilla and espresso bean rum. Our Walled Garden apricot jam and black cardamom vodka, a triumph of a drink, was the sweet product of a bitter day in January.

From the New Year, while everyone else detoxes, exercises and diets in a cloud of resolve and perspiration, we are preparing the biggest event in our calendar, our annual Wassail. For us, the Wassail is a festival fix during the cruellest part of winter. We feel we have recaptured a lost part of our country's heritage and richly updated it. On this cold evening, we never fail to enjoy the magical rituals of eating, drinking and working together.

By the end of January, we are the ones paying penance for our alcohol consumption and excess. Work begins, or rather continues, after a little break. All the fruit trees are pruned, the dividing hedges that are mature and ready for laying are confronted with billhooks and axes, the formidable hedge outside our cider barn is due to be laid next year. We are lucky to have the oldest hedging society in the country, the Wrington and Burrington, which was formed after the Enclosures Act came into force in the early 1800s. It still meets regularly just down the road. There are distinctive styles of hedge-laying that vary from region to region. Each style is specific to the local climate and the types of trees and shrubs that will grow in local soil. The area around the Walled Garden is a hedge-laying stronghold, although we suspect few people will have heard of our local celebrity, Uncle Frank, a hedge-laying legend from Butcombe. All the maintenance has to take place before the birds establish their nests. A carefully selected mix of shrubs and trees, well planted, will yield enough fruit to feed plenty of hungry humans and birds. The hedge, framed in the giant doorway to our cider barn, reads like an inventory of our larder at The Ethicurean: hawthorn, sloes, wild damsons, rosehips, crab apples, hazel and cobnuts. Before our resident robin has time to sing for a mate and build a nest, the yew hedges are clipped, offering an early reminder of the garden's cyclical, ordered style and the imminent arrival of spring.

Beetroot Carpaccio with Honeyed Walnuts

Winter is a testing time for even the most hardened proponent of seasonality. An anonymous sigh can sometimes be heard in the kitchen when Mark, the gardener, comes in with yet another basket of beetroot. The audacious pink-and-white-striped Chioggia, the common red Detroit and the unimaginatively named golden beetroot are frequent visitors to The Ethicurean kitchen at this time of year.

However, the chefs relish the opportunity to create an original dish. This one is our play on the classic beef carpaccio. Reminiscent of a stained-glass window, it celebrates the distinctive taste of each of the beetroot varieties that grow on our doorstep. Flavour and spice intertwine with vibrant splashes of colour, brightening a monochromatic wintry day.

SERVES 4

3 beetroot, topped and tailed
300ml red wine vinegar
120g caster sugar
1 clove
3 star anise
12 black peppercorns
a small piece of cinnamon stick
a handful of winter salad leaves (we suggest a mixture of mizuna, winter purslane, land cress and rocket)
flaky sea salt and black pepper

FOR THE HONEYED WALNUTS:

½ tsp butter
25g walnuts
1 tsp runny honey

Put the beetroot in a pan with the vinegar and half the sugar. Pour over enough cold water to cover the beetroot completely, then add the spices and bring to the boil. Cover with a lid and cook gently for about 40 minutes or until there is only a slight resistance when you insert the tip of a knife in the beetroot. Meanwhile, prepare the walnuts. Melt the butter in a small pan, add the walnuts and fry over a medium-high heat until lightly coloured. Add the honey and toss until the walnuts are evenly coated. Decant from the pan into a cool dish.

Drain the cooked beetroot, keeping half of the cooking liquor, and cool them under cold running water. Pour the saved cooking liquor into a clean pan and add the remaining sugar and a pinch of salt. Boil over a high heat until it has reduced by three-quarters; it should have a thick, syrupy consistency. Remove from the heat and leave to cool.

Peel the beetroot and cut them into quarters. Using a mandoline, slice them wafer thin. If you do not have a mandoline, put the quartered beetroot flat-side down and slice lengthways as thinly as possible with a very sharp knife.

To serve the carpaccio, arrange the beetroot on 4 serving plates, then drizzle over the syrupy liquor. Add a sprinkling of sea salt and freshly cracked black pepper, then scatter the honeyed walnuts and the salad leaves on top.

Duck Terrine with Cranberries and Cobnuts

We use Aylesbury-cross ducks from Madgett's Farm to make this terrine. It was through farmers' markets that we became aware of the commendable work Madgett's has been doing for years. Situated near Chepstow, it was originally a dairy and beef cattle farm (and was even mentioned in the Domesday Book), but over the past decade the poultry business has taken off. Like other great family businesses, they care deeply about what they do which, of course, is reflected in the quality of their produce.

This is a very versatile recipe and you could easily substitute chicken or goose for the duck. Careful weighing of the ingredients is key, as you need to compress them evenly into the moulds.

The terrines need a night in the refrigerator before serving. They will keep well for several days because they are sealed by the goose fat. You probably won't need to butter your toast before liberally applying the terrine – although it is pretty tasty if you do.

MAKES 4 SMALL TERRINES

210g goose fat

1 tsp salt

1 tsp ground white pepper

½ tsp ground star anise

465g skinned duck breast, roughly diced

60g dried cobnuts (or hazelnuts), lightly crushed

60g dried cranberries, soaked in cider for 30 minutes, then drained

135g black cabbage (cavolo nero), coarsely chopped and then blanched in boiling salted water until just tender (optional)

sea salt and black pepper

Put the goose fat in a heavy-based pan over a low heat until melted, then add the salt, pepper and star anise. Place the diced duck breast in the fat and cover the mixture with a circle of baking parchment. Cook over a very low heat for 30–45 minutes, until the duck is cooked but still slightly pink inside (a meat thermometer should register 74°C, though we cook ours to 55–60°C). Remove from the heat and leave to cool at room temperature.

Take the breast meat out of the cooled goose fat and put it in a bowl. (You can pour the fat off the cooking liquor from the duck, strain the liquor and use it to add flavour to other dishes.) Add the nuts, drained cranberries and the cabbage, if using, and season well. Line four 150ml ramekins with cling film and put them in a dish to catch any spillages. Divide the duck mixture between them; it should come slightly above the rims. Pour over enough of the cooking fat to fill the gaps, allowing it to sink in before checking the level again. Cover each terrine with cling film and then spike it with a knife tip so the extra fat can run away as the terrines chill. Place a chopping board on top and weight down with 4 heavy tins. Leave in the fridge overnight.

Before serving, dip the ramekins in hot water for about 30 seconds to loosen the terrines and then turn them out on to a board. Leave to come to room temperature so a little of the fat melts away, then transfer them to serving plates. Serve with toasted sourdough and Rowan Jelly (see page 299), if liked.

† It is reassuring to know that the great Mrs Beeton would have approved of our choice of breed. In her *Book of Household Management*, she writes:

> 'The White Aylesbury duck is, and deservedly, a universal favourite. Its snowy plumage and comfortable comportment make it a credit to the poultry-yard, while its broad and deep breast, and its ample back, convey the assurance that your satisfaction will not cease at its death ... this member of the duck family is bred on an extensive scale...in the abodes of the cottagers. Round the walls of the living-rooms, and of the bedroom even, are fixed rows of wooden boxes, lined with hay; and it is the business of the wife and children to nurse and comfort the feathered lodgers, to feed the little ducklings and to take the old ones out for an airing.'

This inspiring extract serves as reminder of the importance of food provenance in Victorian times, when a meal was a family process that stretched beyond sitting around a table.

Tandoor Scallops, Celeriac Purée and Pickled Rock Samphire

Scallops are prized for their sweetness, which comes from the white meat, an abductor muscle that contains very high levels of mildly sweet amino acid. When eaten fresh, the taste is reminiscent of seaweed. You should be able to order hand-dived scallops from a good fishmonger. In this dish, their sweet nuttiness is complemented by the use of celeriac – a savoury, earthy element given more grandeur by being puréeed with a rich chicken stock. The flavour is heightened with tandoor spices and pungent Indonesian long pepper, which add the final elements to this fantastic and relatively simple starter. Samphire and the salad leaf, red frill, work well together on the plate, for reasons of both aesthetics and taste – the two ingredients almost mirror each other and conjure up an image of the marine bed. If you would like to serve the scallop roes, poach them for 2 minutes in a little vegetable stock prior to serving.

SERVES 4

16 diver-caught scallops, orange
    roes removed
1–2 tbsp rapeseed or vegetable oil
a handful of Pickled Rock Samphire
    (see page 190)
a handful of red frill (or other
    winter salad leaves)
a pinch of tandoori spice mix
a pinch of Indonesian long pepper
sea salt

FOR THE CELERIAC PURÉE:

350g celeriac, peeled and cut into
    1cm cubes
95ml brown chicken stock
    (see page 296)
80ml crème fraîche
¼ nutmeg

First prepare the celeriac. Choose a pan large enough to hold a steaming basket and half fill it with cold water. Grate the nutmeg into the water and bring to the boil. Put the celeriac in the steaming basket and set it over the pan. Cover and steam until the celeriac is very soft. Transfer to a blender or food processor, add the chicken stock and crème fraîche and blitz until smooth, scraping down the sides as needed. (For an extra-smooth consistency, strain the purée through a fine sieve after blending.) Season with salt to taste and reheat gently in a pan.

Season the scallops lightly with sea salt. Set a large, heavy-based frying pan over a high heat for a minute or two. Add a thin film of rapeseed or vegetable oil to the hot pan; it should begin to smoke very lightly. Add the scallops to the pan one at a time, starting from the outside and working in a clockwise direction, spiralling towards the centre. By the time you have put in your last scallop, it will most likely be time to turn the first. An inviting golden crust should have formed on the underside. If it is still a little pale, leave for a further 30 seconds. Turn over all the scallops in order, following the clockwise spiral you made. When you reach the centre, return to the beginning and take out the scallops in order, checking that the underside has coloured too. Set aside to rest on a warm plate.

Place a spoonful of celeriac purée on each serving plate. Place 4 scallops on top of the purée, then decorate with the pickled rock samphire, red frill, a light dusting of tandoori spice and a small pinch of long pepper.

SCALLOPS

As we write, the sustainable and environmentally benign practice of diving for scallops is under threat from European legislation. In an attempt to control the toxin levels of scallops, the EU has set these levels extremely low. This means that the test can only be passed if the scallop is shucked prior to sale and this is having a serious impact on the livelihood of divers, if not the entire dived scallop industry. Trawling for scallops, discarding the shells and the parts deemed unfit, then freezing the meat and roe is high-volume stuff. Scallop divers cannot keep up. It's a double whammy and the snapping and closing shell of a live scallop, once a hallmark of careful fishing, is fast disappearing.

The result is that scallops are now more likely to be fished by dredge trawling, which is the equivalent of ploughing a red tractor through a Japanese peace garden. Scallop divers witness the seabed at first hand. They proactively move scallops – most importantly the young specimens – from the paths of trawlers to 'chucky patches'. These are safe areas where the conditions are better for them to flourish, as they are allowed to spawn enough times before they are harvested. This method of fishing is fundamental in allowing stocks to be replenished for the future.

Guy Grieve and his family chose the tranquil and immaculately clean waters of the Isle of Mull to set up a sustainable shellfish company. It pledges to support fishermen who use sustainable methods in the hope that they can contribute towards the recovery of our seas. The awards roll in for this company and we are pleased to be in support.

MONKFISH

Monkfish are great masters of disguise. Their enormous slimy head and body serve as effective camouflage on the sea bed. Looking akin to a rock, they attract prey through the use of a dangling lure from the head. This ability to blend into their surroundings, coupled with their distinct lack of good looks, meant that they were not popular for eating, enabling them to thrive in British waters for many years. Eventually their superb-tasting meat was discovered by hungry humans, which sadly resulted in fisheries adopting beam-trawling methods to meet the high demand. Inevitably this led to a decline in numbers. The species is now recovering but we would still recommend that you source them from fishmongers supporting sustainable fishing methods.

Monkfish Cheeks with Saffron, Cauliflower and Aniseed

This magnificent dish contains some very fragrant spices that together create a symphony of flavours. We are fortunate to be able to buy monkfish cheeks direct from the fishermen via Kernowsashimi, a fishing company in Cornwall. This is the only way we can guarantee that our fish are either line-caught or from static nets. Kernowsashimi's fleet does not dredge-net any of its catch, a process that is harmful to the marine ecosystem.

Monkfish heads are often discarded at sea, as they are considered an ugly fish. This wastes a particularly tasty morsel in the form of the cheeks, but Kernowsashimi is happy to oblige and your local fishmonger should be able to get hold of them too. The cheeks are a good deal cheaper than the tail, which has long since made its epithet of 'poor man's lobster' redundant. This angling fish is a real brute but the meat is exceptional and its firm texture is what makes this dish so good.

Saffron makes a splendid companion to monkfish, with its ionic hints of sea air and fragrance of fishing ports. Mark, the gardener, has been growing the saffron crocus for a few years but it is a labour of love. In autumn the flowers produce three strands each, yet unfortunately for Mark they do not all bloom at the same time. He has to scrutinise every flower to check whether they are ready to pick; sometimes they are left for too long and the strands are blown away.

† Britain has a history of saffron cultivation in the fields of Norfolk and Suffolk; Cornwall also had a saffron-growing industry until the nineteenth century and you can still buy Cornish saffron cake today. There is a commercial saffron farm in Norfolk but, not surprisingly, they regularly sell out before the next season even begins.

SERVES 4–6

500g monkfish cheeks, rinsed and
    patted dry
12 saffron strands
¼ vanilla pod
½ cauliflower, trimmed and
    split into florets, stalk roughly
    chopped
1 tsp ground cardamom
25ml double cream
a little groundnut or rapeseed oil
50g winter purslane (or other
    winter salad leaves)
a pinch of ground mace
4–6 unsmoked streaky bacon
    rashers, cooked, to garnish
    (optional)
sea salt

FOR THE ANISE DRESSING:

40ml cider vinegar
½ tsp dried aniseed (or ground
    fennel seed)
4 tbsp rapeseed oil
1 tsp smooth Dijon mustard
a pinch of salt

First make the dressing. Heat the cider vinegar in a pan for a few minutes over a medium heat. Remove, add the aniseed and allow to cool to room temperature. Strain the vinegar into a bowl, add the oil, mustard and salt and whisk to combine. Taste to check the seasoning and add a little more mustard if it needs it.

Put the monkfish cheeks in a bowl with the saffron. Mix to disperse the yellow saffron and set aside.

Slit the vanilla pod open lengthways, scrape out the seeds and set aside. Place the pod in a pan of water that will take a steamer basket and bring to a simmer. Put the cauliflower stalk in the basket, place over the water, then cover and steam until very soft. This may take 25 minutes. Meanwhile, add the cardamom to a separate pan of water and steam the cauliflower florets over it for 10–15 minutes, until tender. Remove and set aside.

When you are satisfied that the cauliflower stalk is well cooked, transfer it to a blender and add the cream and some salt to taste. Blend, stopping to scrape down the sides of the blender with a spatula, until very smooth. Any remaining lumps can be removed by passing the purée through a fine sieve. Stir the vanilla seeds through the purée. It comes to life at this moment, becoming scented and speckled. Keep warm while you assemble the rest of the dish.

To cook the monkfish, heat a large, heavy-based non-stick frying pan over a medium heat. It will take a good few minutes to warm through evenly, so resist the urge to cook on it until it radiates heat. Add enough oil to the now golden fish to coat it lightly and season with salt. Add the cheeks to the pan and cook for 5 minutes on each side, until lightly coloured and just cooked through. Ensure that the fish is colouring but not burning and adjust the heat if needs be. Remove the pan from the heat. The fish can rest in the heat of the pan while you assemble the dish.

To serve, toss the winter purslane with the anise dressing. Spoon the cauliflower purée on to 4 serving plates along with the florets and stack the fish alongside, with a pile of salad leaves. Dust with a little ground mace and, if liked, top with the crisp bacon rashers.

Roast Partridge with Bread and Cheese

There are two common species of partridge in Britain, the native grey and the French red-legged. The native bird is a rarity these days and its French relative is the one most of us will encounter. At a quick glance, the partridge looks remarkably like a plump, monocled gent – an illusion that is quickly shattered when it flees in a rapid scuttle, preferring to run rather than fly.

Escaped birds from nearby shoots regularly appear around our cider barn and, rather ironically given this recipe, under our hawthorn hedge.

We think partridges are the perfect size for the hungry cook. It is worth following the rule, 'roast the young, pot the rest' – a somewhat brutal mantra but very useful nonetheless. Older birds are wonderful in stews and casseroles, slow cooked until the meat is tender. A young partridge still has a slightly pliable beak and claws and its breastbone will be smaller than that of an older bird. We normally hang partridge for five days or so in a cool, dry place.

The mix of flavours and textures in this recipe might appear overcomplicated but the result is tremendous. Its creation was greeted with nothing less than comic air-punching in the kitchen. The plump bird sits on bread sauce, fragrant with its gentle hint of clove. The fondant potatoes and cavolo nero provide butter and welcome acidity respectively. The hawthorn jelly is clean, sweet and tart; flecks of Ogleshield cheese marry well with the flavour of cloves and the sweetness of the hawthorn. Ogleshield cheese is made in Somerset by Jamie Montgomery, using unpasteurised milk from a small herd of Jerseys. He washes his truckles, leaving a cheese that is very like raclette, only better.

This dish is best enjoyed with a glass of our house Vermouth (see page 124). The botanicals in the drink greet the clove in the bread sauce like an old friend, while the caramel in the hawthorn jelly matches the initial sweetness perfectly. The addition of orange to this recipe came after tasting the vermouth with what we thought was the final version. Having a blood orange handy, Matthew layered hawthorn jelly, bread sauce, partridge, cheese and a pinch of orange zest in a spoon for each of us and we all took it in turns to swig at the vermouth. The flavour combination sparked immediately (we should confess that the negroni cocktail is a favourite here at Barley Wood).

SERVES 4

4 red-legged partridges

a drizzle of rapeseed oil

4 bay leaves

4 slices of sourdough bread

Hawthorn Jelly (see page 299), for
    brushing and to serve

100g Ogleshield Cheese, or other
    raclette-style cheese of the
    highest order, finely shaved

zest of 1 blood orange (or ordinary
    orange)

Fondant Pink Fir Potatoes (see page
    44), to serve

sea salt and black pepper

FOR THE BRINING SOLUTION:

1.5 litres water

90g sea salt

2 tbsp juniper berries

4 cloves

2 tsp coriander seeds

1 tsp black peppercorns

FOR THE BREAD SAUCE:

300ml milk

2 tbsp double cream

60g yellow onion, roughly chopped

2 good pinches of ground cloves

1 bay leaf

½ tsp English mustard

½ tsp salt

75g stale bread, cut into 2.5cm
    cubes

FOR THE CAVOLO NERO:

200g black cabbage (cavolo nero) or
    red kale, roughly chopped

a drizzle of rapeseed oil

1 tbsp cider vinegar

Put all the ingredients for the brine in a pan and bring to the boil, stirring to dissolve the salt. Leave to cool and then chill. Place the partridges in the chilled brining solution, making sure they are completely submerged, and leave them in the fridge for 1¼ hours.

Drain the birds and discard the brine. Pat them dry on kitchen paper and set aside. (While we are on the subject of chilling, the vermouth ought to be in the fridge by now.)

To make the bread sauce, put all the ingredients except the bread in a saucepan and bring to a simmer. Cook gently for 10–15 minutes, until the onion is completely soft. Remove the bay leaf and cloves, transfer the mixture to a blender and blitz until the onion is incorporated into the milk. Add the bread and allow the bread to soak for a couple of minutes before blitzing until smooth. Taste and add more seasoning if necessary. For a very smooth bread sauce, pass it through a fine sieve, gently pressing with the back of a small ladle. Keep warm until ready to serve.

Heat the oven to 200°C/Gas Mark 6. Lightly coat the partridges in oil, then season with salt and pepper. Place a bay leaf in the cavity of each bird and put them on a baking tray, resting each one on a slice of the bread. Roast in the oven for 12–15 minutes, until lightly coloured – they should still be pink inside. Brush a light glaze of hawthorn jelly over the birds and return them to the oven for 3 minutes. Leave the birds to rest in a warm place for 10 minutes before serving.

For the cavolo nero, heat a frying pan and add a film of oil. Add the cabbage and season with sea salt. Cook over a medium-high heat, tossing regularly to prevent scorching, until the leaves start to wilt. Add the cider vinegar and cook briefly until evaporated. Remove the cabbage from the pan and set aside.

To assemble the dish, spoon some bread sauce on to each serving plate. Flake over shavings of the Ogleshield; they will melt as they land on the sauce. Place the birds on top, then add the cavolo nero, along with dollops of hawthorn jelly. Scatter over the orange zest and serve with the fondant potatoes. Admire your dinner for no longer than it takes to pour the vermouth tableside.

WASSAIL

Our annual Wassail takes place in early January. The Celts viewed this time of year as the gateway from darkness to light, when all of nature awakes. As recently as the early twentieth century, whole villages – elders and infants alike – would congregate in the orchards and sing, shout and bang out rough music on pots and pans to wake the tree spirits from their winter slumber and ward off the evil spirits that might harm the trees' fertility. It was a chance to throw aside the accepted hierarchies, and a sense of chaos prevailed. Central to this event was the Wassail cup, a communal drink of mulled cider and spice that was passed from hand to hand to toast the apple tree. One drink that we ritually pass around when we wassail is Lamb's Wool (see page 30).

Lamb's Wool

Wassail is a curious evening at Barley Wood, a mix of food, music, fire and gnarled apple trees. One drink that we always serve at Wassail is a concoction called lamb's wool – a rich, smooth combination of ale, apples and spices that pre-dates, and outstrips, mulled cider and is perfect for cold outdoor evenings.

This drink, like many recipes that have been passed down and around, has a misty parentage but the name seems to originate from the Celtic *lamh's suil*, meaning hand and eye. We can only imagine that this alludes to the co-ordination you will need to make this drink; its frothy top looks just like lamb's wool.

SERVES 4

6 large Blenheim Orange apples (or Bramleys), cored and left whole

1.5 litres Box Steam Brewery Dark and Handsome, or other dark beer

250g demerara sugar

½ nutmeg, grated

1 thumb-sized piece of fresh ginger, peeled and finely sliced

1 cinnamon stick

1 star anise

Heat the oven to 160°C/Gas Mark 3. Place the apples on a baking sheet and bake for 1 hour or until soft. Remove and leave to cool.

Put the beer and demerara sugar in a deep pan and bring to a simmer, stirring to dissolve the sugar. Add the spices and simmer for 10 minutes. Squeeze the apple flesh from the skins and pass it through a fine sieve. Remove the spices from the beer, then whisk in the apple pulp over a high heat. Bring to the boil, stirring all the time. The hard whisking will create the woolly top on the lamb's wool.

Serve in glasses, silver tankards or the communal Wassail cup – if you have one!

For us, the Wassail is a chance to celebrate the diversity of our orchard, an acknowledgement of the magic of apples, a rebellion against the cold, dark depths of winter. It is a crucial part of our relationship with the land and we feel it is important to involve and engage everyone, city dwellers and country folk alike, with the seasons. For that reason, we have ended up with a beautiful and completely mad festival that centres on food, friendship and happiness. Restoring this ancient tradition to Barley Wood has been a great success, with hundreds of locals and Bristolians joining us each year. It was our friends and artisan cheesemakers, Tim and Angela of Homewood Cheeses, who guided us through our first Wassail.

Wassail night is, without fail, one of the coldest nights of the year at the Walled Garden. The frost forms silently over the orchards and vegetable patches. At first we don't notice it. Torchbearers lead the Wassail procession, taking us to the oldest tree in the orchard. It is then that we look around and realise we are surrounded by shimmering ice. Then the ceremony begins.

Janet's Jungle Juice Ice with Cheddar 99 Flake

We are very fortunate to be situated right in the middle of one of the most prominent cider-producing areas in Somerset. We have a great number of so-called cider apples in our orchard and have had a fair shot at making our own cider. The best results have come from using one of our favourite varieties, Morgan Sweet.

Despite a few good attempts, though, we can honestly say that we are yet to match the cider produced by West Croft in Brent Knoll, Somerset. It is responsible for the delectable beverage aptly named Janet's Jungle Juice or, as we lazily call it, JJJ. This cloudy cider has proved extremely popular at our annual Wassail. It is made from traditional English cider apples collected from West Croft's own orchard, where many of the trees pre-date the First World War. They are all traditional Somerset cider apples: Kingston Black, Morgan Sweet, Sheep's Nose, Brown Snout, Chisel Jersey, Yarlington Mill, Dabinett and Michelin. West Croft does not add sugar to make JJJ stronger and then water it down, as many cider makers do. Instead, it is made from 100 per cent cider-apple juice. We rarely have any left by the end of Wassail evening, which is why we always keep back a supply 'for staff'. It helps focus the mind when all the guests have left and we are faced with a major clear-up in the early hours of the morning.

We came up with this frozen dessert in the week following our first Wassail. It seeks to encapsulate some of the main elements of Wassail evening, allowing us to continue the festivities for that little bit longer, albeit in a more refined and subdued manner.

SERVES 6–8

1 litre Janet's Jungle Juice (or good rough, dry scrumpy cider)

60g caster sugar

65ml cider brandy

150g Keen's Cheddar, cut to rectangular '99' flake shapes

mint leaves, preferably apple mint, to garnish

Put a shallow metal tray in the freezer to chill. Combine the cider, sugar and cider brandy in a bowl and stir until the sugar dissolves. Pour the mixture into the chilled tray and place in the freezer. Leave until it is beginning to freeze around the edges and then stir thoroughly. Every 30 minutes or so, stir with a fork, crushing any lumps, until the ice is firm but not frozen solid – this will take about 3 hours. Transfer to a container with a lid and store in the freezer.

Serve the ice in teacups or glasses, with the Cheddar 'flakes' added, garnished with mint leaves.

Rabbit Confit with Lovage Breadcrumbs

Making a confit, or cooking slowly in fat, is a traditional way of preserving meat (see page 36). At the Walled Garden, we do it primarily in autumn to preserve the legs of the game that comes in. This carries us through until winter, when produce is more scarce.

Shortly after we arrived at the Walled Garden, we discovered to our dismay that there was no lovage growing there. So Mark planted lovage seeds along the west wall in the already diverse herb garden and we waited, but the plants failed to appear. We soon found out that, like all good things, lovage needs time to develop. For a year, Matthew harvested it from the plant overrunning his own garden at home and brought it in to service the restaurant. This plant has been uprooted during two house moves – a process that left Matthew's hands reeking of lovage for a week afterwards.

Lovage is very versatile, and easy to grow once established, so do give it a go. The seeds are full of character and flavour and can be dried and preserved, while the leaves add a new dimension to salads and stocks. This recipe is an ideal way to use the valuable seeds, which have celery tones that match the sweet rabbit flesh – if you don't have any lovage seeds, you could try celery seeds instead. Making the rabbit into a confit keeps the sometimes-dry flesh chin-drippingly juicy. For perfectly crisp breadcrumbs, you need to think in terms of even drying rather than toasting. Follow the method below for success every time.

SERVES 4

2 Confit Rabbits (see page 36)

150g stale bread, cut into 2.5cm
  cubes

15g lovage seeds, roughly crushed
  in a pestle and mortar

2 egg yolks, lightly beaten

toasted sourdough bread, to serve

baked onions (see method), to serve

mixed salad leaves, to serve

Dark Plum Chutney (see page 298),
  to serve

Heat the oven to 180°C/Gas Mark 4. If you have made the confit rabbit in advance, warm the jar in a pan of lightly simmering water so the fat becomes liquid, then remove the legs and lay them on a baking tray.

Blitz the bread and lovage seeds together in a food processor to make fine breadcrumbs. Spread the crumbs evenly on a baking tray and place in the oven. Cook for 6–10 minutes, removing the tray every 2 minutes and turning the crumbs. It will quickly become apparent where your oven has hot spots and cooler areas. Continue until the crumbs are evenly dried and lightly coloured.

Brush the rabbit with the beaten egg yolk and coat with the pungent breadcrumbs. Place in the oven for 8 minutes, then remove and leave to rest for 2 minutes.

Serve the rabbit with lightly toasted sourdough bread and, if you like, some baked onions (place whole, skin-on, onions in the oven for an hour, until tender), salad leaves and Dark Plum Chutney.

CONFIT

This technique is so invaluable, so simple, so versatile and, once you master it, there will always be something robust and epicurean in the fridge to heat up at the last minute in an emergency. Confit is a French technique that was developed before refrigeration and translates as 'preserved'. Alongside curing, smoking and drying, it is invaluable to anyone who wants to eat with the seasons. Game can be preserved through the winter months well into spring. Tougher cuts, such as duck legs, benefit from the long cooking process, while the fat in which they are cooked can be used afterwards. A layer of pork fat seals the top completely and confit can be stored in a cool cellar with no risk of spoilage. The fat can also be reused again and again, reheated with a little more salt added. Containers such as tall-sided preserving jars, canning jars and Kilners are best; to reheat just warm the jar in a pan of lightly simmering water to loosen the fat, remove the duck legs and bake in the oven for 8–10 minutes.

If you're serious about your confit a small investment of thirty quid can buy a home vacuum sealer. Wrapped in polythene bags, meat needs only a tablespoon of fat around it and the air is sucked out of the packaging. This recreates the same airless environment as that of the fat storage method, above, while requiring less space in the fridge and less of the raw ingredient.

Salt and spices are used first to draw moisture from the meat. Follow the spice guide below for suggested seasonings but do try your own blends. The weight of salt is the one constant to adhere to, set at 4g per leg; scale according to this. Blend or crush the salts and spices together, leaving the woody bay leaves whole. Cover your chosen cuts in this salt mixture for a minimum of 12 and maximum of 36 hours. Wash the meat under cold water to remove the residual salt and herbs. Place about three kilos of goose fat in a tall-sided, ovenproof pan. Heat the fat to loosen it and lay the legs in it. Add more fat if needed as the legs need to be fully submerged. Set the oven to 90°C (or the lowest possible oven setting) and cook for 5–6 hours. The oil shouldn't bubble at this temperature so turn down the temperature by five degrees if that's happening.

Opposite are our recommended quantities for different types of meat, using the cooking instructions given above. We have also given a recipe for confit tomatoes, as this cooking method concentrates the flavours in spectacular fashion.

Confit Meats

FOR CONFIT DUCK:
3kg goose fat
12 duck legs
48g fine sea salt
12g star anise
6g black peppercorns
3g clove powder
6g fennel seeds
6 bay leaves

FOR CONFIT CHICKEN:
3kg goose fat
12 chicken legs
48g fine sea salt
12g juniper berries
6g black pepper
3g clove powder
6 bay leaves

FOR CONFIT RABBIT:
front and hind legs from 4 rabbits
3kg goose fat
48g salt
12g lovage seeds
6g black peppercorns
3g fennel seeds
8 dried lavender flowers
6 bay leaves

Confit Tomatoes with Ruffle Basil

Tomatoes are blimmin' marvellous when cooked like this. Although not submerged in fat they are cooked over a layer of rapeseed oil with a little more drizzled over them, essentially preserving them with fat.

6 tomatoes
rapeseed oil
basil or thyme
sea salt

Preheat the oven to 120°C/Gas Mark ½.

Cut a cross in the bottom of the tomatoes and drop them into simmering water for a couple of minutes. Remove with a slotted spoon and peel off the skins. Quarter the tomatoes, scoop out the flesh and seeds (you can retain these for making tomato essence, see below), and you are left with tomato flesh shards.

Line a baking sheet with foil. Brush with rapeseed oil and place the tomatoes on top. Dust with salt and your chosen herb. Place in the oven for 90 minutes. Check them at the end of this time and turn them over; they need to be mostly dry but still pliable. Return to the oven for a further 10 minutes if needs be.

To make tomato essence: place the seeds in a fine sieve and squash through with a spoon. Place the liquid over a low-medium heat to boil slowly; it will reduce and reach the consistency of passata. Add a pinch of salt and sugar to this intensely flavoured savoury sauce. Use as a garnish for any food that pairs with tomato.

Beef Brisket Slow-roasted in Coffee Sauce with Valor Mash

Using the humbler cuts of meat is an Ethicurean prerequisite. Brisket is a relatively inexpensive cut, allowing us to maximise the beast's worth and minimise our costs, while eating exceptionally well. Ask your butcher to bone and roll it, with all its lovely collagen and fat intact. Collagen will only break down at around 70°C, so brisket needs a long, gentle cook. A meat thermometer will help no end in perfecting this roast. Moisture is also vital, and this creates ample opportunity for seasoning with ales and sauces.

The roasted, smoky richness of coffee makes it one of beef's closest, yet largely overlooked, allies. Our coffee supplier is Extract, run by three enthusiasts who roast all of their coffee in a vintage 1955 cast-iron Probat roaster. Sam, David and Mark rebuilt and conditioned this fine contraption themselves and it looks as if it could have been built by Wallace and Gromit. We regularly take our staff to Extract to see the entire process from raw bean to cup, and to lose a few hours in conversation with experts.

SERVES 4

1.5kg beef brisket, rolled and tied
a little oil
a small bunch of thyme
sea salt

FOR THE COFFEE SAUCE:

140g tomato purée
500ml water
100ml espresso coffee
2 tbsp cider vinegar
½ tsp smoked paprika
1 tbsp paprika
1 tsp ground cumin
1 chipotle chilli, deseeded and
    crushed

FOR THE VALOR POTATO MASH:

1.5kg Valor potatoes (Desiree,
    Remarka and King Edward also
    work well), peeled and cut into
    even-sized chunks
125ml milk
125g butter

Heat the oven to 220°C/Gas Mark 7. Rub the brisket with oil and sprinkle the thyme leaves over. Place it in a shallow roasting tray and roast for 30 minutes, until coloured slightly. Remove from the oven and lower the temperature to 140°C/Gas Mark 1.

Meanwhile, mix all the sauce ingredients together. Transfer the brisket to a deep roasting tin and pour over the sauce. Cover the tin tightly with foil, using 2 layers if necessary to create a tight seal. Return to the oven and cook for about 4 hours, until very tender; if you have a meat thermometer it should register 70°C.

For the mash, put the potatoes in a pan of cold water with a tablespoon of salt and bring them very slowly to a simmer. Cook until very soft but not falling apart. Drain through a colander, place the colander over the pan and return the pan to the switched-off hob – the residual heat from the cooker will allow the potatoes to steam dry. They can be left for 10 minutes or so while you heat the milk and butter.

Place the milk and butter in a pan with ½ teaspoon of salt and heat gently until the butter has melted. Pass the potatoes through a potato ricer into the warmed butter and milk (a potato ricer is an invaluable tool for creating light, even-textured mash; once you've tried one you'll wonder why you ever made mash any other way). Stir to combine, then taste to decide whether you would prefer a little more salt.

When the beef is ready, remove from the oven and leave to rest for about 15 minutes before carving. Serve with the mash.

Pigeon Breasts with Beetroot Pearl Barley and Bordelaise Sauce

The irony of serving pigeon and pearl barley together is not lost on many of our customers, particularly the farmers who eat with us. They have seen many a greedy wood pigeon feasting on their barley crop. Bordelaise sauce is a slowly reduced mix of stock and red wine. We like to use Detroit beetroot with the pearl barley as it contains the most molecules of geosmin, the smell that we recognise as moist soil.

SERVES 4

4 wood pigeon, breasts removed and skinned (save the carcasses to use for stock, if you like)

a little oil

4 large handfuls of kale, large stalks removed

a knob of butter

sea salt and black pepper

smoked salt, to serve (optional)

FOR THE BEETROOT PEARL BARLEY:

300g pearl barley

1 medium beetroot, peeled and cut into 1cm cubes

200ml brown chicken stock (see page 296)

FOR THE BORDELAISE SAUCE:

400ml red wine

35g shallots, finely chopped

60g carrots, finely chopped

40g mushrooms, finely chopped

1 tbsp chopped parsley

2 sprigs of thyme

8 peppercorns

1 bay leaf

500ml beef stock (see page 294)

Rinse the pearl barley in a sieve under cold running water for a few minutes to remove excess starch. Place in a saucepan, cover with cold water and bring to the boil. Drain and rinse under cold running water again. Return the barley to the pan and cover generously with water. Bring to the boil, reduce the heat and simmer for 15 minutes. Add the beetroot and cook for 20–30 minutes, until the beetroot is al dente and the barley tender. Drain and return the barley and beetroot to the pan. Add the chicken stock and cook over a medium heat for 5–10 minutes, stirring regularly, until the barley has absorbed the stock and is glazed in appearance. Season with salt to taste.

Meanwhile, make the bordelaise sauce. Put all the ingredients except the beef stock in a saucepan and bring to a simmer. Cook until the liquid has reduced to about 2 tablespoons. Add the stock and simmer for 10–15 minutes, then strain into a pan. Cook over a medium heat until the sauce lightly coats the back of a spoon. Season with salt to taste.

Heat the oven to 200°C/Gas Mark 6. Lightly oil the pigeon breasts and season on both sides. Place a large, ovenproof frying pan over a high heat. Once the pan is smoking hot, add a thin film of oil. Place the pigeon breasts in the pan, skinned-side down. Leave for 15 seconds or until lightly browned underneath, then turn them over, gently press down with a fish slice and transfer the pan to the oven for about 3 minutes; the meat should still give a little when you press it with a finger. Remove and transfer to a warm plate to rest for 10 minutes. Meanwhile, cook the kale in a large pan of boiling salted water until tender (no more than 45 seconds). Drain well, being sure to strain off as much liquid as possible, and toss with the knob of butter.

Spoon the barley on to 4 serving plates and arrange the kale around it. Slice each pigeon breast into 3 and place on top. Pour the sauce over and sprinkle with a little salt or smoked salt.

Steamed Lemon Sole with Fondant Pink Firs, Golden Beetroot and Nasturtium Remoulade

The delicate flesh and subtle flavour of lemon sole are best preserved by steaming. In an attempt to protect the younger fish and prevent depletion of the species, Cornwall has enforced a byelaw that only lemon sole longer than 25cm can be fished. There are no such restrictions in the EU, so you should try as far as possible to buy sole that have been fished sustainably. Whenever you buy fish, it's worth checking the Marine Conservation Society's online guide to seafood (www.fishonline.org), which rates the sustainability of each species on a scale of one to five.

We had, for a while, been debating what were the best accompaniments to fish, with all of us agreeing that capers featured high on the list. Unfortunately, they tend to grow only in warmer climates, and we wanted to use a homegrown alternative. Nasturtium seeds fitted the bill perfectly. If you don't have nasturtiums in your garden, you could, of course, use capers.

Remoulade is a mayonnaise-based sauce, typically made with finely diced cornichons or other gherkins. Using what we have available can sometimes prove a challenge but in this instance it produced a unique sweet, golden beetroot sauce.

SERVES 4

2 lemon sole, filleted
400g purple sprouting broccoli
sea salt

FOR THE GOLDEN BEETROOT AND
NASTURTIUM REMOULADE:

1 small golden beetroot
215ml cider vinegar
1 tsp ground fennel seeds
1 egg yolk
1 tablespoon orchard honey
1 teaspoon English mustard
1 tsp sea salt
350ml rapeseed oil
1 tbsp Pickled Nasturtium Seeds
    (see page 299), chopped
1 tbsp chopped flat-leaf parsley

FOR THE FONDANT PINK FIRS:

1 tbsp rapeseed oil
500g Pink Fir Apple potatoes (or
    other waxy potatoes), cut into
    4cm pieces
250g butter, cut into cubes

First make the remoulade. Peel the beetroot, cut it into 1cm cubes and salt it generously. Leave for about 10 minutes to draw out a little moisture. This will aid the crunch. Rinse the beetroot briefly and put it in a bowl. Bring 200ml of the vinegar to the boil with the ground fennel, pour it over the beetroot and leave to cool. (The vinegar, which will have an earthy flavour from the beetroot, can be saved for salad dressings.)

Place the egg yolk, honey, mustard, salt and the remaining 15ml vinegar in a bowl and whisk either with an electric whisk on full speed for 1 minute or by hand for a little longer. This will allow the acids to go to work on the egg proteins. Add the rapeseed oil in a very slow trickle and watch to make sure it is being fully incorporated while the mixer continues to spin or your arm is a blur. Once the mixture has emulsified, you can pour the oil in a little faster. Eventually the mixture should have a thick, wobbly consistency. Drain the beetroot and stir it in, together with the pickled nasturtium seeds and parsley. Chill until ready to serve – it will keep for a couple of days in the fridge.

For the fondant potatoes, heat the oven to 200°C/Gas Mark 6. Place a large, ovenproof frying pan over a medium heat until hot. Add the oil, followed by the potatoes, and cook, stirring, until the potatoes are golden all over. Season with salt and add all the cubes of butter plus a splash of water. Allow the butter to melt,

† Nasturtiums are a valuable plant to have in any garden. The leaves attract blackfly and slugs, which means that these unwanted visitors leave other nearby plants and veg alone. The whole plant is edible, with the flowers tasting more magnificent than wild rocket. Their peppery taste makes them worthy of their name, which means 'nose twist' (Pickled Nasturtium Seeds, pictured, see page 299.)

then cover the contents of the pan with a disc of greaseproof paper. Place in the oven and cook for 30–35 minutes, until a knife will pass through the potatoes with little resistance.

Season the sole fillets, roll them up and spike on 4 skewers (see photographs opposite). You will need a tall pan with a lid to cook the fillets on their spikes. Bring a few centimetres of water to a simmer in the pan, then stand the skewers in it. Cover and cook gently for 7–8 minutes, until the fish is just cooked through. Remove from the pan and keep warm.

Cook the broccoli in a pan of boiling salted water for 3–4 minutes, until just tender, then drain. Carefully remove the sole from the skewers and serve on the fondant potatoes, accompanied by the broccoli and splashes of the remoulade.

Sea Robin with Fennel Butter Sauce and Herbed Pink Firs

Gurnard used to be so unprofitable for fishermen that it was mostly used as bait or discarded. Thanks to environmental campaigners and chefs, however, the species has recently been successfully championed as food, and it is indeed superbly tasty. It is widely thought of as an ugly fish, but we think that its pouting mouth and big black eyes would not be out of place in a cartoon.

The gurnard's ancient name of 'sea robin' made its inclusion on our menu essential, as it seemed so pertinent to our location. Legend has it that robins are the guardians of the orchards. Sea robins gained their name due to their ability to produce sounds with their swim bladders and attached muscles. It seems that they are as relentlessly vocal as our land robins, which sing all year round.

The delicate-tasting skin of this fish makes a superb match for the liquorice hint of fennel seeds. Fennel can be seen flowering between July and October in central and southern areas of England and along coastlines in Wales. The seeds can be kept and used all year round. You will appreciate that aniseed addition to your food in the depths of winter, when other interesting ingredients are scarce.

The sauce is a variation on a classic hollandaise, made with roughly half the usual amount of butter. We like to serve this with kale (see page 41).

SERVES 4

2 gurnard, scaled and filleted
a drizzle of oil
a knob of butter
fine sea salt and black pepper

FOR THE FENNEL BUTTER SAUCE:

100ml fish stock (see page 297)
75ml white wine
1 tsp fennel seeds
185g cold butter, cut into 1cm cubes
a dash of cider vinegar
3 egg yolks

FOR THE HERBED POTATOES:

600g Pink Fir Apple potatoes (or
    other waxy potatoes), cut into
    4–5cm pieces
1 tbsp rapeseed or groundnut oil
a knob of unsalted butter
a handful of parsley, chopped

Ensure the gurnard fillets are as dry as possible before scoring the skin with a sharp knife, with cuts 1cm apart. (See opposite for our tip on drying the fish fillets.)

To make the sauce, put the fish stock, white wine and fennel seeds in a small pan over a medium-high heat and boil until the liquid has reduced to 3 or 4 tablespoons. Strain it into a heatproof bowl to remove the fennel seeds and leave to cool for 5 minutes.

Add the egg yolks to the reduced stock and whisk until fully incorporated. Sit the bowl over a pan of barely simmering water, making sure the water doesn't touch the base of the bowl. Whisk the mixture until it becomes airy and thick – look for soft peaks, as you would with egg whites. At this stage, whisk in the butter a piece at a time, ensuring each is fully incorporated before adding the next. After a while, larger quantities of butter can be added each time. Season with fine sea salt and vinegar to taste. Take the pan off the heat, but leave the bowl over the water while you cook the fish and stir the sauce regularly to prevent a skin forming.

Cook the potatoes in boiling salted water until tender, then drain. Place a large, heavy-based frying pan over a high heat. When it is hot, add the oil, quickly followed by the potatoes. Toss to coat lightly with the oil and season with fine sea salt.

Liquids high in acidity, such as citrus juice and vinegar, can be used as flavour enhancers, much like salt. It's not necessarily the taste of vinegar or citrus that we want in the sauce, but they lift rich, heavy flavours, providing a welcome acidity and a cleaner taste. When used as a seasoning, vinegar should not be noticeable. If it is obvious, then you've used too much.

Cook, stirring, until golden all over, then add the butter and parsley. Toss through and remove from the heat.

Heat a large, heavy-based frying pan over a medium-high heat. Very lightly oil the skin of the gurnard fillets and season with a light, even layer of fine sea salt and cracked black pepper. Pour a thin film of oil into the hot frying pan and add the gurnard, skin-side down. Cook over a medium heat, without turning or moving the fish, for 2–3 minutes, until the skin turns golden brown. Flip the fillets over, take the pan off the heat and add a large knob of butter. Leave to rest for 5 minutes – the fish will finish cooking in the heat of the pan. To serve, spoon the herbed potatoes into the centre of each plate and press down with the back of the spoon to crush them slightly. Place the gurnard fillets on top and spoon a generous amount of the sauce around the potatoes.

To achieve a crisp skin on the fish, as much moisture as possible must be removed before cooking. Lay the fillets skin-side up on a board. Run a knife blade, angled slightly, down the fillet from the head end to the tail end, using the knife as a squeegee to push the moisture down and out of the skin. Use kitchen paper to wipe off the moisture that collects on the knife and at the tail end of the fish. Repeat until the skin feels dry to the touch. Flip the fillets over and, with a sharp knife, cut each one in half at a slight angle. Turn the fillets skin-side up again and score the skin with cuts 1cm apart. A very sharp knife or a scalpel will come in handy here. Be sure not to cut into the flesh – it's only the skin you want to score. This helps stop the fillets curling in the heat of the pan.

Pineapple, Turmeric and Ginger Glazed Ham with 'Piccalilli'

Salads do not get much better than this one. Gammon and pineapple have been a familiar combination on pub menus for decades. There is science behind this pairing, as we often find when we analyse classic food combinations. Pineapple contains the enzyme bromelain, which is a natural tenderiser for meat. Mexico also has a bromelain and pork love affair, as can be seen at the *tacos al pastor* stands. This outrageously scoffable street food comprises small corn tacos filled with shavings of pork that has been grilled under pineapple. The juice drips on to the meat as it cooks, caramelising and tenderising it in the process.

In the UK, the pineapple used to be a symbol of wealth and hospitality. Particularly during the eighteenth century, possession of this spiky fruit was so prestigious that there was a proliferation of pineapple pits in country houses across Britain. A pineapple pit was a demonstration of tremendous growing skill and dedication. The energy needed to grow this tropical fruit is monumental – the process involved a mixture of moist heat from fermenting oak bark or horse manure in the earth around the pineapple and an intricate set of furnaces and chimneys for additional heat. There are the ruined remains of a pineapple pit on privately owned land very near Barley Wood. It belonged to the slave-trade abolitionist William Wilberforce, a friend and ally of our Barley Wood benefactor, Hannah More, who built Barley Wood House in the late eighteenth century.

During December, pineapples from the Caribbean are in season. Try to find Fairtrade fruit that smells sweet at the base. This indicates that it has been picked close to ripeness, as pineapples do not ripen further after being picked.

SERVES 8 GENEROUSLY

1 large pineapple

250g golden granulated sugar

3 tbsp ground turmeric

50g fresh ginger, peeled and finely diced

1–2kg free-range cooked ham

FOR THE PICCALILLI:

200g cider vinegar

100g caster sugar

20 coriander seeds

½ tsp dried chilli flakes

100g shallots, topped and tailed, sliced in half through the tops and separated into individual layers

1 tbsp ground turmeric

100g cauliflower florets

100g Glazed Star Anise carrots (see overleaf)

Heat the oven to 200°C/Gas Mark 6. Top and tail the pineapple and cut away the spiky skin. Cut the flesh away from the core and place in a blender or food processor. Pulse till smooth, then strain the mixture through a sieve, pressing with the back of a spoon to extract the juice. Reserve 35ml of the juice for the salad dressing (you won't need the rest). Put the pulp in a bowl and mix with the sugar, turmeric and ginger. This is the glazing mixture for the ham.

Place the ham flat-side down on a baking sheet and spread the glazing mixture thickly over it. Cook for 30–40 minutes, until the glaze is caramelised. Set aside to cool.

For the piccalilli, heat the vinegar to boiling point, add the sugar and stir until dissolved. Add the coriander seeds, chilli flakes and shallots and bring back to a simmer. Remove the shallots with a slotted spoon and set aside to cool. Add the turmeric to the hot liquid, followed by the cauliflower florets. Bring to a simmer, then stir well. Remove from the heat and leave the cauliflower to cool in the yellow vinegar. It will pick up the colour of the turmeric as it cools.

FOR THE SALAD DRESSING:

85ml cold-pressed rapeseed oil or
    groundnut oil
25ml cider vinegar
35ml pineapple juice
1 tsp ground star anise
1 tsp Dijon mustard
2 pinches of salt

FOR THE SALAD:

200g Miike purple giant leaves (or
    other mustardy salad leaves)
100g salad leaves (we use a mixture
    of red frill, watercress and land
    cress)
100g winter lettuce leaves
a bunch of coriander
a bunch of chrysanthemum leaves,
    if available

To make the dressing, place all the ingredients in a blender and blend until emulsified.

Arrange all the salad leaves on serving plates, reserving a few of the smaller red frill for garnish. If it helps to cut the Miike purple giant down, then do so. Slice the ham and place a couple of slices on top of the leaves, intertwined with pieces of the deconstructed piccalilli. Finish by lightly drizzling over the dressing and garnishing with the reserved leaves.

Glazed Star Anise Carrots

300g carrots, peeled and cut into
    2.5cm chunks
20g salted butter
2 star anise
1 tsp sugar
pinch of fine sea salt

Heat a pan over a medium heat. The pan should be big enough to hold the carrots in a single layer. When the pan is hot, add the butter (the butter should sizzle but not burn). The second the sizzling subsides, add the star anise and carrots. Toss the carrots through the butter to coat evenly, then add the sugar and salt. Add about 330ml cold water to the pan (enough to almost cover the carrots), and turn the heat up to high. It may take 5–10 minutes for the water to almost fully reduce, and then the carrots will begin to sizzle again. Stir the carrots vigorously so that they begin caramelising evenly on all sides. When they are an even, golden colour, remove from the pan and serve straight away.

† A number of apples tasting remarkably like pineapple can be found in British orchards. Examples in our orchard are Ribston Pippin and Blenheim Orange. Pitmaston Pineapple was most likely grown from a Golden Pippin seedling by John Williams in 1845 at Pitmaston House in Worcester. This small, sweet and russet apple has remarkable pineapple tones and yellow flesh.

WINTER SALADS

Mark, the gardener, grows his winter salad leaves in polytunnels at the bottom of the walled garden. They're on a raised platform hovering over the field below. During winter, we can usually tell whether Mark is in by a trailing plume of smoke from the little stove that heats his kettle. He also throws together an excellent vegetable stew that will often sit cooking on the stove for most of the morning. The view through the tunnels and out of the open door is a wonderful sight: overlooking the field below, it gives the impression of an entrance to another world.

The tunnels are planted with a number of leaves that provide fresh succulence and a welcome vitamin injection to the short, chilly days of winter. In the salad on page 52 we use Miike purple giant (*Brassica juncea*). This leaf is classed as a vegetable and in some cultures is boiled and steamed. We prefer to eat it raw and relish its hot, mustard flavour. It is also an indicator of the weather, as it turns a deeper purple as the temperature drops. Opposite, Mark has planted winter purslane (*Claytonia perfoliata*). A native of North America, it is also known as miner's lettuce, as it was eaten by miners to fend off scurvy. It has a lily-pad-like top and a tender trailing stem. Mature

leaves see the blooming of a tiny flower that pierces the centre.

In recent years, Mark has taken to growing chrysanthemums for their leaves. They have a distinctive tang that resembles pineapple. Prising it from Mark's muddy fingers is a tricky business but well worth it. Adding more mustard heat and colour is red frill – a jagged variety containing two excellent compounds, sinigrin and gluconasturtiin. When the sinigrin in the leaf is exposed to compounds in the air, it reacts and creates mustard oil. It is this very mustardy oil that gives the dish on page 50 its fire, a perfect complement to the sweet, tender ham.

Eccles Cakes with Dorset Blue Vinny Sauce

The relationship between sweet and savoury is an interesting one. Salt makes sweet ingredients taste less one-dimensional, so you perceive them as being more flavourful than they really are. Perhaps the most common example of the combination is our long-standing tradition of eating cheese with fruit. No one would raise an eyebrow if you suggested accompanying a nutty Russet apple with a slice of Cheddar. In Yorkshire – and in some parts of America – serving apple pie with a piece of cheese is commonplace.

This dish sprang from the British tradition of pairing Eccles cakes with a slice of Lancashire cheese. We started experimenting with an Eccles cake recipe when we were trying to find suitable puddings for a sherry and game night at the restaurant. We thought Dorset Blue Vinny would be a worthy local alternative to Lancashire cheese, as it is equally creamy, yet has more depth. Having worked out the correct cheese-to-sherry ratio for the sauce, we poured it over the Eccles cakes that had just come out of the oven, hoping the result would be more than palatable. It worked remarkably well, and has become our West Country version of the traditional northern dish.

We feature this dessert regularly on our daytime menu and find that some customers approach it with a degree of nervousness. But we are yet to meet anyone who does not thoroughly enjoy its well-balanced quirkiness. The sauce has become so popular that customers often request it as an accompaniment to whichever cake happens to be on the dessert menu. We must observe that not every cake is entirely compatible with the sauce, but who are we to curtail our customers' inventiveness?

MAKES 14 CAKES

50g butter

90g dark soft brown sugar

1¾ teaspoons ground mixed spice (see page 303 if you'd like to make your own)

270g currants

50g Candied Peel (see page 303, or use good-quality bought peel), finely chopped

1 quantity of Flaky Pastry (see page 301) or good-quality shop-bought puff pastry

1 egg, lightly beaten

demerara sugar, for sprinkling

To make the sauce, put the cream, sugar, cheese and sherry in a pan (include half the currants, if you want to enrich the flavour of the Eccles cakes) and heat gently until the cheese has melted and the sauce is smooth. Strain through a sieve and set aside (reserve the currants for the Eccles cakes). The sauce can be kept in the fridge for up to 2 weeks.

To make the Eccles cakes, place the butter, sugar and mixed spice in a saucepan and heat through gently, stirring occasionally, until the sugar has melted into the butter. Remove from the heat and stir in the currants (including the ones used for the sauce), and the candied peel. Set aside to cool.

Heat the oven to 180°C/Gas Mark 4. Take the pastry out of the fridge and set it on a lightly floured surface with one of the short ends nearest you. Roll out to about 3mm thick. Using an 11cm pastry cutter, cut out as many rounds as you can. Divide the filling into 40g portions and place one portion in the centre of each circle of pastry. This may seem like a lot, but it makes sense when you are eating the cakes. Next, you need to enclose the currant mixture in the pastry. This can be quite tricky, but you will find a technique that works after a little playing. We do it by pinching 4 'corners' of the circle together over the currant

FOR THE DORSET BLUE VINNY SAUCE:

250ml double cream

100g caster sugar

40g Dorset Blue Vinny cheese (or
    Stichelton cheese), crumbled

50ml sweet sherry, such as Pedro
    Ximénez or Bristol Cream

mixture and then gently folding in the excess pastry. Where you are pinching the pastry together will be the underside, so as long as the filling is completely enclosed it doesn't need to look perfect. The pastry should seal itself, but if necessary brush it very lightly with water.

Place the Eccles cakes the right way up on the work surface and shape each one into a neat round with a flat top. This may require a small amount of manipulating. Using a sharp knife, slash 3 horizontal lines across the top. Lightly brush the top of the Eccles cakes with beaten egg and dust with demerara sugar. Bake for 18 minutes or until the pastry is golden brown and cooked all the way through. Transfer to a wire rack to cool for 10 minutes, then serve with the sauce. Ding dang doo.

† Made from the milk that is left after skimming off the fat to make butter, Dorset Blue Vinny is a thrifty wartime cheese born out of the need not to waste anything. It retains its creaminess by reintroducing semi-skimmed milk powder to the milk once it reaches the appropriate temperature. Legend has it that the bacteria used to be introduced by dragging mouldy horse harnesses through the milk before adding the rennet and storing the cheese on damp bags next to mouldy boots. Sadly, it is boring penicillin by way of blue-mould solution nowadays.

Milk Stout and Chocolate Steamed Pudding

This recipe is a combination of two of our favourite things: milk stout and a British steamed pudding. When we first opened The Ethicurean, we drank Bristol Beer Factory's chilled milk stout on the lawn overlooking the garden. It had the most remarkable balance of sweetness and roast malt that we had ever tasted. Since this boozy summer evening, 'milk stout on the lawn' has become shorthand for, 'Hurry up, let's go and have a beer.'

Milk stout was first brewed on the Bristol Beer Factory site in the 1900s and its recent revival was an excellent move. During the brewing process, unfermentable lactose sugar is added, giving the beer a residual sweetness.

This pudding, served with an inappropriate amount of double cream, should be regarded as a new British classic.

SERVES 6

160ml Bristol Beer Factory's milk
  stout
150g butter, cut into cubes
235g caster sugar
45g cocoa powder
160g plain flour
85ml soured cream
1 large egg
2 tsp vanilla extract
1½ tsp bicarbonate of soda
double cream, to serve

Place the milk stout and butter in a saucepan over the lowest possible heat and whisk until the butter has just melted. It is important not to overheat the mixture or the butter will split, resulting in an oily pudding. Add the sugar and stir until dissolved.

Sift the cocoa powder and flour into the mixture in 2 lots, whisking thoroughly after each to blend well. Set aside.

Lightly whisk the soured cream, egg, vanilla and bicarbonate of soda together until combined. Add this to the stout and flour mixture and whisk briefly to incorporate once more.

Thoroughly grease a 1.2 litre pudding basin with butter. Add the pudding mixture. Take a piece of foil large enough to cover the top of the basin generously, folding a thick pleat in the centre (this will allow the pudding to expand during steaming), and place it on the basin, tucking the edges firmly under the rim. Put the basin in a steamer basket and set it over a pan containing about 10cm boiling water. Cover and steam over a low heat for 2 hours, checking the water level every 30 minutes and topping up when necessary.

Remove the basin from the steamer and leave to stand for 5 minutes. Take off the foil, run a knife around the edge of the pudding, then turn it out on to a plate. You'll need plenty of cream, as this pudding is seriously thirsty!

Pedro Ximénez and Whisky with Vermouth Smoke

Every year we hold a sherry and game night pairing various sherries with a tasting menu of game. Pedro-Ximénez (PX) is always the favourite sherry and we love pairing it with Eccles cakes (see page 54). This velvety sherry is the colour of dark wood and with its raisin and caramel flavours, tastes almost like Christmas pudding in liquid form. Combining PX with a whisky such as Macallan 10 Year Old Fine Oak and a little vermouth smoke creates a totally unique cocktail. Even after the last few drops have been drunk many customers ask for the decanter to stay on the table, so that they can breathe in the last of the treacle smoke.

SERVES 2
100ml PX (we like Bodegas
Gutierrez Colosia Pedro Ximénez)
50ml whisky (we like Macallan 10
    Year Old Fine Oak whisky)

TO MAKE ICE SPHERES:
Wash long balloons out before filling them with water. Tie off the balloons and then use string to separate them into the size of sphere that you would like. Remember that they will expand as they freeze. Using distilled water will mean that the ice is completely clear; but they still look impressive when made with tap water.

Jack uses a smoke gun to make this drink. Chill the PX and whisky by stirring together with ice in a mixing glass. Next fill a decanter with smoke: Jack uses oak chips that have been used to oak our Vermouth (see page 132) and then dried. Pour the chilled liquid into the decanter and pop in the stopper. The smoke should gradually form a dense cloud. Pour into small glasses filled with plenty of ice (we like to put an ice sphere in each glass, see left).

If you do not have access to a hand smoker you can make this drink in a barbecue smoker (see Tin Can and Soldering Iron Approach, page 85). Place the drink in a container with as much surface area as possible and leave to smoke for 1 hour.

NOTE: We have experimented with upscaling this recipe and bottling larger quantities, then leaving to mature (the Negroni on page 140 also upscales wonderfully). We reuse Sipsmith's gin bottles (thanks, Sipsmith). At the time of writing we have a bottle of this cocktail that was mixed three months ago. We have noticed a real development in the complexities of flavour as the elements begin to feather in; it becomes difficult to sense where one component ends and another begins.

Fennel Seed and Ginger Hot Chocolate

We first tasted this combination of chocolate, herb and spice at the Abergavenny Food Festival. Our stall happened to be next to that of the chocolatier Paul A. Young, and he very kindly gave us a few of his creations to taste. We were struck by the sweet, fragrant, almost medicinal quality of his milk chocolate with fennel seed and ginger. Once the cold weather caught up with us at The Ethicurean, we experimented with a few hot chocolate recipes and settled on this one, which we think captures the essence of Paul's idea.

Romanesco fennel seeds are harvested at Barley Wood when the seed heads turn brown. The whole heads can be put in a paper bag to dry. After a few weeks, a strong shake will deposit the seeds at the bottom of the bag. These seeds are at their absolute best when they are still a little green. To make the fennel sugar, whiz equal quantities of granulated sugar and fennel seeds together in a blender or food processor. It can be added to all sorts of desserts.

SERVES 2 COMFORTABLY

400ml milk

100g dark chocolate with 70–73 per cent cocoa solids, grated, plus a little extra to finish (we use Original Beans chocolate)

1 tsp ground ginger

20g dark muscovado sugar

a pinch of salt

2 tsp fennel sugar

100ml double cream

Gently heat half the milk in a pan and add the grated chocolate, ginger, muscovado sugar, salt and most of the fennel sugar (save a pinch for sprinkling). Stir until the chocolate has melted into the milk, then whisk in the remaining milk and the cream. Do not allow the mixture to boil but bring it to a comfortable drinking temperature. If you have a hand blender, substitute this for a whisk; either way, for a frothy head a good amount of whisking is needed.

Serve sprinkled with the remaining fennel sugar and a few shards of chocolate.

If you have access to an espresso machine, combine the grated chocolate with the ginger, sugar, salt, fennel and just enough milk to make a thick paste, then heat it using the steam wand. Warm 2 mugs and pour the thick, spiced chocolate into them. Steam the remaining milk with the cream in a metal jug, using the steam wand. The trick is to introduce enough steam near the surface of the milk to create a whirlpool; this should generate very little noise.

Keep a hand cupped around the steaming jug. When it is too hot to hold comfortably, stop steaming. Tap the jug on the worktop several times to pop any surface bubbles and then swirl to minimise any separation between foam and liquid. Pour this glossy milk on to the thick chocolate. After a little practice, it is relatively simple to create a few patterns. This steaming process will create the micro-foam needed to make a silky hot chocolate.

SPRING

S PRING in the Wrington Vale has a unique feel. There is a sense of imminent activity, that moment before somebody tells you something they have kept secret for a long time.

Colour comes first, and the daffodils are still out in late March, between the outside wall and the lower orchard, thick yellow carpets in the shadows of the apple trees. Jack is out stalking roe deer with Alan Down, a good friend and experienced stalker, before the new shoots and leaves provide too much cover. During spring mornings before service, Matthew and Iain roll down the sleeves of their chef's whites and pick young nettle shoots with gloved hands. Carried up through the garden in apple crates, the nettles are carefully cleaned and end up as a bright green soup. Lumps of Gorwydd Caerphilly are floated on the surface, melting to an irresistible, gelatinous texture.

Kale, radishes and rainbow chard are all ready. We fry the kale in a hot pan with plenty of cider vinegar and salt. Mark plants the radishes as a companion plant between the rows of garlic. We slice these red roots into salads – some are fiery and need a cooling something to subdue their heat. The ruby chard requires little cooking and is smothered under a generous measure of hollandaise as a breakfast treat.

As spring continues on its path, the bluebells flower, replacing the yellow daffodils. They are a deep violet blue. Not many people know that the Victorians would stiffen their collars with crushed bluebells.

Next the blossom comes, a sure sign of the new season, each blossom a potential fruit. First up are the plums and damsons. These guard the west wall, sprayed outwards on their caned espaliers. Pears and cherries quickly follow, while apples are slower, blossoming in April. Quince comes next; we are proud of our single tree, which provides us with enough fruit for membrillo all year long. Medlars are last, cream-coloured flowers that will become ugly fruit but with excellent flavour. Paula can be found walking between the trees forecasting our future crop, and the bumblebees are out for nectar.

April can mean only one thing: the asparagus season. We patrol the beds at Barley Wood, keen eyes hunting for the first elusive spears to push up their tight, crisp tips. This precious crop is devoured with poached eggs or straight from the pan with plenty of butter.

St George's Day marks the time to look for St George's mushrooms. The only foraged mushroom safe to be eaten raw, it has a natural flavour companion in the form of ribwort plantain. This seed head found in our orchard is a firm favourite of ours, and the two together make a wonderful seasonal delicacy.

May heralds the yellow flowers of meadow vetchling and creeping cinquefoil, favourites of the grizzled skipper butterfly. Primroses are also flowering in the shade of the Bramley trees.

In June the herb garden looks beautiful. We pinch out the new growth to make botanical teas for our house vermouth. Mark's strawberries begin to crop and we use up the last jar of the previous season's jam in our rose lemonade steamed pudding. The jam pan is set firmly back on the stove.

Nettle Soup with Caerphilly

This soup's striking emerald colour (nettles have one of the highest levels of chlorophyll in the vegetable kingdom) might lead you to think of it as a light starter. Do not be fooled. It is an extremely wholesome soup that could help you run a marathon. Roman soldiers are said to have brought their own supply of nettles to Britain as a rich source of protein to fuel long marches in the cold, wet climate. Perhaps that is why this soup is so popular with staff at the restaurant when, on busy spring days, you will catch us all sipping a mug of it to keep us going.

The Caerphilly adds a creamy texture. We favour Gorwydd Caerphilly, made by our friends, the Trethowan family, at their farm situated between Lampeter and Aberystwyth. It is one of our all-time favourite British cheeses and we consider its Welsh rabbit capabilities to be unrivalled (see page 82).

Oysters pair remarkably well with nettles, and we'd recommend serving this soup with oysters dropped into it at the last moment. There is an ionic quality to them both that just sings when they are eaten in combination. A chunk of bread with a pat of salted butter is also an excellent addition.

SERVES 4

a little vegetable oil
500g onions, thinly sliced
250g celeriac, cut into small cubes
250g carrots, cut into small cubes
1 litre fish stock or vegetable stock
   (see page 297)
100–120g nettle tips, freshly picked
   (they must be very young)
200g Caerphilly cheese, preferably
   Gorwydd, cut into small cubes
rapeseed oil, for drizzling
sea salt

Place a large pan over a medium heat. Add a thin film of vegetable oil, followed by the onions, celeriac and carrots. Cover and sweat for about 5 minutes, until the vegetables have started to soften but are not coloured. Add the stock, bring to a simmer and cook until the vegetables are soft. They should be soft enough to blitz easily; anything beyond that, however, and the flavour will begin to dull.

Transfer the soup to a blender, in batches that fill it no more than half full, and blitz until smooth, adding the nettles with the final batch. Pour through a fine sieve into a clean pan. Check the consistency of the soup; if you would prefer a looser finish, stir in a little more stock. Season with sea salt to taste and reheat very gently; if the nettles are heated for too long they turn a very unappealing shade of dark green. Serve in large bowls, garnished with the cubes of Caerphilly and a tiny drizzle of rapeseed oil.

† The base to this soup is what is known as a mirepoix. A mirepoix refers to onions, celery (or in this case celeriac) and carrots, in the ratio of 2:1:1. It is a very classic starting point in cookery and results in an overall taste that is greater than that of its worthy ingredients. We often use this ratio of vegetables for stocks and bases of sauces.

MUSHROOMS

When we opened the restaurant, we relied on several professional foragers to bring us steady supplies of mushrooms. We cannot emphasise enough the importance of using experts in your own learning process. If you are ever in doubt about the type of mushroom you have found, do not take a chance. The consequences can be fatal.

It is a common mistake to forget one of the finest wild mushrooms native to Britain – St George's mushroom. They are found around 23 April, St George's Day, and are available until early June. Their distinctive aroma has been aptly described as the smell of British fields. This makes perfect sense, as they often form in a ring, completely hidden under long grass. If you find their smell overwhelming, please don't give up on them. We are convinced that they taste best when eaten raw, so try the smaller ones first, as the smell develops with age and you might find them less pungent. Failing that, if you cook them, their scent is greatly camouflaged. We have heard that some restaurants feel nervous about having them on the menu, yet with expert identification there really is no reason to deprive yourself of such an interesting delicacy.

St George's is the only foraged mushroom that can be served raw and we would always advise you to cook other varieties. Initially, raw St George's taste of fresh cucumber but the flavour develops into something more akin to melon towards the end. We serve them with asparagus and ribwort plantain, another foraged plant that is easy to find, as it grows commonly on lawns and green areas. Sadly, it is now considered a weed, but please help us reintroduce it to British cooking. It is easy to identify: the bulbs have elongated, kernel-like tips and, once you spot it, it is impossible to miss. It initially tastes slightly bitter but this develops into a nutty, woody flavour – often likened to that of cep mushrooms – that ties in perfectly with the earthy, woodland notes of the St George's. For more of our thoughts about mushrooms, see pages 224–5.

St George's Mushrooms with Asparagus, Ribwort Plantain, Mushroom Jelly and Apple Jelly

We used to forage for mushrooms as often as possible before moving to the Walled Garden. Always laden with too many books on the subject, we would set out with our lurcher, hoping to train her to find some delicacies. Our lack of experience must have rubbed off on her, as she was more interested in sticks, pine cones and squirrels. Gradually we learned to identify chicken of the woods, parasols and beefsteak fungus. Foraging became one of our favourite autumnal activities. At first we travelled further away than we needed in our quest to become amateur mycologists. With time, though, we learned the valuable lesson that the best ingredients are usually to be found on your doorstep.

SERVES 4

a bunch of asparagus

20 small ribwort plantain flower heads

1 tsp mint leaves, preferably spearmint

12–16 summer purslane leaves or other salad leaves

fine sea salt

FOR THE MUSHROOM JELLY:

250g St George's mushrooms

a pinch of salt

½ tsp agar agar powder

FOR THE APPLE JELLY:

250g apple juice

½ tsp agar agar powder

First make the mushroom jelly. Remove the stalks from the mushrooms and set the caps aside. Clean the stalks thoroughly and then chop finely. Put them in a pan, cover with 250g water and simmer for 15 minutes. Strain the cooking liquor through a fine sieve into a clean pan, pressing with the back of a spoon to extract it all. Discard the stalks. Measure the cooking liquor and add a dash more water if necessary to take it back up to 250g. Season with salt, remembering that, in this instance, a little goes a long way. Return the pan to the heat and stir in the agar agar until dissolved. The liquor needs to boil briefly to hydrate the agar and activate its gelling properties. Pour into a small plastic box. We use one that gives a final depth of about 1cm so we can cut the jelly into cubes, but feel free to experiment. Leave to cool, then place in the fridge until set. It will keep for 4 days.

For the apple jelly, heat the juice in a pan, stir in the agar agar and bring to the boil until dissolved. Leave to cool and then set in a plastic box as described above.

Trim the asparagus by finding the natural point where the stalk snaps close to the base and breaking it off. Have a pan of fast-boiling salted water ready and a bowl of iced water too. Cook the asparagus in the rapidly boiling water for up to 2 minutes, but no more. Remove the spears and chill them in the iced water; they will retain their bright green colour.

Finely slice the reserved mushroom caps and lay them on 4 plates. Dust with fine sea salt. Lay the asparagus spears on top of the mushrooms. Cut the jelly into small cubes and add a teaspoon of each flavour to each plate, along with the ribwort flowers, mint leaves and purslane. Encouragement for all amateur mycologists.

Sweet-cure Mackerel with Morels, Spelt Soda Bread and Horseradish

The combination of mackerel, aniseed and horseradish offers a wide range of flavours. The cure stops the mackerel in its tracks, preserving a fresh, ionic snapshot of the ocean. Horseradish is a familiar companion to mackerel, since its warmth is good with oily fish. Interestingly, fish are attracted to the smell of aniseed as well as tasting superb with it.

Mackerel are a delicate fish that spoil quickly, so choose line-caught ones and make sure they are very fresh. The small ones with the brightest eyes are best and are often cheaper than the larger fish.

The flavour of morel mushrooms is extraordinary – reminiscent of the richness of beef. The mushrooms release spores that are picked up and carried by the wind. Searching for morels is a deeply engrossing task, so watch out for low hanging branches as you hunt. We have found them under ash and sycamore; they favour dying and dead elms. They have hollow fruiting bodies and a honeycomb structure. Beware of false morels, known as Elfin Sandals.

The horseradish sauce is a useful standby that comes out whenever we have leftover sirloin or brisket. It's also very good on cold lamb, smoked fish and ham, and exemplary eaten with Salt-baked Baby Beets (see page 191) and ox tongue. Dig up the root of a healthy horseradish, wash away residual soil and peel the root. You will likely be left with 50–100g. (A jar of grated horseradish is a fine substitute.) When grated, horseradish releases a compound called sinigrin, and enzymes it meets in the air immediately break this down to form mustard oil. The aroma is guaranteed to have you in rabbinically intense tears. Our small kitchen becomes a riot of faux wailing and laughter whenever we prepare this. The task is now seen as an aid to camaraderie and team building.

SERVES 4

4 mackerel fillets, pin bones removed

10g dried morel mushrooms (or ceps)

400ml cider vinegar

1 tablespoon aniseed

300g caster sugar

fine sea salt

FOR THE SPELT SODA BREAD:

200g brown spelt flour

200g white spelt flour

50g fine oatmeal (or use porridge oats that have been blended until fine)

1 tsp bicarbonate of soda

1 tsp salt

1 tbsp honey

Lay the mackerel fillets flesh-side down on a bed of fine sea salt and chill for 2 hours to cure, then rinse. This gives a firmer-fleshed result.

Rehydrate the mushrooms by steeping them in near-boiling water with a splash of the vinegar for 10 minutes. Strain, reserving the liquor, and then check each one is free of soil and sand. The liquor that remains will be delicately smoky and truly flavoursome.

Warm the aniseed through in a dry pan until it spits and cracks, then carefully pour the mushroom liquor into the pan, leaving any residue of soil or sand behind. It will boil up rapidly as it hits the hot pan, so take care at this point. The evaporation will intensify the flavour of the mushroom stock. Add the vinegar and heat through then add the sugar and stir until dissolved. Add the morel mushrooms and remove from the heat. Allow this mixture to cool, then pour it over the fish fillets. Place in the fridge for at least 2 hours and up to 6 hours. The simple-to-make spelt soda bread can fill this gap quite comfortably.

375ml buttermilk (if unavailable, mix 25ml white vinegar with 350ml milk and leave to rest for 5 minutes)

25g butter, melted

FOR THE HORSERADISH SAUCE:

1 horseradish root, finely grated

2 tbsp cider vinegar

4 tbsp crème fraîche or soured cream

1 teaspoon chopped chives

1 teaspoon chive flowers

sea salt

Heat the oven to 200°C/Gas Mark 6. Mix all the dry ingredients for the bread together in a large bowl, then make a well in the centre. Add the honey, buttermilk and melted butter to the well and mix with a wooden spoon until well combined. Put the dough into a 900g loaf tin (or a 23cm springform cake tin) lined with baking parchment and place in the oven. Bake for 15 minutes, then reduce the oven temperature to 160°C/Gas Mark 3 and bake for 30 minutes longer. Turn the loaf out on to a tea towel and tap the base; it should sound hollow. If necessary, return to the oven for a few minutes longer. Cool the loaf on a wire rack, covering it with a tea towel if you prefer a soft crust.

Combine the grated horseradish, vinegar and a pinch of sea salt. Strain through a sieve, discarding the liquid, then combine with the crème fraîche or soured cream. Season to taste with salt and top with the chives and the purple-hued chive flowers. The sweet anise and morel mackerel can now be lifted from its souse and served with chunks of buttered soda bread and the irresistible horseradish.

Asparagus with Toasted Sesame and Hollandaise Sauce

In a quiet corner beyond the garden walls, sheltered on one side by a set of imposing cobnut trees and guarded on the other by dense Victorian bay hedges, you will find one of our favourite ingredients, growing silently in its sandy bed. For most of the year, the asparagus beds look desolate and grey, like miniature dunes in some foreign land. Their drab appearance means that they are often overlooked by visitors to the Walled Garden. However, they are regularly disturbed by squirrels trying to bury the cobnuts they have laboriously collected from the neighbouring trees. When the asparagus spears begin to grow and we see their shy heads starting to poke out, it is an intensely satisfying feeling. The news that the asparagus is ready for picking travels fast, which is probably why it is invariably the item we run out of first on the menu. Nothing really prepares you for the taste of asparagus freshly picked from the garden.

Unfortunately the original asparagus beds at the Walled Garden did not survive the hard years when the garden was allowed to fall into deep disrepair. Replicas of the originals were built in 1999. The beds are unusual because they are raised – a feature that helps stop the roots drowning in sodden clay soil. The variety is unknown but we do know that they were planted with the emphasis on flavour rather than size. Matthew is convinced that, as it has an unusual purple tinge to the tip and white base, it must be Formby asparagus, from Formby in Merseyside. We think he just misses the northwest a little but they do both love sandy soil, so perhaps he is on to something. To be able to cut fresh asparagus from the corner of the garden every morning and share it with our customers is one of the things that makes us feel very lucky to be alive. We choose to scatter toasted sesame seeds over this dish, as they add a soft, nutty crunch to a delicate ingredient.

People are often put off by the seeming complexity of hollandaise sauce but the method overleaf offers an easy way to achieve a consistent result every time. We flavour it with vintage cider vinegar instead of the more traditional lemon juice and find it adds a new depth and a slightly oaky taste. We also use salted butter rather than unsalted. Our favourite is Maryland, which is produced in Shepton Mallet, relatively close to us, and is quite salty, with roughly two per cent salt. We find that the saltiness of the butter balances the inherent acidity of the vinegar. Alternatively, you could use an unsalted butter and season to taste with fine sea salt.

SERVES 4

2 tbsp sesame seeds

4 sprigs of tarragon

20 asparagus spears, trimmed

FOR THE HOLLANDAISE SAUCE:

3 egg yolks

1 tbsp vintage cider vinegar, such as
    Ostler's

125g chilled salted or unsalted
    butter, cut into 1cm cubes

sea salt

First make the hollandaise sauce: fill a saucepan two-thirds full with water and bring to a rapid boil. Put the egg yolks and vinegar in a heatproof bowl and whisk for about 1 minute, until pale and fluffy. Take the pan of boiling water off the heat and set the bowl over it, ensuring the base of the bowl is not touching the water. Quickly add all the butter to the bowl and whisk steadily with a balloon whisk until the heat from the water melts the butter and cooks the eggs. After a few minutes of constant, gentle whisking, the hollandaise will thicken. When it is the consistency of a thin custard, take the bowl off the pan and continue whisking until the consistency changes to that of an immaculate, velvety custard.

Toast the sesame seeds in a frying pan over a low heat until they are light golden brown. Once they begin browning they can burn very easily, so keep your eye on them and stir regularly for an even colour. Remove from the pan and leave to cool.

Place the tarragon in a pan large enough to fit a steamer basket on top. Add 7–8cm of boiling water, place on a medium heat and put the steamer basket on it. When the water is simmering, add the asparagus to the basket, cover and steam for 3–4 minutes, until the spears are tender but retain a bit of bite.

To serve, place the spears on 4 serving plates, pour over the hollandaise and garnish with the toasted sesame. Poached eggs (see page 81) would make a worthy addition to this delightful starter.

Clear Ham Hock Broth with Poached Eggs

This broth is a marvellously nourishing, clear and balanced liquid. To achieve such clarity we need to act like water: following the path of least resistance, exercising patience, we get where we need and the reward is twofold, with stock as clear as water from a babbling mountain brook and as deep as Poseidon's realm in flavour. When the poached egg yolk is broken, the dish changes before your eyes and a new depth of richness becomes obvious to the tongue.

The broth must be made well in advance, as it has to be frozen soon after its 5 hours in the pan and then defrosted overnight in the fridge. This may seem a long process but once you've experienced the rewards and know what's in store, the next time will be a breeze. You will end up with more stock here than you need for this dish but it keeps well in the freezer. We cook haricot beans in it and use it to rehydrate dried morels (see page 72), amongst other things.

The only way to get perfect poached eggs is to use eggs as newly laid as possible. Within one or two days is best, so befriend someone with their own peep of chickens or consider aiding the commendable work of The British Hen Welfare Trust by rehoming some battery chickens yourself and having access to truly fresh eggs every day.

SERVES 4

4 very fresh organic eggs
cider vinegar
150g rainbow chard, cut
    horizontally into 2.5cm strips
1 lovage leaf, finely sliced
sea salt and black pepper
4 wild vetch tips or pea shoots, to
    garnish

FOR THE HAM HOCK BROTH:

1 ham hock
1 bay leaf
1 clove
1 star anise
2 peppercorns
2 coriander seeds
4 lovage seeds (or fennel seeds)
2 parsley stalks
100g onions, diced
50g carrot, diced
50g celeriac, diced

First make the broth. Wash the ham hock well under cold running water and place it in a large pan. Cover with cold water, bring to the boil, then immediately discard the water and rinse the hock once more. This will remove impurities that might cloud the stock later on. Put the hock back in the pan, fill with plenty of water, covering the hock completely, and bring back to a good rolling simmer. Add the bay leaf and spices and simmer for 2½ hours, regularly skimming off any impurities that rise to the surface. Top up with more water if necessary to keep the hock covered. Makes sure the stock is simmering well so the temperature is high enough to extract the gelatine from the meat.

After 2½ hours, add the vegetables and cook for another 2 hours, maintaining a healthy rolling simmer and topping up the liquid level as necessary. Reward your patience with a little snippet of the meltingly soft hock once it is removed from its cooking liquor. Worth the wait. Set the hock aside to cool a little and strain the stock through a fine sieve into a large baking tin – the wide surface area will allow it to cool rapidly. When the hock is cool enough to handle, prise the meat away from the bones and break it into manageable pieces. Lay these pieces out on a similar shallow tray to cool quickly, then cover and refrigerate.

You should have about 2 litres of stock. Freeze it in 4 tubs, then a day or two before you plan to make the soup, turn out 2 of the frozen blocks and wrap them in 2 layers of muslin. Place them in a sieve set over a bowl large enough to hold the thawed stock, then put them in the fridge. The gelatine, impurities and fat will stay solid in the muslin at fridge temperature, while the stock will run clear below. Resist the urge to squeeze the muslin; it will drain dry eventually. This technique yields about half the initial frozen weight of stock in finished clarified stock. In our experience this is a little too concentrated and will take about a third extra water.

The eggs can be poached in advance of serving. Bring a pan of water to a light simmer, then turn off the heat and leave for 2–3 minutes. The water can drop as low as 80°C and still cook the egg. Crack an egg on to a large slotted spoon and shake it gently so the watery albumen drains off and the tightly bound albumen remains on the spoon. Gently drop the egg into a ramekin and repeat with the remaining eggs, putting each one in a separate ramekin. Submerge the base of each ramekin in the hot water, then turn the ramekin over and tip out the egg. Let the eggs sit undisturbed for 3½–5 minutes, depending on size. The aim is to cook the white while keeping the yolk runny. Remove the eggs, using a slotted spoon, in the same order they went in and lower them into a bowl of iced water. This will stop the cooking. The eggs can be poached in advance and kept in the fridge for 2 days.

Commend yourself, as the building of the dish begins. Heat the broth through, diluting it to taste with about a third of its volume in water if necessary and seasoning with a splash of cider vinegar and some salt. To keep the broth clear, we recommend reheating the hock and cooking the chard separately in simmering water. Add the ham to a pan of salted water and cook at a gentle simmer for about a minute, then drain. Blanch the chard in the water for about 30 seconds, then drain well. If you have poached the eggs in advance, reheat them by bringing a pan of water to a simmer, removing it from the heat, then dropping the eggs in and leaving for 1 minute. Arrange the ham, chard and eggs in 4 bowls and garnish with the lovage leaf and a pinch of salt on each egg. Gently pour the hock broth over them, crack some black pepper over the dish and dress with the vetch tips or pea shoots.

Caerphilly and Cider Welsh Rabbit

This is a staple at The Ethicurean and the smell in the morning as the rabbit is made is intoxicating. Served alongside a pile of Mark's salad leaves, the flavours are acidic, sweet, salty, rich and, foremost, savoury. Many recipes call for the inclusion of stout or porter-style beers. Ours is very much a West Country affair and we choose Perry's Morgan Sweet cider on account of its sweet acidic fruitiness, but any good medium-sweet cider will suffice. Cider pairs very well with Caerphilly. While beer would dominate this cheese's citrusy and mushroomy earthiness, the cider sings in chorus.

The science behind using Caerphilly or a mature Cheddar is very straightforward: we don't want a stringy Welsh rabbit. Cheeses such as Emmental contain casein molecules that are linked by calcium, forming long fibres – essentially the string in stringy cheese. Gorwydd's citrus flavour indicates a high level of acidity, which removes some of the calcium. Its unctuous texture means a higher moisture content that will separate casein molecules. All in all, it's the perfect cheese for rarebit. Mature Cheddar is a good alternative. The ripening enzymes are rather partial to casein and they devour it, preventing any long, string-like fibres forming.

SERVES 6

a large, unsliced white tin loaf
100g very soft salted butter (or 100g beef dripping, melted)
150ml medium-sweet cider
100ml single cream
2 tbsp vintage cider vinegar, such as Ostler's
2 tbsp Worcestershire sauce
2 pinches of smoked paprika
250g Gorwydd Caerphilly (if you can't get Gorwydd, an aged Cheddar makes the best substitute), coarsely grated
2 egg yolks (omit if using Cheddar)

Heat the oven to 200°C/Gas Mark 6. Cut the ends off the white loaf and then divide the loaf into 6 slices. The thickness of the slices is one of the factors that makes this rabbit so perfect, with a crunchy exterior that gives way to a brilliantly soft, white interior. Using a pastry brush, lightly brush the very soft butter (or the melted dripping) on both sides of the bread. Put the slices on a baking sheet and bake for 8 minutes, turning them over half way through. Both sides should be very lightly golden. Leave on a wire rack to cool.

Put the cider, cream, vinegar, Worcestershire sauce and paprika in a non-stick saucepan, place over a medium heat and cook, stirring regularly, until the mixture has reduced to the consistency of double cream. It should be a deep shade of brown. Lower the heat and add the cheese and the egg yolks, if using. Stir until the cheese has melted, then whisk the sauce until very smooth and glossy. Leave to cool and thicken to a paste consistency.

Spread the mixture edge to edge on the toasted bread. Return them to the oven for 4 minutes, then place under a hot grill until evenly browned. Enjoy with a generous helping of dressed salad leaves. As the local Bristolians would say, 'Gert lush!'

† Resting between Lampeter and Aberystwyth on the Ceredigion coastline is Gorwydd farm, the place where one-time archaeologist Todd Trethowan developed his recipe. He began his cheese career after learning from the great West Country cheesemaker Chris Duckett. Finally he moved his camper van home during his 'cheese apprenticeship' and returned to the family farm to make Gorwydd Caerphilly. There are two distinct types of Caerphilly: the first and oldest was the cheese made by hand using excess milk that would have otherwise turned bad. It was a farmhouse cheese to be eaten after a day in the fields. The second brings us back to Somerset and to the Cheddar makers, who desired a quick-maturing cheese that would enable healthy cash-flow during the long maturation periods of their Cheddar.

SMOKING

Humans have always been drawn to the hypnotic and tranquil qualities of fire. There are few things that we love more than sitting around a fire with the closest of friends and family, putting the world to rights over a bottle of wine.

Fires mean smoke, and smoked food was perhaps a by-product of drying (see also curing, page 197), when food was hung over fires and allowed slowly to dry, thus preserving the meat from rotting. Nowadays foods that are to be smoked undergo a preliminary step of curing before being smoked. Smoking is used as an additional form of preservation but not an essential one. These days smoking is used for its application of flavour.

There are two methods: hot smoking and cold smoking. With the former, hot smoke from a fire is either directed into a sealed chamber that houses food, or a chamber can be directly placed over smoking logs. The main goal of hot smoking is to cook and pasteurise the meat. Temperatures inside the chambers used to house the food commonly reach 80–110°C.

Cold smoking, as the name suggests, uses cold smoke to flavour the food. Traditional methods use a sealed container with hooks from which to hang food; however, the heat source is separate. Usually the fire is housed in a separate chamber, joined to the food chamber via some piping. Smoke escapes from the fire box into the pipe and travels into the food chamber. The further the smoke travels, the more it cools on its journey.

The goal of cold smoking was originally to dry food. Giving microbes less water inhibits their growth. Foods used to be cold smoked for long periods of time, at temperatures somewhere around 20–30°C; however, this posed a large risk for the safety of food, as these are perfect conditions for microbial activity. Curing salts were often used to prevent this from happening. Thanks to the invention of the trusty fridge, the primary reason for cold smoking (preservation) is less important and we can now utilise it purely for the flavour it adds.

The point just *before* wood ignites is the perfect point for smoking food, as this is when the temperature is high enough to remove the more unpleasant elements that can be in the smoke. Wood smoking at cooler temperatures can often tarnish foods with an acrid, less favourable flavour. Any higher than this and the wood will ignite.

Smoking is a delicate balancing act, and takes skill and experience. If you have never experimented with smoking before, then we recommend trying a few of the techniques listed here. Be warned that it is an incredibly addictive hobby and once you begin to realise the variables and different methods, it can become an all-consuming obsession – something that Matthew and Iain know only too well. Since they started smoking whatever they could lay their hands on, there is often something smouldering away in the kitchen under close scrutiny. Iain can often be seen wielding a large blowtorch, with a slightly exhausted, manic look in his eye, while Matthew takes a few steps back, covering up his chest hair from the naked flame.

We will introduce you to a few basic smoking methods that are great for the home smoker, and we will highlight the pros and cons for each. There are entire books devoted to this vast and fascinating subject, and if these methods pique your interest we can strongly recommend purchasing one.

Tin can and soldering iron approach:

Jack has experimented a lot with this method. It is one of the easiest and most accessible to the home user; however, it does have its drawbacks. First, this has to be done outside. You need a tin can that is not lacquered on the inside: old condensed milk tins are perfect. Pack dry wood chips into the can and at the base of the can, on the side, make a small incision with a screwdriver – it should be large enough for the tip of a soldering iron. Place the tip of the soldering iron in the hole and turn on. Then put both the can and the iron in the base of a small Weber-style barbecue, with the barbecue shelf placed over the can. Point the can so that the opening is close to the wall of the barbecue and away from the meat. Place the food you want to smoke on the wire shelf, on the opposite side to the can, and pop on the lid. Close all of the vents on the barbecue. If you are smoking meat or fish, we recommend doing it in half-hour increments. You can check on the internal temperature of the barbecue with a thermometer. Take the meat out, try a little and see what you think. If you want more smoke then place back in for another 30 minutes.

Foods that need to be cooked before they can be eaten (raw meat, fish etc.) should never be smoked for more than four hours, but then it is very unlikely that small cuts of meat or fish will require this length of smoking in any case. If smoking these types of foods, place a large bowl of ice under the wire rack, on the opposite side to the can, directly under the foodstuff. This will cool the smoke down some more. If smoking for long periods of time, the chips in the tin can will need replacing every 6–8 hours to ensure you get the best from this technique.

Some people advocate the use of a combination of damp and dry wood chips, but we would strongly recommend, if using this method, that you use only dry chips. Even this method does not achieve high enough temperatures to burn the main carcinogenic components of smoke, and combining damp wood lowers the pyrolysis temperature (the temperature at which molecules in the wood are broken down) and results in even more acrid and acidic components flavouring the food.

If you are attempting this method, set up the barbecue close to a doorway or on a patio. The optimum time for smoking like this is during winter, as the cooler temperatures mean safer conditions. If smoking on a sunny day then keep well shaded. This is a fairly experimental approach, and one that not too many people know about. Considering how easy it is, we'd like to get people hooked on smoking through these basic techniques before encouraging further experimentation with some of the techniques overleaf.

Blowtorch and ice method:

Again, this is practical for the home smoker and allows plenty of scope for experimentation. In a small-to-medium-sized lidded roasting tray, place wood chips or sawdust on one side of the base. On the opposite side of the tray place a bowl of ice. Ignite the chips or dust thoroughly using a blowtorch. Culinary blowtorches will not cut the mustard on this one, as they do not give off enough heat; you will need a plumber's one (ask for a copper brazing torch at your local plumbing supplier). Be sure not to buy a torch that runs off MAPP Gas: these contain a dangerous type of fuel that is not suited for culinary use.

Start the wood smouldering before placing a wire rack on top, with the food on, then covering with the lid. Weigh down the lid if it does not form a tight seal and leave for 30 minutes. Remove from the smoker and test the food to see if it is smoky enough for your taste.

You can also use different types of wood for this method. The boys in the kitchen have experimented with smoking butter with fresh bay leaves. Not all of our experiments have been successful – in fact, some have been appalling, but you never know until you try. While this method does achieve a hotter temperature than the tin can, it is still not as effective at burning carcinogens and acrid components of smoke as some other, slightly more complex techniques.

Hot pan method:

Although this essentially hot smokes your food, you could try combining it with the previous technique – it saves buying a blowtorch. Heat up a large pan until smoking hot. Add a thin layer of wood chips and get them smoking too. Decant the chips into one end of a lidded roasting tray, with a bowl of ice at the other end. Following the remaining steps for the previous method.

Smoke gun method:

A smoke gun is a hand-held device that houses a small chamber, similar to that of a smoking pipe, and contains a fan. You load the chamber with sawdust or wood chips, light them, and then turn the fan on. The fan pulls air through the chamber and feeds oxygen to the fire. Coming out of the smoke gun is a rubber tube that allows you to direct where you want the smoke to go. This method, for the home user, is incredibly effective. Pack the base of the chamber with sawdust and light until smouldering. When smouldering, top with wood chips of your choice and light the wood chips. While you do this, turn the fan on. The smoke from the wood passes through a hot base layer of sawdust that burns any acrid components of the smoke. What you are left with is essentially 'good smoke' that will flavour your food in a positive way. The only company we know of that manufactures a smoke gun is PolyScience. Smoke guns retail around the £50 mark and are available online.

Ultimately, experimenting with food and techniques should be fun. The carcinogenic nature of smoke, however it comes, is not healthy to human beings, so we advise taking care and limiting the amounts of smoked foods you eat. That said, some truly spectacular flavours can be achieved, and as always, we urge you to get creative, learn the basics and then play. You may just stumble across a combination or technique that shapes the future of cooking.

Smoked Chipotle Chillies

The chipotle chilli is a jalapeño that has been left to ripen on the plant; it is then smoked and dried. We all developed a love for this chilli through Paûla who regularly receives dried packages of them from Mexico. Her grandmother's chipotle pickle is absolutely incredible. We smoke the whole chillies with the seeds in, but you can take them out if you prefer a milder sauce.

20 jalapeño chillies (or any type of
    ripe chilli)

We recommend using about 1.5kg of fine wood chips – oak or apple are good, but avoid resinous woods as they will taint the flavour.

When you are ready to smoke, begin by washing the jalapeños. Follow the instructions for the tin can and soldering iron smoking method on page 85. Arrange the jalapeños on the opposite side to the smoking can and then close the barbecue lid. Ideally you want to smoke the jalapeños for 16 hours until dark and crisp. Every few hours check the level of wood in the can and top up as appropriate. You can also finish drying the chillies in a fan oven on about 50°C with the door slightly ajar; fan-assisted ovens are perfect for this task. (Please consult operating instructions – disclaimer!)

Store the cooled smoked chillies in an airtight container in a cool, dry place. The chillies can be rehydrated in hot water; the flavour is very strong so little is needed.

Smoked Roe Deer Loin with Wild Rocket, Clamped Carrots, Honeyed Walnuts and Wood Sorrel

Curing the loin makes the most of this precious cut. We also cold smoke it, adding extra complexity to the end result. This stage can be left out if you prefer. Either way, you need to prepare the loin well in advance, as it has to sit in the cure for five days.

The oak chips impart a flavour that complements the black cardamom, a spice that tastes smoked because the pods are dried over open flames. The sweet walnuts balance the savoury meat. Wood sorrel grows in carpets on the woodland floor and has a citrus tang that adds acidity. It also grows in the deer's habitat, making it a very fitting addition indeed.

SERVES 4, WITH PLENTY OF SPARE
LOIN FOR THE LARDER
1 roe deer loin, weighing 1kg, silver
    membrane removed (ask your
    butcher to do this for you)
2 handfuls of oak chips for smoking
    (or use the smoke gun method
    on page 86)
200g wild rocket
a little cider vinegar
50g Honeyed Walnuts (see page 16)
2 tablespoons wood sorrel (or
    cultivated sorrel)
½ tsp finely chopped crushed
    juniper berries

FOR THE CURE:
6 star anise
6 black cardamom pods
2 tbsp juniper berries
1 tbsp black peppercorns
35g fine sea salt
15g dark muscovado sugar

Blitz all the ingredients for the cure together in a food processor or spice grinder. Lay the roe loin on a large piece of cling film, cover with the cure mixture and rub it in thoroughly, leaving it in an even coating. Tightly wrap the loin in the cling film and place in the fridge for 5 days, turning it every day or so.

Remove the loin from the cure mix and rinse under a cold tap, making sure you wash off all the spices. Hang the meat in a warm, well-ventilated area (a warm part of the kitchen or in the airing cupboard will do) for 12 hours or until it is completely dry to the touch – a temperature of 25°C is ideal, so adjust the time you hang the meat accordingly.

In the meantime, prepare your smoking box following the Blowtorch and Ice method on page 86.

Place the oak chips to one side of the baking tray. On the opposite side, place a bowl of ice with a wire rack stood directly above it. Place the loin on the rack. Using a blowtorch, heat the chips, stirring with a metal spoon to heat them evenly. When the chips are properly on fire, cover with the foil and weight down to prevent smoke escaping. Leave for 30 minutes. The time that the loin sits in smoke is a variable that can be played with. If you prefer a smokier flavour, then repeat the process with fresh wood chips. Once you have smoked the meat to your satisfaction, remove from the smoker and chill until needed.

For the carrot and black cardamom purée, half fill a pan with water, add the cardamom pods and bring to a simmer. Put the

FOR THE CARROT AND BLACK
CARDAMOM PURÉE:

4 black cardamom pods (seek
    these out in Asian supermarkets,
    as the smokiness is very valuable
    to the chef)
200g carrots (for clamped carrots,
    see opposite), sliced
1–2 tbsp honey
sea salt

carrots in a steamer basket, place on top of the pan, then cover
and steam for 35 minutes, until the carrots are very tender
indeed. Purée in a blender or food processor. Mix in the honey
and salt to taste, remembering that this is the sweet component
of this dish. Thin the purée with a little of the steaming liquor
and blend again to give a velvety texture. Leave to cool, then
chill until required.

Slice the roe loin finely at an angle to maximise the length of
slice. Dress the rocket in cider vinegar alone; the carrot purée
will provide ample moisture and sweetness, so no oil is required.
Place the rocket on 4 serving plates and arrange the roe loin,
walnuts and sorrel on top, then dot teaspoons of the smoked and
honeyed carrot purée throughout. Sprinkle the juniper berries
on top to finish this saporific dish.

WOOD SORREL

Oxalis Acetosella; Old English *Alleluia*. This delicate-looking plant has a heart-shaped leaf with
a fold down the centre; these cordate leaves occur in groups of three. Flowers appear around
April to May; they are lilac coloured with darker veins of the same colour. As the sun disappears
wood sorrel's amorous leaves fold together to make a small tent shape. At first light they open
once again. We are lucky to have several good spots in the West Country where wood sorrel can
be found: moist and shady places in, typically, deciduous woods. Wood sorrel likes to shelter
under moss and bracken, or the odd fallen log. It is almost lemon in flavour and the oxalic acid
it contains has the effect of stimulating the salivatory glands. Do not pick the root but make sure
you eat the whole stalk as we believe it to be better tasting than the leaf itself.

CLAMPED VEGETABLES

Clamping is an age-old method of preservation. It saves the autumn crop of root vegetables and has the benefit of increasing flavour and nutrient content. As an example, carrots will increase their vitamin A during six months of storing away from heat and light. Chefs are ever so fond of these clamped roots for two reasons. The increase in flavour and sweetness is obvious, but most importantly they have vegetables to make valuable stocks through the months of February to May.

To clamp carrots, beetroots, parsnips, turnips, swede, celeriac, kohlrabi or potatoes a few important steps need be followed. You will need a frost-free shed or concrete floored garage, some wooden trays and a good quantity of damp sand. Harvest by carefully forking up the roots on a dry day in October. Pick out the larger, thick-cored and unblemished roots and trim back only the leaves. In the case of beetroot, twist the leaves rather than cut to prevent 'bleeding' and don't cut back any green carrot tops as they need to remain whole. Remove any soil (rubbing with sand is effective) and send any damaged or broken specimens to the kitchen post-haste. Lay sand into the wooden tray and place the roots in layers, tessellating but not touching. Cover with sand and repeat until all are stored. Uncover the roots as needed, taking care to cover any remaining ones again. A certain amount of carrots can be left in the ground until spring prompts their growth again but there is often the risk they may turn woody and crack. If your crop warrants leaving in the ground then cover well with straw to ease their lifting during frosts. Given the benefits for flavour and mineral content, clamping is the better option.

HUNTING DEER WITH ALAN

We regularly stalk with our friend Alan. He is a horticulturist, a country man: he reads the landscape and whispers the names of the things that grow, crawl, run and sing. He has a wonderfully clipped accent. 'Jack!' he will say. 'Let's concentrate on the first course, shall we?', as the sight of St George's mushrooms often causes distractions on a spring stalk.

Deer are most active during dawn and dusk, meaning early starts and late finishes for the stalker. Mornings provide a crystalline beauty as we walk through the last few frosts of the year. Evenings give us ethereal sunsets and the chance to watch the land settle down for the night. All the deer in our area are roe. They are a native British species (Old English *Raha*) and are spread widely across Britain. Particularly in the south of England these deer were thought to have been all but wiped out during the Middle Ages. They are found predominantly in small groups or alone, although larger groups will feed together during the winter months. Roe will feed on berries, leaves, grass and young shoots. They particularly like young bramble shoots and newly coppiced woodland.

Even in the failing light Alan's grin is perceptible. He nods to the silhouette of a roe buck as it traces the skyline with its pin-like legs, its ears flicking independently. We must wait for it to disappear over the brow of the hill, hoping that it will provide a clear shot with a safe backstop on the other side. At this time roe deer look pretty scruffy, their winter pelage is giving way to their summer coat of chestnut red. Merlin the labrador is unconcerned by our potential quarry, preferring to push her large head into the nearest palm for a scratch.

The roe buck has stepped down from the skyline and has presented itself broadside with a safe backstop for a shot. From our position, bodies pressed against the ground, we can see the buck lean forward and taste the air, its lips seeking a warning scent. Alan stops for an instant, takes aim and slips the safety catch back. Before the buck has a chance to turn there is a bang and it falls to the ground.

Curd Cheese, Cucumber, Flat Bean, Aniseed and Sesame

According to the British Cucumber Growers Association, if all the cucumbers grown in the British season were laid end to end, they would go almost right round the world. Yet despite the great number available to us, as with a lot of fruit and vegetables, most cucumbers are flown in from Europe or beyond. It seems a shame when the reality is that they are relatively easy to grow in the UK. Having said that, growing cucumbers commercially takes a lot of skill. The crops are susceptible to damage from pests, making them difficult to grow organically. The organic cucumbers we get come from The Community Farm, where the team ensures that we are rarely short of seasonal produce. Their location in Chew Magna, just 7 miles away, is very good news for us.

Other than a quick cucumber pickle and a dressing, this salad is made to order, highlighting the way fresh produce at its best marks the start of a productive summer. Here we make use of cucumber and flat beans, both of which grow splendidly early in our glasshouses. These will be available for those growing outdoors in late spring to early summer. The aniseed dressing works harmoniously with the juicy cucumber and delightfully sweet flat beans.

SERVES 4

100g flat beans, chopped

1 tsp sesame seeds

3 young cucumbers

1 tsp aniseed (or fennel seeds)

100ml cider vinegar

100g caster sugar

8 tbsp ewe's curd (or goat's curd or a fresh young cheese)

50g cheese rind, the older and drier the better, finely grated (the rind of unwaxed ewe's milk cheese is ideal)

fine sea salt

12 borage flowers and a few watercress leaves, to garnish

FOR THE WATERCRESS DRESSING:

70ml buttermilk (if unavailable, stir 1 tsp vinegar into 65ml milk and leave for 5 minutes)

35g mayonnaise (see Paprika Mayonnaise on page 96 if you would like to make it from scratch, omitting the paprika)

Blanch the flat beans in fast-boiling salted water for 2 minutes, until just tender, then drain and leave in iced water. Toast the sesame seeds in a dry frying pan till they turn golden, then tip them out of the pan on to a plate to prevent burning. Cut one cucumber into 5mm dice and sprinkle liberally with salt. Leave to drain in a sieve for 20–30 minutes to give the finished pickle a crunch. Heat the aniseed in a dry pan till it spits and crackles. Take the pan off the heat, carefully add the vinegar and then stir in the sugar until dissolved. Allow this to cool somewhat while you rinse the salt from the cubed cucumber. Put the cubes in a bowl and cover with the warm vinegar mixture. Leave to cool. This will keep in the fridge for 5 days should you choose to make it in advance.

To make the dressing, put all the ingredients in a blender, keeping back a few of the watercress stalks, and pulse until the stalks are very finely chopped. The mixture should be no thicker than single cream and a beautiful pale green colour. Taste and add more of the stalks should you want to increase that fresh green pepper taste from the mustard oil within. Season with salt and set aside.

Trim the ends and 2 long sides from the other 2 cucumbers and peel into strips with a Y-shaped vegetable peeler – or on a mandoline should you want super-tidy slices. Lay these on each

a bunch of watercress stalks
mustard powder
sea salt

serving plate, curling the strips over, and dress with a little fine
sea salt. Spoon scoops of ewe's curd and roll them in the grated
cheese rind. Place these amongst the strips of cucumber. Add
a few cubes of pickled cucumber and a teaspoon of the aniseed
marinade to each plate. Scatter the flat beans over the plates
and then spoon over the watercress dressing. Finish with the
delicate blue borage flowers, a few small watercress leaves and
the toasted sesame seeds. Marvellous colours and tidy on the
taste buds.

Crab Salad with New Potatoes, Pickled Carrot and Smoked Paprika Mayonnaise

We have often wondered why crabmeat is not more popular in Britain nowadays. Most crab caught in British waters is sent straight to Europe, where it is in high demand. Perhaps we simply don't know how to cook them, less still how to eat them. Admittedly, preparing a whole crab takes practice and can be a messy and time-consuming affair. However, if you surround yourself with a group of friends, furnish yourselves with a good loaf of bread and a couple of beverages, preferably of the alcoholic variety, you will see how much fun it is to practise. The native brown crab is delicious and the spider crab ranks higher than lobster in taste for many, us included. It is truly adored in Spain, commanding the highest shellfish prices. If you need more good reasons to eat British crabmeat, remember that it is relatively inexpensive and has better sustainability credentials than most fish you find in the supermarket.

The quantities given for the smoked paprika mayonnaise make more than you need for this recipe but it is very versatile. Serve it with other salads, smoked fish and as a general substitute for bought mayonnaise. We guarantee that it tops anything you can buy in a shop.

SERVES 4

200g new potatoes, scrubbed clean and cut into 5cm chunks

1 live brown crab or 2 live spider crabs

200g spring salad leaves

80ml The Ethicurean Salad Dressing (see page 298)

a few pinches of ground mace

bronze dill or fennel fronds

100g Pickled Carrots (see page 299)

a few edible flowers (optional)

FOR THE SMOKED PAPRIKA MAYONNAISE:

1 large free-range egg yolk

½ tbsp honey

½ tbsp Dijon mustard

½ tbsp smoked paprika

1 tsp fine sea salt

about 450ml rapeseed oil

1 tbsp cider vinegar

First make the mayonnaise. Using a stick blender, electric whisk or freestanding electric mixer, combine the egg yolk, honey, mustard, paprika and salt. Whisk on full speed for 30 seconds or until smooth. With the whisk or blender running on full speed, very slowly start adding the oil. After a third of the oil has been mixed in, add the vinegar, then continue in the same fashion with the rest of the oil. Be sure to pour in a very fine, steady stream to begin with; if you add too much oil early on, the mayonnaise will split. As the oil is being incorporated, the mayonnaise should start to thicken to a thick, orangey-red emulsion (you may not need all the oil). Check the taste and season with more salt and vinegar, if necessary.

Cook the potatoes in boiling salted water until tender, then drain and leave to cool.

Cook and prepare the crabs as described overleaf. Place some of the salad leaves on 4 serving plates with the potatoes. Add more leaves, intertwining them with the crabmeat. Dress each layer as you go with salad dressing, while trying to maintain height in the dish to keep it looking attractive. The claws of the crab look great when extracted whole, so combine these with the flaked white crab meat for extra visual appeal. Spoon on as much of the smoked paprika mayonnaise as you wish, then finish with a few pinches of mace, the bronze dill or fennel fronds, pickled carrots and any edible flowers you may have. Serve immediately.

PREPARING CRAB

How to cook a crab

The first step in cooking a crab is knowing how to kill it humanely. Our head chef, Matthew, who worked for many years as a fishmonger, is convinced that the only way to do this is to put the crab in the freezer for 2 hours or so first. The effect is to numb the crab and ensure that the pain is minimised when it is killed. When you take the crab out of the freezer, turn it on its back, lift the tail away and locate the dimple right in its centre. Take a sharp skewer or other sharp, thin implement and push it through the dimple, then, as it meets the top shell, move it from side to side. Do the same between the crab's eyes, pushing the skewer through and easing it from side to side.

The crab should be cooked immediately after killing. It will need 15 minutes per kilogram in a large pan of well-salted boiling water – we allow a tablespoon of salt per litre. If you are cooking two crabs, calculate the time based on their individual rather than combined weight.

How to prepare a cooked crab

1. Turn the crab on its back and twist off its legs and claws.

2. Separate the top shell from the bottom shell by placing your finger under the top of its tail. Pull both shells apart, using a heavy spoon to crack along the line that is there if it doesn't come away easily.

3. Now, don't be put off by what you see when the shell is fully open. You will need to do a bit of tidying up before you are able to appreciate the full potential of this crustacean. Start by getting rid of the pointy, grey pieces of meat in the shell (called dead man's fingers) and the bony bits. These are all inedible. You will need to remove the stomach sac just behind the eyes and mouth too. The creamy brown meat to either side of the head is, for some, the tastiest and most supremely edible, so don't discard it.

4. Using a skewer or some tweezers, you now need to remove the white meat from the middle part of the body. This is where the first glass of your beverage of choice will come in handy, as the process does take some time. So pour yourself a drink and start by cutting the body in two so it is easier to access the meat inside. Carefully remove all the white meat from the shell. What makes this task quite laborious is that some of the desirable white meat is attached to hard, bony sections and it is difficult to differentiate between the two. Be patient.

5. Finally, crack the claws open. DIY tools will probably be more effective than kitchen utensils here – a small hammer works well, or you could try the back of a heavy knife. Extract as much white meat as possible with your tweezers or skewer and don't forget to open the whole of the claw. There is much precious meat in the lower parts of the claw, which is often forgotten about. Do the same with the legs. With practice, the whole process will take you less and less time, and, we guarantee, it will never cease to be enjoyable.

Spring Radishes with Anchovy Crème Fraîche

This simple anchovy dip pairs beautifully with fresh radishes. We like to sit around eating this in the garden on a sunny spring evening, while drinking a glass of Limney (a fantastic organic wine produced in Sussex) and enjoying the first real warmth of the year. What's great about radishes is that as the weather begins to warm, so does their inherent fiery-pepperiness.

SERVES 4–6
2 bunches of radishes

FOR THE ANCHOVY CRÈME FRAÎCHE:
a little rapeseed or groundnut oil
1 spring onion, finely sliced
1 head of wet garlic, finely sliced (or
   2 cloves of dried garlic)
35g marinated white anchovy
   fillets, finely chopped
75ml crème fraîche
sea salt and black pepper

Heat a splash of oil in a small frying pan, add the spring onion and garlic and fry over a medium heat until soft. Add the anchovies and cook for a couple more minutes. Transfer the mixture to a small bowl and leave to cool. Stir in the crème fraîche and season to taste.

Thoroughly clean the radishes and their leaves, keeping the leaves attached. Holding the leaves allows you to dip the radishes into the anchovy sauce, before biting them clean off their greenery. There are few simpler or more delicious ways to enjoy these peppery delights.

Trout with Kelp and Shiitake Mushroom Stock, Rice, Flat Beans and Sea Kale

Finding the best local ingredients is one of the most rewarding tasks for us at The Ethicurean. So we were delighted when Tessa Tricks, part of the Ethicurean family, described how committed her father was to fishing in the local area. Her family's freezer, we were informed, was always up to maximum capacity with rainbow or brown trout, caught in the nearby Chew Valley or Blagdon Lakes. It was no surprise to hear that they referred to trout as 'the Trick's family currency'. Charlie Tricks started fishing at the age of 10 in the River Yeo. He now prefers to fish at the banks of the lake, as he can move around and choose his spot. Bank fishing is more of a challenge but this adds to the excitement when you do eventually succeed in catching something worth cooking.

The Tricks eat trout at least once a week and have developed an impressive catalogue of recipes over the years. It was our task to offer them something new that would fit with our menu. This recipe requires two Japanese-style stocks, which need preparing a day in advance. Unlike European stocks, which often require long cooking, Japanese stocks are quick, lukewarm-water preparations that use umami-rich ingredients such as mushrooms, dried fish and seaweeds (see page 123 for more about 'umami'). The simplicity, freshness and seasonality of Japanese food are qualities that we often try to replicate. Kelp is frequently used in Japanese stocks and in this instance we used native kelp, dried in a very low oven. You should be able to find kelp, labelled as kombu, in oriental markets and healthfood stores.

When Charlie and his family tried this dish, we worried that the delicate ingredients accompanying the fish would not stand up to it, but the table was alive with talk of ribonucleotides in mushrooms, guanylate compounds in umami, and seaweed stocks. By the end of their dinner, the Tricks were committed to attempting brining at home.

SERVES 4

300g basmati rice

40g sea salt

1 rainbow trout, weighing 800g–1kg
    filleted, with pin bones removed

6 tbsp mirin (rice wine)

100g onions, finely diced

50g celeriac, finely diced

50g white mushrooms, finely diced

2 star anise

1 tsp fennel seeds

200g flat beans, trimmed and cut
    into 2cm slices

500g sea kale (or kale), stalks
    removed, cut into 3cm strips

First prepare the stocks (see ingredients overleaf). For the mushroom stock, wash the dried shiitake, then soak in 600ml cold water overnight in a glass or metal bowl. Don't worry if your kitchen smells as if there is a gas leak; the pungent shiitake will be the cause. The following day, strain the stock through a piece of muslin and chill.

Rinse the dried kelp of any sand or residue in a bowl of cold water. Be brief, so as not to lose its concentrated flavour. Put 1.2 litres water in a saucepan, set it over a low heat and look out for tiny bubbles appearing on the base of the pan. Turn off the heat, add the kelp, then cover the pan and leave for an hour, switching the heat on again for 3 minutes half way through to maintain the temperature. If you have a thermometer, the temperature should hold close to 60°C. Anything higher will release sulphur compounds, iodine and aldehydes from the kelp, which will taint the sweet and delicate stock. Strain the stock through muslin, leave to cool, then chill.

FOR THE MUSHROOM STOCK:
50g dried whole shiitake
    mushrooms (the ready-sliced
    dried ones are much stronger,
    so reduce to 10g if that is what
    you have)

FOR THE KELP STOCK:
20g dried kelp (kombu)

Combine the 2 stocks, then measure out 750ml. Set both portions of stock aside.

Wash the rice in a sieve under plenty of cold running water. The aim is to remove all the starch, so keep going until the water runs completely clear. This may take 10 minutes or more but gives perfect rice every time if this step is followed. Stir the rice, rubbing it gently with your fingertips to loosen any remaining starch, then leave to drain. Basmati will absorb one and a quarter times its weight in water during cooking. Even if you don't possess a rice steamer, beautiful fluffy rice can be achieved with a saucepan and well-fitting lid. Put the drained rice into a fairly wide pan, add 375ml water, then cover and set aside.

To make a brine, add the 40g sea salt to the 750ml mixed stock and stir until it has dissolved. Cut the trout fillets into 4 even portions per side. Add these to the brine and refrigerate for precisely 20 minutes, then drain. In the meantime, heat the remaining stock to a simmer and then taste it. It will be ever so subtle and delicate but your tongue will register something specific, something complex yet hard to pin down. The elusive umami taste, the essence of Japanese cooking is present, yet very delicate. Add the mirin and then add salt, a pinch at a time. Taste again and notice how the sweetness and salt have added depth. Season gradually until you are pleased with the balance.

Put the pan of rice over a high heat and watch for it to come to the boil. The moment it does, add a teaspoon of salt and stir. Cover the pan tightly and reduce the heat to low. Cook for 10 minutes, resisting the temptation to peer into the pan. The idea is to try to mimic a rice steamer, so the steam needs to be trapped by the lid. After 10 minutes, turn the heat off but leave the lid on for a further 10 minutes. Continue to resist the temptation to peer in!

Heat the oven to 120°C/Gas Mark ½. Boil a kettle and pour the water into a deep baking tray to a depth that will cover the fish fillets comfortably. Add the onions, celeriac, mushrooms, star anise, fennel seeds and the drained fish fillets. Place in the oven and leave for 10 minutes.

Blanch the flat beans in a pan of boiling salted water for 2 minutes and the sea kale in a separate pan for 1 minute, then drain. Run a fork over the rice to loosen the perfectly cooked fluffy grains, then divide it between 4 serving bowls and arrange the greens around it. The fish will be delicately poached by this point. Put the fish fillets on top of the rice and pour the clear stock around the outside. A five-stage palate pleaser for certain.

FRESHWATER FISH

Being island-dwellers, we have been exposed to more waterways than many other places around the world and we have had the time and opportunity to develop better fishing practices. In recent years, freshwater fish has been labelled as having an unsavoury muddy quality to it. This is not a totally unfounded comment, especially if the fish comes from high silt content waters that are relatively stagnant. Given the strain that the fishing industry is imposing on the marine environment though, freshwater fishing is a good sustainable alternative. Moreover, not all freshwater fish taste muddy. Trout in season, for example, does not. If caught shortly before or after its breeding period, the fish are full of milt or eggs, which will make them deceptively larger in appearance and contribute to that 'muddy' or 'gritty' taste. Be warned.

We like the fact that the trout we have on our menu comes from a man who has been fishing in the local area for over 50 years. We are convinced that his experience and knowledge trickles down in some form or other and leads to a better dish. When we asked him how fishing in the local area had changed over the years, he believed the biggest difference to be in the fly variation. Forty years ago, large numbers of big red sedge flies, which the trout devoured, were commonly seen in midsummer. Nowadays, sedges are much smaller so the trout is more difficult to entice. No doubt, this adds to the challenge and makes it even more worthwhile to get a catch.

Goat Meatballs, Mash, Lovage Butter and Mustard Greens

Before we found the Walled Garden, we usually ate goat's meat only at St Paul's Carnival in the centre of Bristol. The rule was that we would locate the stalls with the longest queues and devour as many Caribbean curries as necessary in our quest to find the best. It was at this calypso-infused event that we had our annual intake of succulent goat's meat.

Goat's meat was commonplace in the UK until the mid-seventeenth century. Now most of it is imported from eastern Europe, off the back of the dairy industry there, and is rarely free range. The meat is certainly flavoursome but it tends to be tough, which means that slow cooking is essential. From an ethical point of view, using what would otherwise be a by-product of the dairy industry makes perfect sense. Many farmers see the male kids as a drain on their resources. Once they are born, they serve no purpose, so they have to be killed. This seems a terrible waste considering the energy devoted to breeding them. Our goat's meat supplier is Cabrito, based near Wellington (see also our Cheeseboard, pages 280–3). It does not breed goats specifically to sell on. Instead, it buys the billies from small-scale farmers, raises them as free-range meat and sells them to restaurants. It's worth asking your local butcher whether they can track down some British goat's meat. We have no doubt that it will begin to become more popular and more easily available soon. It would be fantastic if, in 50 years time, a food historian wrote of the return of goat's meat to the British diet in the first part of the twenty-first century.

The response we have had from customers to this dish has been overwhelming, though not surprising: the meat is succulent and sweet; it is high in protein and iron and contains less fat than pork, beef or lamb. We find that most people are intrigued by these meatballs and want to know more about goat's meat.

SERVES 4

50g bread
1½ tsp salt
1 tsp lovage seeds (if not available, omit the salt and use 1½ tsp celery salt)
1 tsp coarsely ground black pepper
½ tsp dried chilli flakes
1 tsp cumin seeds
550g goat's meat, finely minced
1 large egg, lightly beaten
rapeseed oil
50g onion, finely diced
25g carrot, sliced into half moons
25g celeriac, finely diced
250ml brown chicken stock (see page 296)
200ml medium-sweet cider
a bunch of large mustard greens, cut into strips 2–3cm wide

Heat the oven to 180°C/Gas Mark 4. Blitz the bread, salt and spices in a blender or food processor to make fine crumbs. Put them in a bowl, add the minced goat's meat and egg and mix thoroughly. Divide the mixture into 12 and shape into balls. It helps to rub a little cooking oil on to your hands to stop the meat sticking.

Heat a little rapeseed oil in a small saucepan, add the onion, carrot and celeriac, then cover and sweat over a low-medium heat until the vegetables are beginning to soften. Remove from the heat and set aside.

Put the meatballs in a deep baking tin in which they just fit in a single layer. Pour over the chicken stock and cider and add the softened vegetables. Cover with foil, place in the oven and roast for 30 minutes. Take off the foil and roast for 10 minutes longer, until the meatballs are nut brown in colour where they sit above the liquid.

Meanwhile, make the lovage butter: put the stock, lovage seeds and wine in a saucepan and boil until reduced by two-thirds its

½ tsp English mustard

Valor Potato Mash (see page 38),
   to serve

sea salt

FOR THE LOVAGE BUTTER:

100ml brown chicken stock (see
   page 296)

2 tsp lovage seeds (or a handful of
   lovage leaves)

75ml white wine

3 egg yolks

185g cold unsalted butter, cut into
   1cm cubes

a dash of vintage cider vinegar, such
   as Ostler's

volume (if using fresh lovage, add it after the liquid has reduced and leave to infuse for 20 minutes). Strain the mixture through a fine sieve into a heatproof bowl and allow to cool slightly. Whisk in the egg yolks. Place the bowl over a pan of simmering water, making sure the water does not touch the base of the bowl. Whisk until the mixture becomes thick and airy. At this point, start whisking in the butter, one cube at a time, waiting until it has completely melted before adding the next piece. After a few pieces of butter have been added, you can start adding 2 or 3 cubes at a time. The more butter you incorporate, the more you can add each time. Season to taste with sea salt and a dash of cider vinegar if you wish.

Place a frying pan over a medium heat. When it is hot, add a film of rapeseed oil, followed by the mustard greens, mustard and salt to taste. Cook, stirring frequently, until the leaves have wilted.

Serve the meatballs immediately with the mash, wilted greens and lovage butter.

† When we researched the eating of goat meat in this country, we found that it was commonplace until about 1650. Lucius Columella, the prominent Roman agricultural writer, recommended that even sick goats would be fit for human consumption if they were salted and dry cured. In the Elizabethan era, the physician Thomas Moufet maintained that old goats should be eaten by tenderising them. By contrast, roast kid was a favourite seventeenth-century springtime dish. In the eighteenth century, the Welsh naturalist Thomas

Pennant reported that kids were a 'cheap and plentiful provision in the winter months', while dried and salted goat haunches, known as 'hung venison', were eaten instead of bacon. In his book of British zoology, he claimed: 'This makes an excellent pasty; goes under the name of rock venison, and is little inferior to that of deer. Thus nature provides even on the tops of high and craggy mountains, not only necessaries but delicacies for the inhabitants' (*British Zoology*, 1776).

Ox Tongue with Swede, Parsley and Cider Vinegar

Tongue should be regarded unsqueamishly as an excellent cut of meat, suitable for use in a diverse range of dishes. In Victorian times, it certainly would have made an appearance on the cold table. One combination that dates back to the fourteenth century, described by Dorothy Hartley as 'always popular with the menfolk', was a rich, thick and creamy mustard sauce poured over slices of ox tongue.

This recipe and the following one require you to brine your own tongue. Patience really is a virtue in this case: a week of brining, followed by a comparatively short time in the pot and you are left with a delicious piece of meat. Tongue is great in salads, in a sandwich or roasted with vegetables. We could go on.

SERVES 4, WITH LEFTOVERS
1 ox tongue
200g swede, peeled and cut into
   2.5cm cubes
5 star anise
50ml double cream
a bunch of radishes, finely sliced
50g flat-leaf parsley leaves
rapeseed oil
a little cider vinegar
sea salt
smoked sea salt, to serve (optional)

FOR THE BRINE:
200g caster sugar
300g sea salt
6 juniper berries
3 cloves
3 star anise
6 black peppercorns
6 lovage seeds (or fennel seeds)
2 bay leaves

FOR COOKING THE TONGUE:
100g onion, finely diced
50g carrot, finely diced
50g celeriac or celery, finely diced
10 parsley stalks
2 bay leaves
10 peppercorns
4 star anise
2 cloves

Put all the ingredients for the brine in a large saucepan, add 2 litres of water and bring to the boil, stirring occasionally to dissolve the sugar and salt. Remove from the heat and leave to cool, then place in the fridge and chill until the temperature is below 5°C. Put the tongue in the brine and weight it down with a non-reactive item – something wooden, plastic or ceramic will do the trick. Make sure the tongue is completely submerged. Cover and leave in the fridge for a week.

Drain and rinse the tongue, then put it in a large saucepan with 2 litres of water and all the ingredients listed for cooking the tongue. Bring to a simmer, cover and cook very gently for 4 hours, checking the water level hourly and topping it up as necessary. Remove the tongue from its cooking liquor and leave until cool enough to handle, then peel it. It is important to peel it while it is still warm, otherwise the fats solidify, making this task much more difficult.

To cook the swede, place the star anise in a saucepan a quarter full of water and set a steamer basket over the top. Bring to a simmer. Place the swede in the basket, cover and steam for 35–40 minutes, until tender. Transfer the swede to a blender or food processor, add the cream and blitz until completely smooth. Season with salt and leave to cool.

Thinly slice about 200g of the tongue. Spoon the swede purée on to 4 serving plates and top with the tongue, sliced radishes and parsley. Lightly drizzle a little rapeseed oil over the parsley and finally add a few splashes of cider vinegar and a sprinkling of smoked salt, if you have it.

† In England the use of oxen, castrated males, both for draft, pulling carts and ploughing, and for beef, was once general practice. Four pairs of oxen would pull a plough, each animal aged with a year between. Staggering the pairs meant that each year, two would be fattened for beef and sold, thus paying their way. The Enclosures Acts of the late eighteenth and early nineteenth centuries, which reduced field sizes, hastened the end of the ox's use as the teams of eight needed enough space to turn at the end of each furrow. By the beginning of the twentieth century, the more high-maintenance horse was favoured for its speed and manoeuvrability, and eventually replaced the dependable ox. Today we are not eating the draft cattle that our ancestors would have known but in fact beef cattle and, in some cases, calves.

Ox Tongue with Cauliflower, Gilliflower and Hazelnuts

In her book *Food and Drink in Britain*, C. Anne Wilson refers to the practice of eating tongue with gilliflowers, more commonly known as carnations. They have a flavour that very closely resembles clove. This pairing has been all but forgotten about. Apparently if a witch tries to kill you, you should hand her a red carnation, as she will have to count the petals, giving you enough time to finish your ox tongue and gilliflower dinner and escape any nasty spells.

SERVES 4

1 cauliflower, divided into florets

2 tbsp plain flour

¼ tsp ground cloves

2 eggs, lightly beaten with a pinch of salt

30g butter

200g ox tongue, brined and cooked as in the recipe on page 108, then cut into 12 slices

50g hazelnuts, toasted in a dry frying pan and then dusted with ¼ tsp ground cinnamon

1 tablespoon roasted cobnut oil (or walnut oil)

FOR THE GILLIFLOWER SYRUP:

a bunch of organic carnations (be sure to use ones that haven't been sprayed)

100ml cider vinegar

100g icing sugar, plus 2 tbsp

You will need to prepare the gilliflower syrup a few days in advance. Cut the petals from 3 carnations and put them in a bowl. Cover with the cider vinegar and then stir in the 100g icing sugar. Weight down with a plate and set aside for 3 days at room temperature.

On the day you want to serve the salad, trim the petals from 2 flower heads, rinse them and spin dry in a salad spinner. Dry the petals on a tea towel to catch the last drops of moisture, preventing any flavour loss. Strain the gilliflower syrup and taste it. There will be notes of clove and pepper, though it may need sweetening a little further with icing sugar to mellow the vinegar. Set 2 tablespoons of the syrup aside, adding the 2 tablespoons of icing sugar to it. Reserve this to caramelise the ox tongue before serving.

Cook the cauliflower florets in lightly simmering salted water for about 10 minutes, until al dente. Drain, cool in ice-cold water and drain again very thoroughly. Mix the flour with the ground cloves. Dust the cauliflower florets in this mixture and then dip them into the beaten eggs. Heat the butter in a frying pan and fry the cauliflower in it in small batches till golden.

After frying the cauliflower, clean out the pan with kitchen paper and place it over a medium-high heat. Brush the ox tongue slices with the caramelising syrup and place in the hot pan. Cook, without moving them, until you can see them browning at the edges, then turn and colour the other side too.

Assemble the dish by arranging the cauliflower, ox tongue and petals on 4 serving plates. Drop the cinnamon-dusted hazelnuts on top and dress with the gilliflower syrup and roasted cobnut oil.

Salt Marsh Lamb with Tidal Greens

In England, the benefits of salt-marsh grazing have been known since the thirteenth century, yet for many years the vast majority of the meat has been exported to France, where it is recognised as a delicacy. In *English Food* (Michael Joseph, 1974), Jane Grigson wrote: 'People living around Romney Marsh ... have to look across at flocks of sheep feeding on the salt marshes, and know that the meat will bypass *their* butchers and be served to tourists in Normandy, Brittany and Paris, as *agneau pré-salé, specialité de la maison*, price to match.' However, salt marsh lamb is once again becoming available here. Farmers with coastal pasture bring their flock to the sea marshes in spring when the weather improves, so the sheep can graze close to the water's edge, feeding on sea vegetation such as samphire, sorrel, sea lavender and thrift.

We took a foraging course that ambled through the salt marsh on the Severn, where the lamb we buy for the restaurant graze. We learned about edible sea grasses, sea kale and sea beet and realised that we had some new greens to serve alongside this prime lamb shoulder. We also serve it with fat hen, a common plant, often considered to be a weed, which grows in gardens, roadside verges and hedgerows.

SERVES 6–8

1 tin of anchovies, drained

1 shoulder of salt marsh lamb, boned, weighing about 2kg

rapeseed oil

4 onions, cut into quarters

4 large carrots, peeled but left whole

4 spears of rosemary

a bunch of parsley

1 head of garlic, cut in half through its equator

200ml dry vermouth

1kg new potatoes

a knob of butter

a small bunch of mint, chopped

FOR THE SALT MARSH GREENS:

a bunch of sea arrow grass or Pickled Samphire (see page 190)

a bunch of sea arrow grass

a bunch of sea beet (can be replaced with spinach or kale)

a bunch of sea kale (can be replaced with purple sprouting broccoli)

a bunch of fat hen (can be replaced with spinach)

a knob of butter

Heat the oven to 160°C/Gas Mark 3. The first task is to get the anchovies into the meat: spike the lamb in several places with a small knife, working it under the top layer of the flesh laterally rather than downwards. Push the anchovy fillets into the incisions. They will dissolve during the long cooking process, seasoning the meat and negating the need to salt the joint further. Even if you are not keen on these rich, salty and umami fish fillets, we urge you not to omit them. The final flavour will not be of fish but of seasoned lamb.

Heat a thin film of rapeseed oil in a large, heavy-based frying pan, add the lamb shoulder and sear over a high heat until browned all over. Put the onions, carrots, rosemary, parsley and garlic in a roasting tin and place the lamb on top. Pour in the vermouth, cover with foil and place in the oven. Roast for 3½–4 hours, until you have a tender roast of the highest order. Remove from the oven and leave to rest for at least 20 minutes.

Scrub the potatoes and cut them so they are all roughly the same size as the smallest ones. Cook in boiling salted water until tender, then drain well and toss with a knob of butter and the mint.

Wash the greens and then blanch them whole in fast-boiling, well-salted water for 1 minute. Drain well and toss with a knob of butter. Serve the lamb with the greens and potatoes.

† At the restaurant, we usually source a breed called Suffolk Cross Charollois. The breed was first imported from France in 1976, originally from the town of Charolles in the Saône Loire region of France where it grazes alongside the famous Charollais Cattle. Our butcher buys our lamb from farms based on the banks of the River Severn near Frampton on Severn. They are slaughtered at Stonehouse, Gloucestershire and so have less than 5 food miles attributable to them. The wild sea plants on which our lamb feed are high in salt levels and iodine, making the muscle cells in the flesh retain more moisture. The meat is consequently sweeter, juicier and not as pink as mountain lamb.

Steamed Rabbit Pudding

Rabbit has historically been regarded as poor man's game. It was one of the only wild animals that commoners were allowed to hunt, the rest being reserved for the crown or the gentry. Today, people are sceptical about cooking with rabbit but it is undoubtedly growing in popularity. At The Ethicurean, we cook only wild rabbits, favouring their firm texture and gamey flavour. Much of the rabbit available in shops is farmed. Please avoid buying this, as it tends to be bland and altogether uninteresting. Instead ask your butcher to order you a young wild rabbit.

It is a good deal easier to identify the age of a rabbit that has the pelt (fur) still attached. An old, tough rabbit will have a scruffy, patchy coat, worn claws, tough ears and broken and damaged teeth. There is little to do with these in the kitchen but slow roast them. A young rabbit should have a glossy, healthy coat, good strong claws and pliable ears.

In this recipe we employ a great British tradition, the steamed suet pudding. Before sealing the rabbit in the pastry, we pressure-cook it whole in Morgan Sweet cider from the lower orchard. We have seen the odd apple drop and land on a rabbit's head. The irony is not lost on us.

SERVES 4

8 spring onions, outer layer and
    roots removed
1 rabbit, skinned, kidneys removed
1 bottle (330ml) Perry's Morgan
    Sweet cider, or other good sweet
    cider
5 sprigs of thyme
5 black peppercorns
sea salt

FOR THE SUET PASTRY:

300g self-raising flour
a pinch of salt
150g coarsely grated beef suet
butter for greasing

Place a griddle over a high heat and leave for a few minutes to get very hot. Add the spring onions and cook, turning occasionally, until they are charred and tender. Place them in a pressure cooker with the whole rabbit, cider, thyme and peppercorns. Attach the lid and place on the highest heat until it is at full pressure, then turn the heat down and cook for 1½ hours. Remove from the heat and leave to cool to room temperature before removing the lid. (If you don't have a pressure cooker, cook the rabbit in a covered pan over a low heat for 3 hours, checking the liquid level every hour or so and adding more cider if necessary.)

Take the rabbit out of the cooker, reserving the liquid. Thoroughly flake all the meat from the bones. Place the meat in a saucepan, strain the cooking liquid through wet muslin or a fine sieve and cook over a medium-high heat until the liquid has almost completely evaporated. Season with salt to taste.

To make the pastry, sift the flour into a bowl, add the salt and suet and mix well with a knife. Slowly add 200ml water, stirring it in to make a dough. Turn out on to a floured surface and knead lightly for a couple of minutes, then roll out to 5mm thick. Grease a 1.2 litre pudding basin well with butter, then line it with the suet pastry, reserving about a quarter for the lid. Fill the basin with the rabbit. Roll out the reserved pastry to fit the top of the basin, then put it over the filling and pinch the edges together. Trim off any excess pastry.

Take a piece of foil large enough to cover the top of the basin generously and fold a 2–3cm pleat in the centre to allow room for expansion. Cover the basin with the foil, tucking it under the rim to seal. Place on a wire stand inside the pressure cooker and add a couple of inches of water to the pan. Attach the lid to the pressure cooker and place over a high heat to bring it to full pressure. Reduce the heat and cook on full pressure for 1¼ hours. (Alternatively, you could steam the rabbit in a conventional steamer for 2½ hours.)

Remove from the heat and allow to cool a little, then turn the pudding out on to a large serving plate. Dive right in.

Pork, Juniper and Black IPA Pie

In Britain, the relationships between apples, beer, pork and pies are as old as the hills. There is much to celebrate on our little island and the pork pie should be worshipped, at the very least, once a week. A little smudge of mustard, a slice of pie balanced on the knee, with a good pause between each bite. This is a pie that must be eaten outdoors and helped on its way with a good best bitter or dry cider.

We must confess that the eccentricities of this recipe evolved from the great French tradition of making coarse pork terrines. We love juniper – its heady, resinous fragrance is the delight of gin drinkers, and it is truly at home with pork. The French – and the late, great Keith Floyd – would tumble in a claret, saving the last third of the bottle as a cook's perk and another to enjoy during baking. We forgo wine here for an India Pale Ale (IPA), and a black IPA at that. This isn't merely for patriotic effect but because of the wonderfully hopped nature of an IPA and the roasted, malty base that comes from the inclusion of dark malt. Moor Beer, based in Pitney in Somerset, makes a very good black IPA called Illusion. Justyn, the head brewer, refuses to add finnings to clear his beer, saying, 'Why would I want the swim bladders of fish in my pint purely for clarity?' He has a point. If you cannot find a black IPA, a good regular IPA will do very well indeed.

Even if you are unfamiliar with the name, hot-water crust pastry, you will undoubtedly have eaten it if you have ever indulged in a good pork pie. It is commonly used for making hand-raised pies and is an important part of Matthew and Iain's infamous 'pie offs'. The two are rarely competitive, but when it comes to hand-raising pork pies (rather than taking the easier option of making them in a mould, as below), we will often hear the words, 'It's on', from the kitchen – then deadly silence ensues while the two meticulously go about shaping their pies. Once the pies are in the oven, the banter and teasing begin: 'Waaah, your pie's definitely going to crack!' 'Whatever! Yours is so wonky it's not even gonna stand upright!' It is a pastry that contradicts traditional methods of pastry making, needing to be used warm so it can be shaped. Do not let this intimidate you – this is a very easy and fun pastry to work with.

† We do enjoy a splash of Somerset Cider Brandy in our pie. Julian Temperley has made a success of distilling cider, along with the help of his two continuous stills, Josephine and Fifi. This is no poor relation of Cognac, but a formidable spirit that has a floral spice and a depth that has been brought to life on the Somerset levels. Julian's experiments with blends, barrels and ageing have furnished our restaurant with enough marvellous drinks to keep any Somerset cider farmer rosie-cheeked.

SERVES 8

FOR THE FILLING:

1.3kg pork belly, minced on a coarse
  setting (ask your butcher for the
  bones)

200g pig's liver, cut into 1cm cubes

200g minced beef

10 smoked streaky bacon rashers,
  cut into 2cm pieces

2 garlic cloves, finely sliced

15 black peppercorns, plus 1 tsp
  freshly ground black pepper

17 juniper berries, lightly crushed

½ tsp ground mace

250ml black IPA (or regular IPA)

75ml Somerset cider brandy

1 tbsp fine sea salt

FOR THE JELLY:

the bones from the pork belly

3–4 pig's trotters

1 large carrot, finely sliced

1 large onion, finely sliced

1 bay leaf

5 sprigs of thyme

12 black peppercorns

2–3 lovage leaves (or celery leaves)

sea salt

FOR THE HOT-WATER CRUST PASTRY:

450g strong white flour

½ tsp salt

1 tbsp icing sugar

1 egg

80g lard, diced

80g butter, diced

1 egg, lightly beaten, to glaze

First make the jelly. Put all the ingredients except the lovage and salt in a pan, add 1.5 litres of water and bring to the boil. Reduce the heat to a simmer and cook, uncovered, for 2 hours, meticulously skimming off any scum that rises to the surface. Strain through a fine sieve into a clean pan and bring to the boil. Boil until reduced to a quarter of its volume, then remove from the heat. Now it's time to test whether it has reduced to the correct consistency. Put a tablespoon of the liquid on a plate and leave it in the fridge for 20 minutes. Push your finger through the middle of the liquid. If the liquid begins to crinkle, then it's ready. If not, continue to reduce it over a high heat for a few more minutes, then test again. When the correct consistency is achieved, bring the liquid to the boil, add the lovage leaves and turn off the heat. Leave the lovage to infuse for 20 minutes, then remove and discard. Taste once more and season with sea salt accordingly.

You could make the stock for the jelly in a pressure cooker. Follow the instructions above but cook at full pressure for 80–90 minutes. Remove from the heat and allow to cool to room temperature before removing the lid. Then strain, reduce and test as above.

Put all the ingredients for the filling in a bowl and mix with your hands until thoroughly combined. Set aside while you make the pastry.

Heat the oven to 180°C/Gas Mark 4. To make the pastry, mix the flour, salt and icing sugar together in a large bowl. Make a well in the centre and add the egg. Cover the egg with the flour. Put the lard and butter in a saucepan with 200ml water. Gradually bring the water to a simmer and leave until the fats have melted. Slowly pour the water and fat into the flour. Cut together with a knife until a dough has started to form, then turn out on to a floured surface and knead lightly until glossy and smooth – a couple of minutes maximum. Use immediately.

Set aside a third of the pastry for the lid. Roll out the rest on a lightly floured surface to 5mm thick and use to line a 23cm pie mould or springform cake tin. Trim the excess pastry hanging over the edges and put to one side. Spoon in the filling, pressing it down gently so it is evenly distributed. Roll out the reserved pastry 3mm thick to make a lid. Put it on top of the pie and pinch it to the pastry edge so there are no gaps. You can gently shape the rim into a pretty design, should you so wish. Make a small hole in the centre for venting.

Roll out the pastry trimmings to 3–5mm thick. Cut a strip 5cm wide and a similar length to the pie. Cut diagonally into strips all the way down the entire length, and then again the other way, so what you are left with are diamonds in the centre and half diamonds on the edge (see the photo opposite).

Brush the pie with the beaten egg to glaze, then lay the extra pastry in a strip across the top of the pie, in a design of your choice, leaving the vent hole clear. Lightly glaze the extra pastry pieces with egg, then place the pie in the oven and bake for 20 minutes. Turn the oven down to 160°C/Gas Mark 3 and bake for a further 45–60 minutes, until the juices run clear (if you have a probe thermometer, the internal temperature of the pie should be 86°C). If the pie is browning too quickly, which can often happen, cover it tightly with foil.

Allow the pie to cool to room temperature, then carefully remove it from the mould. If the jelly has set, warm it slightly so it is just liquid. Slowly pour the jelly in through the steam vent until the pie is full. Place in the fridge for 2–4 hours to set the jelly.

Pearl Barley with Old Demdike and St George's Mushroom

We love umami-rich foods, and mushrooms and cheese are fantastic sources of it. Umami, or savoury flavour, is now considered to be the fifth basic taste – the others being sweet, sour, salty and bitter. Tomatoes, cheeses such as Parmesan and Cheddar, and mushrooms are packed full of it.

This dish is very similar to the Italian *orzotto*. *Orzotto* is like risotto only pearl barley is used, easily matching the quality of Carnaroli or Vialone Nano rice. When risottos and orzottos are well executed, they are a delight – hearty, soothing and often nostalgic – yet they can be improved upon further with the use of textural contrasts and bursts of flavour, as we do in this recipe. Here, intensely flavoured mushroom jellies add a burst of rich umami and a textural contrast. St George's mushrooms give hints of watermelon and cucumber, while a ewe's cheese crisp adds a fine aesthetic finish to an already stunning dish.

SERVES 4

150g Old Demdike cheese, grated
300g pearl barley
2 tbsp rapeseed oil
200g onions, finely diced
150g carrots, finely diced
200g celeriac, finely diced
250ml red wine
350ml mushroom stock (see
    page 297)
10–15 small St George's mushrooms,
    quartered (if unavailable, use
    oyster mushrooms)
1 tbsp chopped parsley
Mushroom Jelly (see page 68),
    made with smoked salt
    if possible
sea salt

To make the ewe's cheese crisps, arrange 50g of the grated cheese in an oval shape on a piece of baking parchment. Place another piece of parchment on top and roll it out into a thin layer. Turn out into a frying pan and place on a medium-low heat, until the cheese has melted and the bottom has begun to brown lightly. Put the pan under a hot grill and leave until the cheese is an even golden-brown colour all over. Leave to cool, then break into 4 pieces and set aside.

Place the pearl barley in a saucepan, cover with cold water and bring to the boil. Drain well, then repeat. Drain and set aside. Heat half the rapeseed oil in a saucepan, add the onions, carrots and celeriac and cook over a medium heat until they begin to soften. Do not allow them to colour. Stir in the pearl barley, followed by the red wine, and cook until the wine has been completely absorbed by the barley. Add the mushroom stock a ladleful at a time, waiting for it to be fully absorbed before adding the next. Continue for 10–15 minutes, until the pearl barley is cooked but still has a slight resistance to the bite.

Meanwhile, heat the remaining rapeseed oil in a frying pan, add the mushrooms and fry over a high heat until tender and golden brown. Add them to the pearl barley, reserving a few for garnishing. Stir in the remaining grated cheese and the parsley and season with salt. Serve garnished with the remaining fried mushrooms, the mushroom jellies and the cheese crisps.

Rhubarb and Custard

Most people credit the eccentric Victorians with placing jellies firmly on the British gastronomy map. After all, it was the Victorian aristocracy who excelled at using decorative jellies at banquets to display their power and social standing. In fact, jellies had been around for centuries previously and savoury jellies were common at medieval feasts.

We created this dessert in honour of Robert May, a seventeenth-century cook who introduced fruit jellies to the English table and met with a surprising amount of resistance. This superbly flavoured jelly consists of two ingredients that we think were meant to be together – rhubarb and custard. You don't necessarily have to layer them exactly as described below. You could make thinner layers or add a border of jelly etc. Get creative! Just be sure to set each layer fully before adding more.

SERVES 6

FOR THE RHUBARB JELLY:

1.5kg rhubarb, cut into 2cm pieces

150g caster sugar

13g gelatine

FOR THE CUSTARD:

600ml double cream

1 vanilla pod

8 egg yolks

200g caster sugar

11g gelatine

FOR THE RHUBARB COMPOTE

(OPTIONAL):

2 large rhubarb stalks, cut into
    1–2cm pieces

a few tbsp caster sugar, to taste

For the jelly, put 650ml water in a pan and bring to the boil. Place a steamer basket over the top large enough to hold the rhubarb. Add the rhubarb to the basket, cover with a tight-fitting lid and steam over a low heat for 1 hour. If too much steam is escaping, put a layer of foil over the pan and put the lid on top of the foil.

While the rhubarb is steaming, make the custard. Pour the cream into a heavy-based saucepan. Slit the vanilla pod open lengthwise and scrape out the seeds. Add the seeds and pod to the cream and bring to just below boiling point, then remove from the heat and cool slightly. Whisk the egg yolks and sugar together in a large bowl until the yolks become pale and the sugar is fully incorporated. Pour the cream through a fine sieve on to the egg yolks, whisk until smooth and then transfer to a clean saucepan. Put the gelatine sheets into a bowl of ice-cold water and leave to soak for 10 minutes.

Heat the custard mixture gently, stirring constantly. After a few minutes it will begin to thicken. It is vital to stir all parts thoroughly to prevent any of the mixture overcooking. (If you have a digital thermometer, then this is a good time to use it; the custard should be no more than 85°C, otherwise it will scramble.) When it has thickened enough to coat the back of the spoon without running off, remove from the heat and place the pan briefly in a bowl of cold water to stop it cooking further. Strain the custard through a sieve into a bowl. Squeeze out any excess liquid from the gelatine and add the gelatine to the custard, stirring until completely dissolved. Cool the custard quickly by placing the bowl in a couple of inches of cold water in the sink, then chill in the fridge.

† The Victorian era was the hey-day of jelly making, though jellies had been around for centuries. In Tudor and Stuart times it was common for the gentry to build summerhouses in their gardens just so that their banqueting guests had somewhere quiet where they could enjoy the final jelly course. As sugar became more widely available, dessert-makers made the most of it. By the seventeenth century, sweet jellies were the norm, seasoned with rosewater and spices. Other creations included transparent puddings in which layers of sliced almonds, raisins, citron and candied lemon were visible through the jelly.

CUSTARD

In a busy kitchen, making custard from scratch is a bit of a treat. A simple job, it is a chance to stand still and focus on one task; it forces you to slow down, physically and mentally. Slowly watching how the viscosity of the custard changes, while stirring constantly, is quite a grounding exercise. It is a moment when you take in the sounds and smells around you, and regain some clarity amidst all the activity.

When the rhubarb has steamed for 1 hour, remove from the heat and discard the rhubarb. All the juice and flavour from the rhubarb will be in the water in the pan underneath, so keep this. Measure out 450ml of the rhubarb-infused water into a clean saucepan, add the sugar and heat gently, stirring, until dissolved. Soften the gelatine in ice-cold water, as for the custard. Squeeze out any excess water and add the gelatine to the pan, off the heat. Stir until completely dissolved, then set aside.

To set the jelly, you will need a 1-litre terrine, jelly mould or bowl. If using a terrine, very lightly oil the inside, using a pastry brush, then line with a layer of cling film. Once the terrine is lined with cling film, it helps to fill the terrine with water, which enables you to remove any remaining air bubbles from the edges of the terrine. Discard the water and gently pat dry with kitchen roll. Ignore this process if using a jelly mould or bowl.

Pour a layer of jelly into your chosen receptacle till about 1–2cm deep. Place in the fridge for 1½ hours or until set firm. Put half the custard in a pan, place over the lowest possible heat and stir continuously until fluid. Pour the custard into the mould over a back of a spoon held just above the rhubarb jelly. This slows its fall, making it less likely to break the jelly apart. Pour the custard over the first layer of rhubarb jelly and return to the fridge. Leave for 2 hours or until completely firm.

Take out the remaining jelly and place in a saucepan over a low heat until fluid. Pour over the set layer of custard (using a spoon as you did before) and return to the fridge until completely set. Then heat the remaining custard until fluid and pour it into the mould over the back of a spoon as before. Leave in the fridge, preferably overnight, until set.

To make the compote, put the rhubarb in a saucepan just big enough to hold it in a single layer and add 2 tablespoons of water. Cook, covered, over a low-medium heat until the rhubarb begins to break down. Stir in sugar to taste and continue to cook until the compote is the consistency of runny jam. Remove from the heat and leave to cool.

Turn the jelly out of the mould and serve, with the compote if liked.

Chocolate and Salt Caramel Brownies with Cherry and Elderflower Sauce

There are countless recipes for chocolate brownies, and initially we thought that perhaps there were too many already. However, given that our local area has such an illustrious history in chocolate production, we felt it was only fair to come up with our own chocolate recipe. We have the industrious Victorians to thank for making chocolate available to the wider public. It was, in fact, a factory in Bristol, owned by J S Fry & Sons, that produced the first chocolate bar in 1847. The company went on to produce some of our childhood favourites, such as Fry's Chocolate Cream and Turkish Delight.

We like to use Original Beans chocolate because of its quality and the company's ethics, which closely match our own. Co-founded by the environmentalist entrepreneur, Philipp Kauffman, Original Beans is renowned for its zero carbon policies and passion for sustainable farming.

The addition of salt caramel is primarily to enhance the sweetness of the brownie, although we have to admit that it does add a lot to the overall presentation too.

SERVES 4, WITH PLENTY OF BROWNIES LEFT FOR TOMORROW

250g dark chocolate, at least 72 per cent cocoa solids

170g unsalted butter

300g caster sugar

3 large eggs, lightly beaten

1 egg yolk

80ml rapeseed oil

60g plain flour

½ tsp baking powder

½ tsp salt

70g organic cocoa powder

50g Salt Caramel (see page 303), plus extra to serve

FOR THE CHERRY AND ELDERFLOWER SAUCE:

100g frozen sour cherries

50g Elderflower Syrup (see overleaf) or elderflower cordial

Heat the oven to 180°C/Gas Mark 4. Lightly grease a 23cm springform cake tin.

Melt 200g of the chocolate in a bowl placed over a pan of lightly simmering water, making sure the water does not touch the base of the bowl. Remove from the heat.

Using an electric whisk, or a freestanding mixer fitted with the paddle attachment, beat the butter and sugar together until pale and light. Change the mixer attachment to a whisk, or continue using the electric whisk. Slowly add the eggs and the extra yolk, no more than a tablespoon at a time, whisking thoroughly between each addition. Slowly add the rapeseed oil and whisk the mixture for a further 5 minutes, until it has a glossy, silky appearance.

Sift in the flour, baking powder, salt and cocoa powder and whisk briefly until incorporated. Using a metal spoon, fold in the melted chocolate. Pour the mixture into the cake tin and smooth the top. Roughly chop the remaining chocolate and lightly push the pieces into the surface of the cake mix. Repeat the process with the salt caramel pieces. Place in the centre of oven and bake for 25 minutes, or until a knife inserted in the centre comes away with a little cake mixture attached; it should not look raw.

If it does, return to the oven, testing every 3 minutes. Remove from the oven and leave to cool on a wire rack.

Allow to cool to room temperature on a wire tray. Meanwhile, put the cherries and elderflower syrup in a small saucepan and cook over a medium heat for about 10 minutes, until syrupy. Leave to cool a little before serving.

The brownies can be served hot or cold. Turn out and slice, then serve with shards of salt caramel broken over each portion and the warm syrup poured over. The brownies can be refrigerated for up to 5 days but you would need a great deal of willpower for them to last that long. Freezing is a good way to lengthen their life and it has the added bonus of increasing the fudginess.

Elderflower syrup

100ml water
100g caster sugar
2 large heads of elderflower

Put 100g caster sugar in a pan with 100ml water and bring to the boil, stirring to dissolve the sugar. Immediately remove from the heat and add 2 large heads of elderflower. Leave to infuse for 20 minutes, then strain through a piece of wet muslin or a sieve. Leave to cool, then store in the fridge for up to a week.

Strawberry and Rose Lemonade Pudding with Saffron and Cider Brandy Custard

This is a marvellous way of using up the last jar of strawberry jam before the summer glut. We have polished off one of these puddings in under 5 minutes between the four of us. The brandy and saffron give the custard complexity and punch and complement the strawberry in a way you might not have expected.

SERVES 6

160ml Rose Lemonade (see page 137 or use Fentimans)

150g salted butter, at room temperature, cut into cubes

235g caster sugar

160g plain flour, sifted

85ml soured cream

1 large egg

2 tsp vanilla extract

1½ tsp bicarbonate of soda

100g strawberry jam

a handful of pale rose petals, to garnish

FOR THE SAFFRON AND CIDER BRANDY CUSTARD:

12 saffron stamens

25ml cider brandy

480ml double cream

1 vanilla pod

6 egg yolks

160g caster sugar

Put the rose lemonade and butter in a pan and warm over the lowest possible heat until the butter almost melts, then remove from the heat. Add the sugar and stir in well. Whisk in the sifted flour in 2 stages until completely incorporated, then set aside. In a separate bowl, whisk together the soured cream, egg, vanilla extract and bicarbonate of soda. Add this to the rose lemonade and flour mixture and whisk to incorporate once more.

Grease a 1.2 litre pudding basin with butter. Put the strawberry jam in the bottom of the basin and top with the cake mix. Take a piece of foil large enough to cover the basin and make a pleat in the centre; this will allow the pudding to expand during cooking. Put the foil over the basin and tuck the edges under the rim. Put the basin in a steamer, cover with a lid and steam for 2 hours, checking the water level every 30 minutes or so and topping up when necessary. (The pudding can also be steamed in a pressure cooker over a trivet with 2.5cm water in the bottom at full pressure for an hour to get it to the table quicker.)

The custard can be prepared as the pudding comes to the end of its steaming. Add the saffron to the cider brandy to infuse their heady scents together. Split the vanilla pod open and scrape out the seeds. Put the seeds and pod in a heavy-based saucepan with the cream and set over a low heat until almost boiling. Remove from the heat and let it cool a little. Whisk the egg yolks and sugar together in a bowl until the yolks turn pale, then pour in the cream through a sieve, whisking to combine. Pour the mixture into a clean pan and set over a low heat. Cook, stirring constantly, until the mixture thickens. It is important not to leave the pan alone at this stage, as wandering concentration will lead to a scrambled egg custard. If you have a digital thermometer, the custard will start to thicken at 70°C and be at its thickest at 85°C – any higher than that and it will scramble. With or without a thermometer, much of the skill lies in being able to see this change. Keep a close eye on the custard as you stir and watch for the moment when there is a clear trail

left behind the spoon on the base of the pan. Chalk up another kitchen skill when you see that velvet sauce completed.

Pass the custard through a fine sieve and stir in the cider brandy and saffron.

Turn the pudding out of the basin and serve with the custard. Saffron and strawberry is a lip-smacking combination and can be bettered only by the addition of a few pale rose petals, scattered over the pudding once it is served.

VERMOUTH

Essentially, vermouth is made with a base wine that has been sweetened with a mixture of grape juice and alcohol. Various botanicals extracts are then added before maturation, filtering and bottling. There are an incredible number of vermouths on the market, at least 40 varieties. Two of the best-known are the French Noilly Prat, which uses 20–30 botanicals, and the Italian Martini Rossi, which contains 30. A 'tea' is made by macerating the botanicals in a high proof spirit in slowly revolving barrels for 10–15 days, then a set ratio of each is added to the base wine. This is ever so slightly more professional than shaking a jam jar.

We were inspired by the flavours of Antica Formula and Punt e Mes and by the subtlety of Bonme, which comes from the Piedmont region of Italy. It is the complexities of vermouth that really captured our attention. It works as an aperitif, a cocktail ingredient, a digestif and as an ingredient in cooking. This is due to the medicinal nature of the botanical ingredients: some stimulate hunger, while others settle the stomach. We wanted to create our own house vermouth that matched our tastes, an expression of our restaurant and our location. Jack had to engage a good deal of grey matter to get his head around the maths when it came to the botanicals. What followed was nothing short of a lengthy process of trial and error. We had bottles and bottles of vermouth, all slightly different as we increased and decreased the proportions of each botanical tea. The Ethicurean was peppered with jars of our experiments. Some were so astringent that they resulted in extreme facial contortions amongst the friends who tried them. We had a good chat with Jekka McVicar, who helped us choose the varieties of herbs best suited to our recipes and to being grown in the Walled Garden. The recipe below is for sweet vermouth but this is by no means a definitive recipe. The pleasure comes from trying out your own combinations. Please feel free to leave out botanicals or add new ones of your own. We have included the option of lowering the sugar content for a drier offering.

Set aside a small area of your kitchen and stack up those jars of macerating botanicals. Try them all individually, noting their flavours, and you will gradually begin to be able to build your own vermouth based on your chosen profile. There may even be the possibility of substituting some wild bittering agents for some of the exotic bitter botanicals. Here is a short list of possibilities:

CHAMOMILE: used in lots of vermouths; adds a good floral flavour
GORSE FLOWERS: alternative bitter flavour
MARITIME PINE NEEDLES: resinous flavour
FENNEL SEEDS: used in some vermouths

EQUIPMENT
• Scales that measure to 0.1 of a gram are crucial for weighing out the small amounts of each botanical tea. They are a great piece of equipment and quite inexpensive.
• A hydrometer is useful for working out the alcohol content of your finished vermouth.
• 20 sterile jam jars for the botanicals.
• A pipette for adding each botanical tea, although a teaspoon will suffice.
• A small tea strainer will help to keep out any pieces of the botanicals when adding the tea to the base wine.

The Ethicurean Vermouth Botanicals

ANGELICA SEEDS (*Angelica archangelica*): Similar in aroma to juniper.

BAY (*Laurus nobilis*): Medicinal qualities. Anti-inflammatory, antibacterial.

BLACK PEPPER (*Piper nigrum*): Hot, wood and floral flavours.

CARDAMOM (*Amomum cardamom*): Aromatic and resinous, digestive. Used to treat infections.

CINAMMON (*Cinnamomum verum*): Laurel family. Sweet aromatic spice.

CLOVE (*Syzygium aromaticum*): Central and Southern Europe, principal ingredient in Angostura bitters, good for digestion. Contains glycosides, one of the most bitter natural compounds known, and eugenol, which has antiseptic and anaesthetic qualities.

CORIANDER (*Coriandrum sativum*): Lemon and citrus flavour. Warm, nutty, spicy, orange.

GENTIAN ROOT (*Gentiana lutea*): Very bitter, used in Angostora bitters.

JUNIPER (*Juniperus communis*): Piney and resinous.

MARJORAM (*Origanum majorana*): Balsamic and aromatic flavour.

NUTMEG (*Myristica fragrans*): Preserving and delicate agent.

ORANGE PEEL: Aromatic, sweet on the nose and, for us, a key element of our vermouth.

ORRIS (*Iris germanica*): Enhances other aromas and perfumes. Violet-like smell, tastes like raspberry.

QUASSIA BARK (*Quassia amara*): Quassin is the bitterest substance in nature.

ROSEMARY (*Rosmarinus officinalis*): Aromatic, warm and slightly bitter.

SAGE (*Salvia officinalis*): contains thujone, a slightly antiseptic-tasting compound. Savoury flavour.

STAR ANISE (*Illicium verum*): A great flavour enhancer. Rich spice.

VANILLA (*Vanilla planifolia*): Adds a flavour of aged oak, which is found in mature vermouths.

WORMWOOD (*Artemisia absinthium*): Very bitter, medicinal properties. Key ingredient for an authentic vermouth.

YARROW (*Achillea millefolium*): Very bitter. Often called arrowroot in the UK, it is regarded as a healing herb.

Vermouth

QUANTITIES FOR EACH BOTANICAL
TEA:

Angelica seeds 15g

Bay leaves 15g

Black peppercorns 10g

Cardamom 1g

Cinammon 8.3g

Clove 0.5g

Coriander 15g

Gentian root 2g

Juniper 15g

Marjoram 5g

Nutmeg 5g

Orange peel 14.6g

Orris 6g

Quassia bark 4g

Rosemary 5g

Sage 15g

Star anise 5g

Vanilla 5g

Wormwood 4g

Yarrow 2g

Your vermouth can be stored in a sterilised bottle with a good seal; vacuum pumping it is a very sensible idea. Store in the fridge and drink within a couple of months; we are sure that it will be gone in a week.

The botanicals listed here can all be purchased online or from Chinese herbalists. We use a crisp dry English white wine from Somerset as our base wine, although in the past we have used a Colombard and Gros Manseng blend. Try out a few white wines and see which one you prefer.

We make our own caramel and add it to the wine. However, reducing the amount of caramel can make very good dry vermouth. Sweet vermouth typically contains 10–15 per cent sugar, while a dry one will contain no more than 5 per cent. It is crucial to raise the alcohol by volume of the wine (this is achieved by adding the botanical teas), as at 13–15 per cent alcohol, the yeast will stop converting grape sugars. This is important as you do not want a bottle that will continue to ferment. A Muscat wine makes an excellent sweet vermouth.

The basic proportions for this recipe are 500ml wine, 150ml in total of the botanical teas, 200g caramel. This yields just under 700ml vermouth.

Take a small jam jar and fill it around a third full with your botanical. Top up to twice the height that the botanical reaches with a high proof vodka. Screw on the lid and leave to macerate at room temperature for 2 weeks.

When making the caramel for the vermouth, follow the instructions for the salt caramel on page 303, omitting the salt. We recommend taking the caramel to a dark amber colour for extra depth and complexity. Heating it to somewhere between 185 and 188°C will do the trick. This can be poured on to a silicone mat and allowed to cool into a solid caramel. It can be stored in the same way as the salt caramel until needed.

When combining the caramel with the wine, add a quarter of the wine (or as little as needed to dissolve the caramel) to a pan and place on a low heat. Add the caramel shards and stir until completely dissolved. Allow the mixture to cool to room temperature, before combining with the remaining wine. Add the botanicals in the proportions given above. Please taste as you add them, as this will give you a sense of what each ingredient adds to your vermouth.

HOW TO OAK YOUR VERMOUTH.

If you would like to try oaking your vermouth, you will need a large, sterilised jar with a wide neck. Place a handful of clean oak chips in the centre of a piece of sterilised muslin and tie with a piece of string. Drop the bag of oak chips into the jar and top up with the vermouth. Try leaving for a week and taste regularly. Some of the best vermouths are matured in oak, this is a great way of simulating that maturation process.

A tip for sterilising the oak chips without removing too much of their flavour and tannins is to steam them. Place in a pan with a drop of water and a lid, turn up to a medium heat and the chips will steam.

Rose Lemonade

We have loved Fentimans' botanically brewed drinks for years. Recently we had a dabble at cooking with some of them, and the winner was rose lemonade. We decided to work out a recipe for our own version. In order to brew it properly, we first had to track down a ginger beer plant (GBP), which is essentially a yeast called *Saccharomyces florentinus* and a bacterium called *Brevibacterium vermiforme*. These two unlikely friends form a gelatinous substance and a symbiotic relationship within which the yeast excretes alcohol and the bacterium consumes it. Yeast has a low tolerance of alcohol, which of course remains low due to the bacterium. GBP is better for making drinks than ordinary yeast because you end up with much better flavours, low alcohol and little chance of dangerous explosions.

We eventually found a supplier online and received a little envelope containing a packet of white, jelly-like substance, yeasty, sweet and alcoholic. Waiting lists, payments, refunds and repayments followed. A little research told us that a very clever chap by the name of Harry Marshall Ward discovered GBP's talent for brewing in 1892.

We used Japanese rose petals, *Rosa rugosa*, as they really do offer the finest flavour. If you can't get these, you could try dried rose petals. Please avoid roses that have been sprayed with chemicals. The general rule is that the paler varieties have a better flavour.

MAKES 2 LITRES
250g caster sugar
juice and zest of 1 lemon
2.5cm piece of fresh ginger,
    roughly chopped
a handful of rose petals
1 tbsp GBP

It is really important to sterilise all the equipment you use, including the muslin and string. You can do this by pouring boiling water over everything and then leaving it to dry.
Put the sugar and lemon zest in a pan with 250ml water. Bring to a light simmer, stirring to dissolve the sugar, then remove from the heat and leave to cool.

Pour 1.75 litres water into a large container (a large, lidded plastic box is fine) and add the lemon juice; this will neutralise the chlorine generally present in tap water, which would otherwise affect the yeast's productivity. Strain in the sugar and water mixture. Put the ginger in a piece of muslin, tie with string and drop it in. Add the GBP, then cover and leave at room temperature for 5 days. Be sure to open the lid briefly every day in order to let out any carbon dioxide that has built up, otherwise it will open of its own accord.

Strain the mixture through a fine sieve into a sterilised 2 litre plastic bottle and put on the top. Save the GBP and give it a rinse; it will have grown. (If you store it in the fridge in a small, sterile container, it will keep for up to 2 weeks). After 2 days the rose lemonade will be ready to drink, although if you desire a fizzier brew, leave it for longer. Refrigeration will halt any further fermentation.

The Ethicurean Cocktail

This cocktail has quickly become a classic at The Ethicurean, a delightful balance of sweet, sharp and savoury. As the days lengthen, it makes a perfect pre-dinner drink in the garden. Thyme has antiseptic qualities, as do honey and lemon, making this an excellent pick-me-up, with or without the vodka.

   Investing in an inexpensive Boston cocktail shaker is a very good idea. It allows you to build and shake drinks containing juice, aerating them, chilling them quickly and forming a pleasing froth. Most bartenders would advise that shaking should be used only when drinks contain some juice. You will significantly lower the temperature by shaking, but expect a small level of dilution from the ice. If all the ingredients are clear, stirring is the better option, preserving the clarity of the drink.

SERVES 1

ice cubes
¼ lemon
2 sprigs of thyme, plus 1 to serve
1 tsp honey
25ml Chase English Potato vodka
100ml apple juice

Fill your glass to the rim with ice.

Squeeze the wedge of lemon into the glass part of a Boston shaker, then drop in the squeezed lemon wedge, together with the thyme. Mash together with a wooden pestle. Add the honey, pouring in just a little warm water to dissolve. Measure out the vodka, there's no harm in a double if the wind takes you, and pour it on to the other ingredients. Add the apple juice and top up to just below the rim with ice. Tap the tin on top of the glass and shake till water condenses on the outside of the shaker. Separate by using the heel of your hand to knock where the glass and tin are touching. Pour those last few precious drops into the tin, then place a Hawthorne strainer over the tin and pour the mixture into your chilled glass. Top up with ice and a small sprig of thyme, then add more juice to taste.

HONEY AND THYME SYRUP

We like to make a half and half syrup to use in the cocktail above. If you are making a few cocktails, it's a good way of saving time.

1 tsp honey per cocktail
1 sprig of thyme for every drink you would like.

Place the honey and thyme in a pan and add 1 teaspoon of water for every teaspoon of honey. Bring gently to a simmer, then remove from the heat and leave to cool. Strain into a sterilised container and store in the fridge; it will keep for 2 weeks.

Negroni

The Negroni is an enduring classic. The preserve of bartenders and restaurateurs, it has a satisfying bitterness that is welcome after a long shift. We find ourselves settled in by the second. This cocktail is more than the sum of its parts and its success rests on its balanced simplicity. We use our own Vermouth (see page 132), but Antica Formula and Punt e Mes make superb ones.

We have also served this drink with a sage leaf as a garnish, as it finds a harmonious place amongst the aromatics in the gin and vermouth.

SERVES 1
1 orange
25ml gin
25ml vermouth (see above)
25ml Campari

Chill a tumbler with ice topped up with water. Take a fine slice of zest from the orange, avoiding the bitter pith. Fill a large glass one third full with ice and pour over the gin, vermouth and Campari. Stir until the outside of the glass condenses, then strain into the chilled tumbler and squeeze a little of the precious flavour from the orange zest. Brush the rim of the tumbler with the orange zest, then pinch and squeeze it over the glass to release the essential oils. Top up with ice to below the rim (above is most uncouth), then slot in a slice of orange.

For a twist, try stirring a couple of lovage leaves into the contents of the mixing glass.

VERMOUTH

Although the earliest references to an aromatised wine crop up around 1250 BC in China and India, it took a while to catch on in England. Purl was a seventeenth-century bitter ale infused with wormwood and a few other botanicals, mainly used to settle the stomach. By 1690 'Stoughton's Great Cordial Elixir', an infusion of 22 botanicals, had become a popular cure for hangovers and gastric ailments: 'Drank by most gentlemen ... to recover and restore a weaken'd stomach or lost appetite .... occasioned by hard drinking or sickness' (*Imbibe*, page 170). Vermouth as we know it today began life in the region around Turin, Italy, in the eighteenth century. Relatively sweet with a full-bodied, herbaceous flavour, this dark-red drink was followed by drier, straw-coloured styles from France, in particular Chambéry in the Savoie region.

SUMMER

SUMMER arrives when the central walkway through the yew hedges has progressed from a carpet to a graduating wall of colour. This is Maddy the flower gardener's favourite time, as the perennials take their place on the stage. There are nepeta, achillea, salvia and geraniums.

On Midsummer's Eve, bonfires can be seen on the Mendips at dusk as the old pagan ceremony of strengthening the sun takes place. In the track through the orchard, the lavender is beginning to flower, some of it destined for marshmallows served toasted to order in the glasshouse. Mark carries up boxes of strawberries still covered in straw, the odd woodlouse scrambling to safety. The wild strawberries, barely a mouthful, are picked as we gather mint and the new, bright-green lovage leaves.

Matthew and Paûla disappear for a day to their samphire spot in South Wales. They return with armfuls of this salty vegetable, not a whisper of the name of the beach. The rope hanging in the dipping pond is a ladder for the first dragonflies of the year taking wing. The pond, once used for watering cans, is teeming with life.

Mark has sown salad leaves that resist bolting in the heat. An hour after he picks them, they sit layered on plates with pickled pollock and red peppers. We roast the deep-red peppers and purple aubergines over an open flame until they change from rich red and purple to ash black. The smell is perfect. They cool before the skin is peeled.

The elder hedge provides us with the first star-headed elderflowers with their tranquil scent. Next come the berries, and some will be picked unripe to be pickled with pepper and salt – we think of them as Somerset capers.

In descending order, tied to fence posts, are raspberries, blackberries, loganberries and white raspberries. These fruits make their way into myriad recipes: set creams, sorbets, jams and vinegars. The white raspberries are muddled in cocktails, providing an acidity that makes lemon redundant. As we fill containers, we are careful not to pick a honeybee. Ivor the beekeeper arrives and opens the hive. The queen's wings are clipped, she is marked and then returned. The espaliers are drooping under the weight of fruit. There are apricots,

greengages and Victoria plums. On the stove sits an ever-bubbling pan of fruit – greengage and vanilla, perhaps, or blackberry with bourbon whiskey.

The artichokes, plump and green with sharp scales, are snipped off above any secondary buds. The kitchen makes a hollandaise and the globes are cooked and placed in a bowl, served with this buttery sauce. Within 20 minutes the rim is surrounded by stripped petals and fingers reach for the heart.

Maddy's flowers are joined by the blooms of campanula, echinacea and potentilla. The border outside the glasshouse is a moving riot of butterflies and honeybees, while the odd one is skilfully freed from the dining room.

By this time, the foxgloves have begun to tumble over, top heavy with blue flowers. Meanwhile, the first apples are starting to crop. Worcester Pearmain, Beauty of Bath and Cheddar Gold are collected in trugs and baskets. The days are shortening and the crops are preserved, pickled and stored.

Figs Wrapped in Pork Belly with Lavender and Buffalo Mozzarella

Compromise is difficult when you are a big fan of figs. They are wonderful when they are ripe but not really worth tasting at any other stage. Unripe figs have got to be one of the most disappointing foods there is. The problem is that they are so difficult to transport that either you have to grow them yourself or be close to a good source. Contrary to popular belief, fig trees do grow well in the UK. Granted, they are no match in size for some European varieties but their freshness makes up for what might initially be perceived as a deficiency.

The fig tree at the Walled Garden never ceases to surprise us, as it seems to be oblivious to the volatility of the British weather. It lives in a blissful state of constant expansion, extending its leafy branches without shame, claiming the front brick archway as its rightful area, ensuring that all visitors passing through the top gate are welcomed by its generous presence. As summer progresses, opening the heavy wooden gate without damaging the tree's branches becomes more and more challenging. It is almost as if it is trying to remind us of its healthy growth every morning. There is no need for such attention-seeking behaviour. It is one of the most watched trees in our garden. The figs are so precious to us that we cannot risk any of them being wasted.

Figs have a natural affinity with salty ingredients and are commonly served with prosciutto. However, we find that in this dish the crunch of the fig seeds is greatly enhanced by the crispiness of the cured pork belly.

Honey and figs is another combination that works remarkably well. We tried it with lavender honey and found that it was even better. It made sense then to use stalks of lavender to attach the pork belly to the fig.

The creaminess of the buffalo mozzarella serves to balance the sweetness of the honey and figs with the saltiness of the pork belly. To have access to British-made buffalo milk mozzarella from Laverstoke Park Farm is as satisfying as having a British-made chorizo sausage (see page 292). Each has so many applications in the kitchen that any chef seeking to use solely local ingredients has much cause to celebrate.

SERVES 4

8 ripe figs

1 buffalo milk mozzarella, sliced into 8 pieces

16 slices of cured pork belly, such as pancetta

16 lavender spears, from lavender in flower

4 tsp lavender honey

Heat the oven to 200°C/Gas Mark 6. Wash and dry the figs, taking care not to damage the skin. Cut a cross 2–3cm deep through the stem of each and open the fig up like a flower. Stuff a slice of mozzarella into each fig, then wrap 2 slices of cured pork belly round the outside. Spike each fig with 2 lavender flower spears to hold the pork in place during baking.

Put the figs in a baking dish, drizzle ½ teaspoon of lavender honey over each one and cook for 10–12 minutes, until the pork belly is crisp and the figs lightly caramelised. Cool slightly before serving.

Caramelised Chicory, Labneh and Macerated Strawberry Salad

The arrival of summer at the Walled Garden often takes us by surprise. The first sign is the quiet murmur of insects from various corners of the garden, then the burst of colour in the herbaceous borders alongside the central brick path. As the insects noisily gather around these flowers, we realise that summer has tiptoed in. There follows child-like excitement from kitchen folk and front-of-house staff alike. The arrival of summer means more ingredients to experiment with and more excuses for forays around the garden.

This salad showcases all that is great about the season. Strawberries are particularly important to the Somerset area. Not far from us, you will find the famous Strawberry Line, an old railway line, now a cycle path, which runs through neighbouring villages. Built in the Victorian era, it took its name from the famous Cheddar strawberries that used to be carried along the line to London. In this recipe, we use chicory as a contrast to the tangy sweetness of the macerated strawberries.

SERVES 4

500g ewe's milk yoghurt

½ tsp salt

120g medium-sized strawberries, hulled and sliced vertically into 3

about 200ml cider vinegar

300g caster sugar

6 large heads of chicory, cut into quarters through the root

icing sugar, for dusting

a little ground cinnamon

a little cobnut oil (or hazelnut oil)

a few borage flowers (optional)

black pepper

Prepare the labneh and strawberries a day in advance. Line a sieve with a piece of muslin or a cloth, allowing the ends to overhang the sieve. Put the yoghurt in and mix in the salt. Cover the yoghurt with the ends of the muslin and then place the sieve over a bowl. Leave in the fridge overnight. The following day, liquid will have collected in the bowl and the yoghurt will be thicker and creamier. Discard the liquid and spoon the yoghurt into an airtight container. Keep in the fridge until needed.

Put the sliced strawberries in a plastic box and pour in enough cider vinegar just to cover them. Cover and leave in the fridge overnight. The next day, strain off the vinegar into a bowl. Add the caster sugar to it and stir thoroughly until dissolved. Pour the vinegar over the strawberries and refrigerate until needed.

Place a griddle pan over a medium-high heat until hot. Lightly dust the chicory with icing sugar and then place flat-side down on the griddle. Cook without moving it until it begins to caramelise underneath and charred lines develop. Turn the pieces on to their other flat side and repeat, then flip them on to their rounded side and cook until tender. Remove the chicory from the griddle pan and set aside to cool a little.

Divide the chicory between 4 plates, spreading out some of the leaves. Dot the strawberries throughout, then add several teaspoons of the labneh. Sprinkle cinnamon over the labneh. Dress with cobnut oil, some of the macerating liquid from the strawberries and borage flowers, if you have any. Coarsely grind some black pepper over the strawberries and serve immediately.

Roasted Tomato and Liquorice Basil Soup

Roasting or caramelising vegetables can transform an average soup into something truly spectacular. Pair it with a little textural contrast and bursts of flavour, as we do here with basil croutons and golden tomato and apple balsamic jellies, and you are going far beyond what most people have come to expect when they hear the word soup.

The flavours you can achieve by roasting tomatoes are glorious. Indeed, it is hard to think of a culinary world without tomatoes. As Paûla, our resident Mexican, will proudly tell you, they are native to Mexico. The Spaniards brought them back to southern Europe for cultivation on a major scale. Drying out some of the moisture from the tomatoes intensifies their flavour and the browning from the roasting process adds a new complexity to one of our favourite ingredients. Tomatoes are a great source of umami (see page 123). When they are combined with mushroom stock in this recipe, we achieve savoury heaven. Add to that a warm infusion of herbs and pieces of the tomato vine, which contains incredibly fresh, aromatic tomato flavours, and we guarantee that this is a soup to rival any you have had before.

We use a strain of liquorice basil in this recipe, as the anise notes make a superb accompaniment to tomato. Mark, the gardener, spoils us with unique heritage or heirloom strains of plants and herbs, each with a richer flavour than the common hybridised strains. He grows cinnamon basil alongside tomatoes to attract pests away from the red fruit plants. Seek out a heritage or heirloom seed company if you are interested in growing herbs, as they will delight from a culinary aspect but will also provide seed for the following years. Genovese basil, mammoth basil and Mrs Burns lemon basil are heirloom varieties well worth searching for.

SERVES 4

1kg vine-ripened tomatoes, vines reserved

2 garlic cloves, peeled

2 bay leaves

10 sprigs of thyme

20g basil leaves (see above)

rapeseed oil

¼ tsp smoked paprika

100ml mushroom stock (see page 297)

100ml white chicken stock (see page 295)

2 dashes of Worcestershire sauce

cider vinegar

1 tbsp tomato purée

sea salt

Start by peeling the tomatoes. The easiest way to do this is to cut a wide cross at the base of each tomato, scoring only through the skin. Have a bowl of iced water at the ready. Put the scored tomatoes in a bowl, pour boiling water over them and leave for no more than 30 seconds; the skins should split where you made the incision. Remove from the water and plunge straight into the iced water. Leave until cold, then peel off the skins.

Heat the oven to 180°C/Gas Mark 4. Slice the tomatoes into quarters and put them in a roasting tray, cut-side up. Add the garlic cloves, bay leaves, half the thyme sprigs and half the basil leaves. Drizzle with enough rapeseed oil to coat the ingredients lightly and add a generous sprinkling of sea salt. Place in the oven and roast for 20–30 minutes, until the edges of the tomatoes begin to blacken. Take out of the oven and leave to cool. Remove the bay leaves, thyme and basil and discard.

Transfer the tomatoes, garlic and tomato purée to a blender with the smoked paprika and blitz on full speed for 1 minute. Add the mushroom stock and chicken stock and blitz for about 2 minutes. Pass

FOR THE GOLDEN TOMATO JELLY
(OPTIONAL, BUT RECOMMENDED):
500g golden tomatoes
¼ tsp agar agar powder

FOR THE APPLE BALSAMIC JELLY
(OPTIONAL, BUT RECOMMENDED):
200ml apple balsamic vinegar (such
    as Aspall's)
½ tsp agar agar powder

FOR THE BASIL CROUTONS
(OPTIONAL, BUT RECOMMENDED):
1 thick slice of sourdough bread, cut
    into 1–2cm cubes
rapeseed oil, to coat
1–2 tsp icing sugar
10g basil leaves
flaky sea salt

through a fine sieve into a saucepan, add the Worcestershire sauce and bring to a simmer. Immediately remove from the heat and add the reserved tomato vines plus the remaining basil and thyme. Leave to infuse in a warm place for 15 minutes. Strain through a fine sieve once more, season with salt to taste and a dash of cider vinegar for a little welcome acidity. If you left the soup to infuse somewhere warm enough, it should still be a good temperature to eat. If you prefer it a little warmer, then reheat quickly and serve immediately – with all or any of the optional garnishes, if you like.

If making the jellies, it is useful to know that agar agar will remain stable up to roughly 80°C. We usually serve our soups around 75°C.

For the golden tomato jelly, blitz the tomatoes to a purée in a food processor for 2 minutes. Place in a fine sieve set over a bowl and leave to drain until you have 200ml liquid. Press gently with the back of a ladle if the tomatoes need a little coaxing. Taste and season with salt to taste. Put the liquid in a saucepan and slowly add the agar agar, stirring constantly. Bring to the boil over a high heat to hydrate the agar agar. Immediately remove from the heat and pour into a square or rectangular Tupperware container that allows the liquid to be 1cm deep. Leave to cool; the liquid will set. Turn out on to a board and cut into 1cm cubes. Store, covered, in the fridge until needed.

For the apple balsamic jelly, put the vinegar in a saucepan and slowly add the agar agar, stirring constantly. Bring to the boil over a high heat, then immediately remove from the heat and pour into a square or rectangular Tupperware container that allows the liquid to be 1cm deep. Allow to cool and set, then cut into 1cm cubes as for the tomato jelly. Store in the fridge. Drop the jelly cubes into the hot soup immediately before serving.

If you want to serve the soup with the croutons, toss the cubes of bread in a little rapeseed oil and flaky sea salt until lightly coated, then sift a fine, even layer of icing sugar over them. Put the bread in a roasting tray with the basil and place in an oven preheated to 180°C/Gas Mark 4. Cook for 5–10 minutes, until golden brown, tossing half way through to ensure even browning. Scatter the croutons over the soup to serve.

WARM INFUSIONS

The flavour of most green herbs dulls after even a short period of cooking. Infusing liquids, stocks and even soups with herbs at the last minute ensures that the green notes of each herb remain as fresh and pungent as when they were picked. The most common way to prepare a warm infusion is to bring about 500ml liquid to the boil, remove from the heat immediately and add a handful of herbs. Leave to infuse for 15–20 minutes, then strain through a very fine sieve, taste and use immediately. We recommend experimenting with this method. Occasionally you will need more herbs than you might expect to get the desired result.

Roasted Courgette and Cobnut Soup with Labneh and Ginger, Turmeric and Mint Dressing

Courgettes are a relatively recent addition to British cooking, becoming widely known only in the mid-twentieth century, as a result of Elizabeth David's writing. Admittedly, they are not the most fascinating of vegetables but labelling them as tasteless or watery is unfair, in our view. Whilst they do have a high water content (they are, after all, related to watermelons and cucumbers), we would urge anyone who thinks they are tasteless to try growing their own. When they are small and fresh, they have a subtle nuttiness unlike any other member of the *Cucurbita* family to which they belong. The addition of toasted cobnuts in this dish emphasises the nuttiness inherent in our fresh produce magnificently.

There is an impressive row of cobnut trees in the lower corner of the Walled Garden. Resembling a group of wisely content elders, these prosperous leafy trees are known for being easy to keep. This is probably why they are loved by all at Barley Wood, particularly squirrels and chefs.

SERVES 8

1kg small, firm courgettes, sliced
    into 2cm pieces
rapeseed oil
500g onions, finely sliced
250g carrots, finely sliced
250g celery, finely sliced
1 tbsp salt, plus more for the final
    seasoning
40g fresh cobnuts, finely chopped,
    then lightly toasted in a dry
    frying pan

FOR THE LABNEH:

500g yoghurt
½ tsp salt
1 tbsp finely chopped marjoram
1 tbsp finely chopped oregano

FOR THE GINGER, TURMERIC AND
MINT DRESSING:

85ml rapeseed oil
50ml cider vinegar
1 tsp English mustard
½ tsp ground ginger
¼ tsp ground turmeric
1 tsp chopped mint

The labneh must be made a day in advance. Line a sieve with a piece of muslin and put the yoghurt in it. Stir in the salt, cover with the overhanging ends of the muslin and then set over a bowl – it should be deep enough to allow the liquid to drain off the yoghurt. Leave in the fridge overnight. The following day, discard the liquid, unwrap the labneh and put it in a bowl. Stir in the herbs. Keep in the fridge until needed.

To make the dressing, blend all the ingredients together until well combined, then season with salt to taste.

Heat the oven to 200°C/Gas Mark 6. Toss the courgettes with a little rapeseed oil until lightly coated, then spread them out in a roasting tray. Place in the oven and roast for 20 minutes. Meanwhile, heat a thin film of rapeseed oil in a large saucepan, add the onions, carrots and celery and sweat for 10–15 minutes, until tender. Stir regularly and do not allow the vegetables to colour. Add the roasted courgettes and sweat for 5 minutes longer. Add enough water barely to cover the vegetables and bring to a gentle simmer. Add the salt and cook for 5 minutes, then decant into a blender, in batches if necessary. Blitz until smooth, then add enough water to take it to your desired consistency; we like it on the thin side. Blitz once more, then pass through a fine sieve for a velvety mouthfeel. Season with salt to taste. (The soup can be kept in the fridge for up to 5 days at this point.) Reheat gently, then pour the soup into serving bowls and finish each one with a tablespoon of labneh, a sprinkling of chopped cobnuts and a drizzle of the dressing. Serve with seeded bread and salted butter.

† Cobnuts are one of the most wonderful, historically rich native nuts we have, yet surprisingly they are greatly underused in British cooking. A variety of hazelnut, the cobnut has been present in our gardens and orchards since at least the sixteenth century. Historically, cobnuts have been instrumental in hedgerow-growing, forming a dense boundary to keep domestic livestock contained. They keep fresh for months and were thus a valuable source of protein for those at sea. The most common variety, the Kentish cob, was introduced around 1830. It was grown so successfully in Kent that cultivation increased dramatically in the Home Counties, from where cobnuts could be quickly transported to London. During the First World War, labour in the UK became more expensive, and the native plants could not compete with imported fruit and nuts. This led to the demise of plants in Kent, culminating in near-extinction by the early 1990s.

Soused Mackerel, Carrot, Fennel and Saffron with Gooseberry and Mint Granita

Mackerel are one of the most stunning fish in British waters. Their stripy, greenish-blue back affords them excellent camouflage from above, while their silver belly gives an impressive, almost ethereal look as they swim at great speed in purposeful shoals.

The best time to eat mackerel is in the summer. It is then that they gather close to shore in search of fry, allowing them to be easily line-caught, a more sustainable fishing method than nets or trawling. It is also when they start to put on the weight that will allow them to live in deep waters during winter. The additional weight is rich in omega-3 fatty acids, and consequently they are one of the healthiest fish you will have the pleasure of eating. When purchasing, look out for firm, shiny flesh and bright eyes as signs of freshness. Sousing, or pickling, mackerel is a great way of preserving it.

Mackerel's pairing with gooseberry is a classic combination that has survived the test of time. The natural partnership between these two ingredients has not gone unnoticed by the French, who named the gooseberry *groseille à maquereau*, or mackerel berry. Sadly, gooseberries are not grown in the Walled Garden, so we get them from our friends at the Community Farm a couple of miles down the road.

For a berry that is regarded by some as a quintessential British fruit, gooseberries are pretty elusive, even when in season in June and July. The fact that they have often been criticised for being too tart might have led to their demise.

† Mackerel has been a favourite fish in Britain for centuries. It formed the basis of the Roman *liquamen*, also known as *garum*, a fermented fish sauce used in cooking, and which they brought with them to the British Isles.

Records show that as early as 1353, Daniel Rough, the clerk of Romney, Kent, and a prominent fishmonger, sold mackerel to the locals. By the 1660s, it seems that mackerel had become popular further inland, as it starts cropping up in breakfast dishes of the period. Such wider availability might have been the result of an Act of Parliament passed in 1669, which finally declared that London's fish market at Billingsgate could open six days per week.

† Contrary to common belief, the gooseberry is not a native berry. Originally cultivated in cooler areas of Europe, it grows so well in British soil that it quickly became naturalised. Records from the royal garden at Westminster show that bushes were planted in the thirteenth century. By the nineteenth century gooseberries were cultivated on a large commercial scale. Competitive gooseberry-growing clubs were established all over the UK, and the quest to find the best and biggest fruit was taken extremely seriously. Unfortunately, in the early 1900s the entire gooseberry crop was wiped out due to a mildew disease brought in from the United States. Luckily for our British palates, the plant was reintroduced, although it never regained the popularity it had enjoyed in the Victorian era.

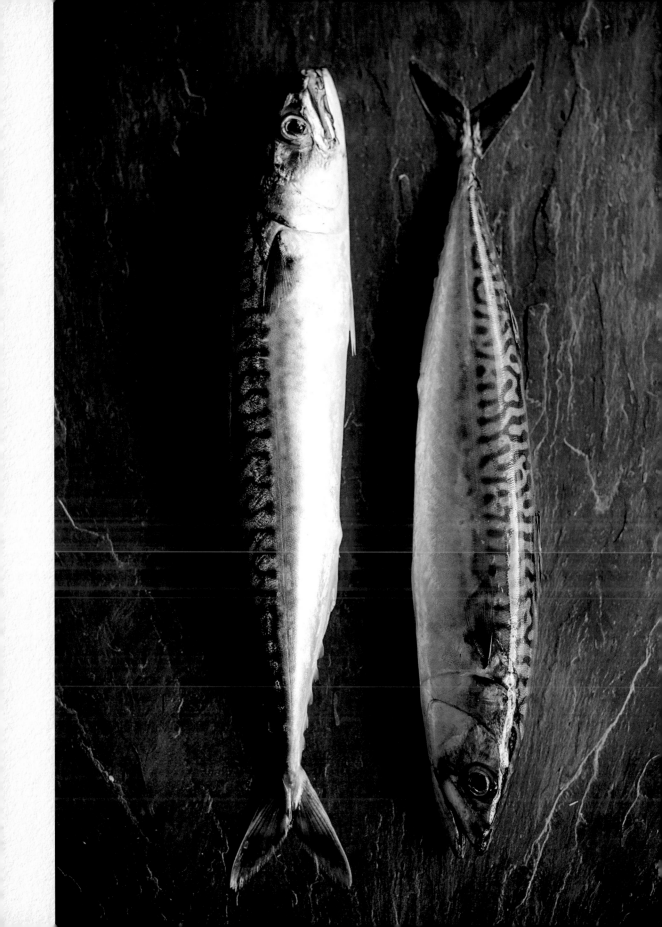

SERVES 4–6

1 x 350–500g mackerel, filleted

8–12 saffron strands

FOR THE CURE:

100g fine sea salt

100g caster sugar

1 tbsp coriander seeds

FOR THE SOUSING LIQUOR:

250ml vintage cider vinegar, such
as Ostler's

100g caster sugar

1 star anise

¼ tsp coriander seeds

¼ tsp black pepper

3 saffron strands

1 shallot, very finely diced

2 carrots, sliced into wafer-
thin long strips, preferably on a
mandoline

½ fennel bulb, sliced wafer thin,
preferably on a mandoline

FOR THE GOOSEBERRY AND MINT
GRANITA:

500g gooseberries, topped and
tailed

100g caster sugar

10g mint leaves

This dish needs to be started at least a day in advance. Remove the bones from the ribcage of the mackerel fillets, using a pair of pliers or tweezers. Next, locate the bones that run down the centre of each fillet. With an extremely sharp knife, slice at an angle down one side of the bones, then down the other side. You will now be able to remove and discard the thin strip containing the bones.

Blitz the cure ingredients in a food processor until the coriander seeds are as fine as the salt and sugar. Spread the cure mix out on a plate large enough to hold the mackerel fillets. Place the mackerel on the cure, skin-side up, cover with cling film and leave in the fridge for 2 hours. Remove from the cure, wash under a gently running tap and pat dry with kitchen paper. Place in the fridge.

For the sousing liquor, put all the ingredients except the carrots and fennel into a saucepan and bring to the boil. Remove from the heat and pour over the carrots, keeping the fennel separate. Allow to cool to room temperature, then chill. Cover the mackerel in the liquor and leave in the fridge overnight.

To make the granita, bring 500ml water to the boil in a saucepan. Put the gooseberries in a steamer basket and place over the water. Cover and steam for 45 minutes. The steam breaks down the gooseberries and their juice drips into the water. The gooseberries are left with little flavour afterwards, so are best discarded.

Remove the pan from the heat, add the sugar to the gooseberry-flavoured water and stir to dissolve. Gently roll the mint leaves between your thumb and finger, then put them in the liquid and leave to infuse for 20 minutes. Rolling the leaves bruises them slightly, without damaging them, so that they give off more aroma and flavour the liquid more effectively. Strain the liquid through muslin or a fine sieve and leave to cool, then chill. Pour into a plastic box and put in the freezer. Leave for 1 hour or until it's starting to set around the edges, then remove from the freezer and rake straight lines from top to bottom with a fork. Place back in the freezer for 30 minutes and then rake with a fork again. Repeat until the granita is completely frozen into ice crystals. It will keep in the freezer for a month.

When the mackerel has had its night in the fridge, remove it from the souse and pat dry. Cut the fillets into 1–2cm strips (the thin tail sections make a tasty snack while you plate up the rest of the dish). The sousing liquor will be a little cloudy after the mackerel has spent some time in it. If you are using this recipe for a dinner party and want to give the extra wow factor, then discard the liquid and make a fresh batch. This will give great clarity to the finished dish.

To serve, bunch some fennel in the centre of each serving bowl and place the mackerel around it. Roll the carrots into ribbons and arrange them around the mackerel. Pour in enough of the sousing liquid just to cover the bottom of each bowl. Place a tablespoon of the granita on top of the fennel and finish with a couple of strands of saffron in each bowl.

Chilled Beetroot Soup, Par-cel, Walnut Ice Cream and Roasted Cobnut Oil

During our first summer at the Walled Garden, we noticed, with some degree of surprise, that whenever there was even a slight indication of sunny weather, customers would ignore the freshly made hot soup on the menu, prepared with vegetables picked from the garden that same morning. This chilled beetroot soup proved to be an acceptable alternative.

The recent success of beetroot in British cooking must be due at least in part to its wonderful combination of sweetness and earthiness. Its earthy aroma comes from geosmin, an organic compound found in beets and the same ionic aroma you get during rain after a dry spell. This scent is detectable by the human nose at very low concentrations. Walnuts are a perfect match for the earthy taste of beetroot, their bitterness balanced by the subtle sweetness of this geosmin gem.

Mark grows a fascinating parsley and celery cross called par-cel. It is so pungent that you need only a small amount as an alternative to celery.

SERVES 6

1kg beetroot, cut into 2cm dice
500g onions, cut into 2cm dice
250g carrots, cut into 2cm dice
1 litre beef stock (see page 294)
2 tablespoons chopped par-cel (or use 250g celery and a handful of parsley stalks)
sea salt
roasted cobnut oil, to serve (we use oil from Hurstwood Farm in Kent, see our list of Friends and Suppliers on page 307)

FOR THE WALNUT ICE CREAM:
225g clotted cream
75g walnuts, finely chopped

To make the walnut ice cream, simply stir both the ingredients together, then freeze in a plastic box. Because of the high fat content, the cream will still be supple when frozen, and beautiful scooped swirls can be made by pulling a spoon over the surface just before serving the soup.

Put the beetroot, onions and carrots into a pan with the beef stock and par-cel, then add enough water to cover the vegetables. Bring to the boil, cover and simmer for 35 minutes or until the vegetables are tender but not falling apart. Pour the contents into a colander set over a bowl and leave until thoroughly drained. Taste the stock and season with salt to taste. It will be a dark, rich colour and heavily red on the spoon. Watch your summer whites!

The soup is the liquid that comes from draining the vegetables, so leave this to cool and then chill. If you need to chill the soup quickly, place ice cubes in a freezer bag, seal it and float it in the liquid. Alternatively, make the soup on the same day as the walnut ice cream and chill it overnight. The vegetables that have been cooked in the stock can be reserved and served as a mash on another occasion (mash the roots and onions, season with salt, butter and chopped tarragon, reheat gently and serve with leftovers; mustard is great to liven it up, too).

Serve the soup chilled, with a spoonful of the walnut ice cream and a smattering of rich roasted cobnut oil, which will shimmer on the surface alluringly.

† Walnuts are one of the most popular nuts in Britain; historical records show that walnut trees were grown in the early medieval period. They are a glutton's delight. Since harvests were uncertain from one year to the next, it was thought acceptable to eat as many walnuts as possible when the harvest was plentiful. Walnuts were thought to help digestion so they were eaten whole at the end of the meal. One can imagine that this belief, despite being totally unfounded, would have encouraged post-meal conversation, which is probably the reason the tradition continued well into the twentieth century.

Ewe's-curd-stuffed Courgette Flowers with Fennel Sherbet

Courgette flowers have never really been popular in the UK. Paûla has fond memories of eating them in quesadillas in Mexico when she was a child. She used to buy them at a stall on her grandmother's street, close to the market where they would arrive every morning in copious amounts, adding a touch of sunshine to an already colourful stall. She talked about them so much that they were one of the first dishes Matthew tried when he travelled to Mexico to meet Paûla's family. Since then, we have wondered whether their lack of popularity in the UK is down to the general view that courgettes do not taste of much at all, and consequently that their flowers don't either. They grow well here, so there should certainly not be a shortage of flowers in the summer. It would be an absolute pleasure for us if the British could adopt the courgette fully into their cooking.

In this dish, the flowers are baked – primarily so that the ewe's curd melts, becoming creamier, but also because they tend to be a little bit spiky when raw. Not only do they look fantastic on the plate but surely few other flowers epitomise summer so effectively. We dare anyone not to think of sunshine when presented with a bright-yellow courgette flower. The fennel sherbet adds a touch of freshness to balance the milky cobnuts.

SERVES 4

1 yellow and 1 green courgette

8 courgette flowers, stamens
    removed

160g fresh ewe's curd

40g fresh cobnuts, lightly crushed

cobnut or hazelnut oil, for drizzling

FOR THE WILD FENNEL SHERBET:

100g icing sugar

2 tsp citric acid

1 tsp bicarbonate of soda

1 tbsp wild fennel seeds (or
    ordinary fennel seeds)

To make the sherbet, put all the ingredients in a blender and blitz until the seeds are finely ground, then pass through a fine sieve. (It will keep in an airtight container for up to a month, and is great with ice creams and sprinkled over other desserts.)

Heat the oven to 200°C/Gas Mark 6. Top and tail the courgettes, then cut them along their length in wafer-thin slices, using a mandoline or vegetable peeler. Stuff the flowers with the ewe's curd. To do this, we fill a piping bag with the curd and place the tip of the nozzle in the flower before filling. Alternatively, you could just gently open up the flowers and spoon in the curd. Place the flowers on a roasting tray and bake for 2–3 minutes, until the cheese has melted and the tips of the leaves are beginning to crisp a little. Remove from the oven and keep warm.

Arrange the courgette ribbons decoratively on 4 serving plates and place the stuffed flowers amongst them. Lightly scatter with the cobnuts, add a drizzle of oil and then dust with the fennel sherbet.

Globe Artichokes with Hollandaise Sauce and Sumac

The inspiration for this dish comes from Paûla. It was the most requested dish in her Mexican grandmother's vast repertoire, and with good reason. She did not always say yes to this particular request, as it was truly a labour of love. It took so long to prepare that she would wait for a special occasion when she knew most of the family would be present. Only then would she start the laborious task of carefully placing a slice of panela cheese between each artichoke leaf. The closer she got to the centre of the artichoke, the harder this became. She would then cover them with a secret mixture involving breadcrumbs and eggs before deep-frying. There was at least one artichoke for each member of the family and, since it was not the smallest family, you can imagine how long the whole process took. For Paûla it symbolises communal eating, with plenty of stories and conversation before you reached the artichoke's heart, eaten with a generous amount of freshly squeezed lime juice and washed down with a mezcal (for those who were old enough).

Globe artichokes are members of the thistle family. Although they are available all year round they are at their best during the summer. The day Mark, the gardener, handed us some globe artichokes straight from the garden, we knew we wanted to replicate the idea of communal artichoke eating. We came up with hollandaise sauce with sumac for dipping the leaves into. It's also pretty good with an anchovy and crème fraîche dip (see page 100), which makes a simpler alternative to the hollandaise, or you can serve them both.

A word of warning is needed here: this is not a dish for the fastidious eater. Using your fingers is pretty much a requirement and it is highly likely that you will need to lick them at the end. Don't bother with serviettes, they will only hamper your enjoyment. Place the artichoke plate, with the bowl of hollandaise in the centre, in the middle of the table and peel off the outer leaves from your artichoke. Dip them into the hollandaise sauce and sumac before eating the tender flesh around the base of each leaf. Paûla's grandmother would no doubt approve.

SERVES 4

4 large globe artichokes, stalks removed
Hollandaise Sauce (see page 77) and/or Anchovy Crème Fraîche Dip (see page 100), to serve
a little sumac, for sprinkling

Using a pair of scissors, cut the tip of each spiky leaf off the artichokes. These spikes are not such fun to eat. Put the artichokes in a steamer and steam over a gentle heat for 25 minutes or until tender.

Meanwhile, whip up the hollandaise sauce or the anchovy crème fraîche dip (or both!). Put them into bowls and sprinkle the hollandaise with sumac.

Remove the artichokes from the steamer and serve on a plate. Have a spare bowl at the side to discard the inedible parts of the leaves. Start peeling the leaves away from the artichoke. The base of each leaf yields a small, fleshy morsel. Dip the base into the sauces and eat straight off the leaf, discarding the rest of the leaf. Every leaf you eat will yield more and more edible flesh until you get to the heart of the artichoke – undoubtedly the best bit – but take care to remove the hairy layer of 'choke'.

Pea, Goat Bacon and Lovage Broth

Bacon and peas has been a classic combination since the 1600s, when, according to Alan Davidson's *Oxford Companion to Food* (Oxford University Press, 1999), they were sold as street food: 'hot grey pease and a suck of bacon'. The peas would have been dried, but we favour fresh peas, which are grown by Mark, the gardener. Instead of ordinary bacon we use our own 'goat bacon', or cured goat loin. It has rich cumin overtones from the simple cure and is pleasantly salty. Lovage and peas work well together.

This is working food – it looks and tastes like a dish that should be eaten after a hard day in the garden. The goat bacon needs to be made several days before required but, once cured, it will keep for two weeks and can be used in the same way as ordinary bacon. Your butcher should be able to order goat loin for you, but if you can't get hold of it, substitute pork tenderloin.

SERVES 4

1kg unshelled fresh peas

rapeseed oil

4 small red onions or 8 spring
    onions, cut into quarters

1 litre white chicken stock (see page
    295)

a bunch of lovage leaves

a splash of cider vinegar, if needed

sea salt

FOR THE GOAT BACON:

2 goat loins, weighing 250–350g
    each, silver membrane removed

20g fine sea salt

10g dark muscovado sugar

1 tsp fennel seeds

2 tsp coriander seeds

1 tbsp cumin seeds

½ tsp black peppercorns

First make the bacon. Tie the loins together with several lengths of butcher's string at intervals of 5cm or so. Place the salt, sugar and spices in a food processor or spice grinder and blitz to a fine powder. Lay the loins on a large piece of cling film, at least 4 times as wide as the loins. Cover with the spice mixture and wrap tightly in the cling film. Place in a large plastic container and leave in the fridge for 5–7 days, turning once a day. Do not drain off any liquid that escapes during this time.

Remove the bacon from the fridge, wash off all the spices under a cold tap and pat dry on kitchen paper. Hang the meat in a warm, well-ventilated area, such as the kitchen or an airing cupboard, for 12 hours or until it is completely dry to the touch – a temperature of 25°C is ideal, so adjust the time you hang the meat accordingly. When the bacon is ready, it should have a distinct, sweet goat smell and be rich in cumin.

Shell the peas, ensuring you have something else to nibble or drink alongside – otherwise you'll be lucky to have any left by the end. Heat a little rapeseed oil in a saucepan, add the onions and fry until lightly coloured. Using a large, sharp knife, cut 15 slices from the goat bacon the thickness of bacon rashers. Add them to the pan and fry till they take on some of the caramel colour from the onions. Add a good splash of the chicken stock, stirring to deglaze the pan. Pour in the remaining stock, then add the lovage leaves and the peas. Bring to a simmer and cook for a couple of minutes, until the peas are tender. Taste the broth and decide whether it requires salt and a splash of cider vinegar. Vinegar will cut through the fattiness of a dish and calm any saltiness. A big bowl of peas for tea. Happy pea days for sure.

Scallops in Puff Pastry with Vermouth and Fennel Cream

This looks like a very simple dish, almost as if it had just been plucked from the shoreline. Choose the curved shell of the scallop to serve them in, rather than the flat one. The pastry cover leaves your guests the task of discovering what you have placed beneath. Since scallops need very little cooking and the shells conduct heat so well, all the ingredients quickly steam under the pastry as it crisps in the oven. The dish can be assembled in advance, kept chilled and then finished in 10 minutes (add a couple of minutes to the cooking time if they've been kept in the fridge).

The sauce is based on a simple reduction. Reducing liquid by boiling it rapidly forces it to evaporate, causing it to thicken gradually. The combination of fish stock, vermouth and cream begins as sweet and rich and ends up with a savoury and satiating bitterness after being reduced. Fennel is an ingredient in some vermouths and has a tried and tested affinity with the botanical flavours in our vermouth (see page 134). The scallops can be served on fennel fronds, those feathery leaves at the top of the fennel bulb.

SERVES 6

150ml fish stock (see page 297)

75ml single cream

50ml dry vermouth (for our house
    Vermouth, see page 134)

6 diver-caught scallops, including
    the orange roe, plus their shells

1 small carrot

1 small onion

¼ small bronze fennel bulb

320g puff pastry (for homemade,
    see pages 301–303)

1 egg, beaten with a pinch of salt,
    to glaze

sea salt and black pepper

Put the fish stock in a heavy-bottomed pan, place over a fairly high heat and let it boil away vigorously until reduced by half its volume. Add the cream and vermouth and continue to boil until the sauce has thickened and reduced by half again. Taste and add salt if needed, then remove from the heat and leave to cool.

Slice each scallop horizontally into 3 if they are thick enough to do so, or in half if they are a little smaller. Cut the carrot into matchstick-sized pieces and finely dice the onion. Cut the fennel bulb quarter into very fine slices. Add a layer of each vegetable to each curved scallop shell and place the scallop slices on top. Pour a couple of tablespoons of the sauce over each scallop and crack some black pepper over them.

Roll out the pastry on a lightly floured worktop to 2–3mm thick. Cut it into 6 squares large enough to cover the scallop shells. Press the pastry on to the edge of each shell, working round it with your thumb so the sharp shell cuts through, trimming off the excess. This will seal the edges at the same time. Cover with cling film and chill until needed.

Heat the oven to 200°C/Gas Mark 6. Brush the pastry with the beaten egg and place the shells in the oven for 8 minutes or until the pastry is lightly coloured.

Pickled Pollack with Flame-roasted Peppers, Cucumber, Pul Biber Chilli and Water Mint

Pollack makes a superb, sustainable alternative to its close relatives, cod and haddock, which have become overfished almost to the point of extinction in some parts of the world. Its flaky texture is very similar to that of the better-known white fish, yet it has suffered a bad reputation in the past and has been criticised for being tasteless. Even the illustrious Jane Grigson in her book, *Fish Cookery* (Michael Joseph Ltd, 1973), relegated it to the quality of a Monday fish rather than a Friday one. We could not disagree more.

The earthiness of the roasted peppers perfectly complements the acidity in the pickled fish, with the cucumber and mint adding a touch of freshness. The dish is finished with a scattering of pul biber chilli. Also known as Aleppo pepper, this is a fruity, medium-hot chilli with cumin overtones, a salty taste and an oily finish. It marries with the mint exceptionally well.

Scallops make a great alternative to pollack in this recipe.

SERVES 4

650–750g pollack fillet

4 tbsp coarse sea salt

2 red peppers

1 cucumber

a handful of water mint (or garden mint)

100g land cress or watercress

juice of 4 limes, mixed with equal parts of cider vinegar

a few pul biber (Aleppo) chilli flakes

The first job is to cure the fish by salting it – this draws some of the water from it. Scatter the coarse salt over a plastic or wooden tray and place the fish on it, skin-side up. Cover with cling film and place in the fridge for 1½ hours, no more. In the meantime, flame-roast the peppers (see page 178) and slice them into strips. Slice the cucumber into long strips by pulling a vegetable peeler down its length, and wash and pat dry the mint and cress.

Remove the fish fillet from the fridge, rinse off any residual salt and pat dry with kitchen paper. It will have firmed up nicely, making the next step easier while seasoning at the same time. With a sharp knife, cutting away from you at an angle, slice thin strips of fish from the skin and place them in the lime juice and vinegar mixture. The acid will effectively 'cook' the fish by lowering its pH level. This forces coagulation in the same way heat does but more slowly. Finely sliced as it is, the fish will need a maximum of 20 minutes for this to happen. You will see it turn white as soon as it lands in the liquid.

Arrange the watercress, cucumber, slices of pepper and mint on the plates. Place the pollack slices amongst the leaves and dust with a few pul biber flakes.

Dorset Blue Vinny and Flame-roasted Peppers with Charred Little Gem

This salad is simple summer food and deserves to be cooked and assembled, in all its parts, outside. Flame-roasting is our favourite way of cooking peppers. The smoke imparts a depth of flavour that acts as a great contrast to their inherent sweetness. We like to cook them on a barbecue when the fire has died away and the coals are searingly hot. The peppers are laid in a spiral formation directly on the coals and turned over in order as their skins turn to slate black. Leaving them on the barbecue for too long will make peeling the charred skin very difficult, so an attentive eye is needed.

We often cook aubergines in the same way, on the barbecue or a gas hob. Once the skins have blackened, make sure that you do not lose any of the precious juice that is contained within the fruit. It has a flavour that must be experienced.

We like coriander seeds here for their gentle, grassy, orange-like flavour, as well as a little ground coriander. We also drop a few coriander flowers into the salad. Their flavour is milder than coriander leaves, and at first glance they resemble cow parsley. Dorset Blue Vinny is a staple in our kitchen. A piece on the riper side is blended with crème fraîche to make a sauce.

SERVES 4 AS A MAIN COURSE, 6–8 AS A STARTER

2 Romero peppers

200–250g new potatoes, cut into 1cm pieces

6–8 Little Gem lettuces

vegetable or rapeseed oil, for brushing

300g mixed lettuce leaves

The Ethicurean Salad Dressing (see page 298)

6–8 coriander flower heads

ground coriander, for dusting

2 tsp coriander seeds, lightly crushed

FOR THE DORSET BLUE VINNY SAUCE:

50g Dorset Blue Vinny, roughly chopped

150ml crème fraîche

sea salt

Begin by roasting the peppers, either on a barbecue as described above or on a gas hob, as follows: turn a gas ring on full, place the peppers directly on the flame and leave until the skin begins to blister and blacken. Using metal tongs, turn the peppers and repeat on the other side. It is possible to overcook the peppers by this method, so care is needed to ensure that only the skin is in contact with the flame. (If you do not have a gas hob, then cut the peppers vertically in half and remove their seeds. Lightly oil the skin and place under a hot grill until the skin blisters and blackens.) As soon as the peppers are blackened all over, place in a small bowl, cover with cling film and leave for 20 minutes.

Meanwhile, cook the potatoes in boiling salted water for about 12 minutes, until a knife tip passes through the potato with little resistance. Drain and leave to cool.

Put the Dorset Blue Vinny and crème fraîche in a blender or food processor and blitz until smooth. Season with salt to taste. If the cheese is too strong for your liking, simply lengthen it with a little more crème fraîche.

With a lightly dampened cloth or hand towel, rub the peppers to remove the blackened skin. Split them in half and remove the seeds. Tear the peppers vertically along their natural 'grain' into strips about 5–10mm thick and set aside.

Place a griddle pan over a high heat. Lightly brush the outside of each Little Gem lettuce with rapeseed or vegetable oil. Put them on the griddle pan and leave, undisturbed, until there are charred lines underneath. Turn and repeat on all sides until the leaves are coloured and tender. Avoid overcooking them, which would result in too dark a colour and a crisp texture. Set aside in a warm place.

Put the charred Little Gem on serving plates amongst the mixed leaves. Scatter the potatoes around and lightly dress the leaves with the salad dressing. Dot the pepper strips throughout the leaves and add drops of the Blue Vinny dressing. Separate the coriander heads into smaller flowers and use to garnish the salad. Dust with ground coriander and a few crushed coriander seeds.

John Dory with Morel Mushrooms, Flat Beans, Haricot Beans and Ham Hock Stock

Morel mushrooms have a natural affinity with fish and make a particularly fine companion to John Dory. Jack can remember prepping this fish during his first job as a kitchen porter. The spines were sharp but the cooked fish was a revelation.

A little fishmongering is required here – it's not at all complicated if you want to give it a go yourself. The fillets on John Dory are connected only lightly and can almost be prised free with thumbs alone once the spine is removed with scissors. The outside of the fish shows a distinct arced line that sweeps in a gentle 's'. This is where the spine runs and is a key identifier in understanding its simple yet beautiful anatomy. If you are new to filleting, just take your time and use your fingers to feel around the bones as you go. A knife should only really be needed to coax the fillets free in some places. By the time you have extracted the four fillets, you will well and truly understand the process. John Dory is one of the first fish we let the young 'uns prepare at the restaurant. We only give them one warning: on any kind of fish, don't rub your hand upwards from tail to head, as they are always spiky this way. There have never been any complications and all come away beaming at having mastered a new skill.

Some fish have delicate skins, which make very good eating. John Dory skin is one of our favourites. The secret to ensuring it is crisp and delicious is to make sure it is very dry before cooking. Remove the fish fillets from the fridge and place them flesh-side down on a board. Run a knife sideways over the skin like a squeegee on a window and a surprising amount of liquid will be freed. Pat this away with kitchen paper and the fish will be ready to cook.

Ham and haricot bean is a classic pairing. Pulses can be cooked with a pig's trotter, which adds gloss and sheen from the gelatine in the bones. In this recipe we use ham hock stock to do the same job.

† John Dory is best eaten when summer draws to a close, as June to August is the breeding season. It has a large, eye-like patch on its flank that confuses both predators and prey, the former fearing a larger fish and the latter mistaking it for a mouth. A popular legend is that the mark on a John Dory is the thumbprint of St Peter, the keeper of the gates of heaven. Though covered in spines and yielding a prehistoric-looking flat body, John Dory is a fearfully tasty native fish.

SERVES 4

300g haricot beans, soaked in 2 changes of cold water for 12–24 hours, then drained

5g dried morel mushrooms

cider vinegar

about 400ml ham hock broth (see page 79)

a bunch of flat-leaf parsley or lovage

200g flat beans (also known as helda beans), trimmed and cut into bite-sized chunks

rapeseed oil

2 John Dory, weighing 500–750g each, filleted (ask your fishmonger to do this, if you prefer)

flaky sea salt

Cover the soaked beans with fresh water and bring to the boil. Reduce the heat and simmer for 35 minutes, until just cooked but still with a little bite. Drain and set aside.

Cover the mushrooms with hot water, add a splash of cider vinegar and leave them to soften for 20 minutes. Morels are typically found on sandy soil and have myriad cavities in which this can get trapped. Gently massage the softened mushrooms to help free any sand or grit, which will sink to the bottom of the water. Once the morels are clean, pour the valuable earthy liquid into a cup, discarding the sandy dregs. Slice the mushrooms.

Put the drained beans in a saucepan, then add the mushroom soaking liquid and enough ham hock broth to cover them just barely. Add the sliced morels, a couple of stalks from the parsley or lovage and the flat beans and bring to a simmer. Cook, stirring occasionally, until the stock has reduced enough to coat the beans. Remove from the heat, season and cover with a lid.

Place a large, heavy-based non-stick frying pan over a medium heat and let it heat up. Add enough rapeseed oil to create a large puddle. It might smoke lightly as it heats; this is a good indicator that it is ready to cook in. Sprinkle flaky salt on the skin side of the fish and lay the fillets skin-side down in the oil. If you can fit only 2 fillets in the pan, cook them in 2 batches, as the skin won't crisp if the pan is crowded. If you have some small ramekins, place one on the middle of each fillet to hold it flat. Resist the urge to move the fillets in the pan. After 3–4 minutes, the fish should have turned white around the edges and through to the top exposed flesh. The extreme edges will also begin to brown a little. Once the band of white at the edge of the fish has worked 1–2cm inwards, then you can lift the fish slightly with a fish slice and peer underneath; the skin should be a light caramel colour. Turn the fillets over and remove the pan from the heat. The residual heat will be more than sufficient to cook the other side within a minute or two.

Serve the fish alongside the cooked beans with chopped flat-leaf parsley or lovage.

Mussels in Cider with Tarragon

Mussels are one of our favourite shellfish. We are truly addicted to them and feel you can never have enough. It is perhaps without much objectivity therefore that we would claim they are one of the most outstanding foods to be found in the British Isles.

We have introduced a West Country twist to this classic recipe with the addition of a medium-dry local cider called Perry's Dabinett, but any good medium-dry cider can be substituted. Rather than using fish stock, we opt for the deeply rich and meaty pressure-cooked chicken stock that is an essential part of our kitchen routine (see page 296). Chicken and cider have a great affinity with each other and you will soon see why the combination works so well in this dish. The 'bridging' flavour is the tarragon. If you don't have any, you can substitute star anise.

SERVES 2 (OR 4 AS A STARTER)

1–1.5kg live mussels
rapeseed oil
3 shallots, sliced into half moons
1 garlic clove, crushed under a knife and then finely sliced
250ml medium-dry cider
250ml brown chicken stock (see page 296)
100ml double cream
4 sprigs of tarragon
sea salt
sourdough bread, to serve

It is important to clean the mussels and check that they are alive before cooking. Rinse them under cold water and remove their 'beards' by pulling them away. Inevitably, a few mussels will be slightly open. Tap them quite hard several times on the work surface. If, after a minute or so, the mussel closes, then you know it is alive. Any mussels that do not close should be discarded.

Heat a splash of rapeseed oil in a large pan, add the shallots and garlic and fry over a medium heat until softened but not browned. Add the cider, chicken stock and cream and turn the heat up high with the lid on. Once the liquid has come to a rapid boil and there is plenty of steam, add the mussels to the pan. Stir once, cover the pan again and cook for 2–3 minutes, until the mussels open. Add the tarragon sprigs and stir the mussels to check that the majority have opened. Any that don't open should be discarded. It is far easier to overcook mussels than it is to undercook them, so resist the urge to continue any longer.

With a slotted spoon, divide the mussels between 2 serving bowls, then taste the cooking liquid and add salt if needed; it will probably already be salty from the mussels. Ladle the liquor over the mussels and get amongst them pronto. An empty mussel shell makes a perfect set of tweezers for removing the remaining mussels from their shells, and decent sourdough bread will thirstily mop up the last drops of the liquor.

Steamed Megrim Sole with Rock Samphire and Sumac-braised Fennel

Rock samphire has complex citrus notes, hints of eucalyptus and a delicate, lingering bitterness that pairs well with fish. We forage rock samphire from the local coastline.

SERVES 2

60g butter, at room temperature, plus an extra knob

1 tbsp chopped mixed flat-leaf parsley, thyme and mint

2 tbsp sumac

4 tbsp cider vinegar

2 fennel bulbs

rapeseed oil

2 carrots

1 megrim sole, weighing 750g–1kg (or 1 witch or 2 dabs)

200g rock samphire or marsh samphire

a glass of white wine

sea salt and black pepper

crusty bread, to serve

Beat the 60g butter with the parsley, thyme and mint, then chill. Bring the sumac and cider vinegar to a simmer in a small saucepan, then strain and reserve the liquid.

Lightly trim the top and bottom of the fennel bulbs. Cut each one vertically into quarters; the core will hold each piece together in segments. Heat the knob of butter in a pan with a splash of rapeseed oil. Add the fennel and cook over a medium-high heat for 5–6 minutes on each side, until browned and lightly caramelised. Add some salt and the sumac vinegar, which should roughly cover the base of the pan. Cover and cook gently for 20–25 minutes; the fennel should still offer a little resistance to the tip of a sharp knife. When it is cooked with the fish later, it will become very tender.

Heat the oven to 200°C/Gas Mark 6. Slice the carrots as finely as you can down their length. If you don't have a mandoline, a y-shaped vegetable peeler will make perfect strips too.

Place a length of thick foil, 2½ times the length of the fish, on a work surface. Put the cooked fennel towards one end of the foil and rest the fish on it. Scatter the samphire and carrots on top of the fish and season with salt and pepper. Pull the edges of the foil up around the fish and then pour in the wine. Cover the fish with the other end of the foil and fold the edges in to seal it tight. Place on a baking sheet in the oven and bake for 12–16 minutes, until the flesh comes away from the spine easily when a knife is inserted near the bone. It could also be cooked on a barbecue with a lid, as the glass of wine steams the fish pretty quickly. The timing will be similar but will depend on the heat of the barbecue.

Drop the chilled herbed butter on to the fish prior to serving. This dish rarely makes it out of the foil at our place, so just needs a warm plate to carry it to the table. Eat with crusty bread to mop up the last of the juices, which are impossible to resist.

SALT AND VINEGAR PICKLING

Salt and vinegar preservation is a great way of storing foraged or garden summer foods. When used as garnishes and ingredients in the winter they will add much to the plate during a season where less grows.

1. Calculating yield and number of jars

Wash all the foraged or garden vegetables thoroughly in a couple of changes of cold water. Weigh the vegetables and make a note of the quantity. Place an empty sterilised jar (see below) on the scales and set them to zero (or 'tare'). Pack the vegetables into the jar, pressing down well, and note down the weight. Divide the total weight of the vegetables by the weight of the vegetables in the jar. (So, if you have 130g in the jar and 1300g total vegetables, you will get 1300/130 = 10 jars.)

2. Calculating quantities of vinegar and salt

Place a pan on the scales and set them to zero (or 'tare'). Add enough pickling or cider vinegar to the jar to cover the vegetables by 1cm depth. Pour off the vinegar into the saucepan and decant the vegetables into a separate bowl. Multiply the weight of vinegar by the number of jars you have lined up and fill the pan with this amount of vinegar. You then need to add ten per cent salt. (So, for 1100g vinegar, you need 110g salt.)

3. Sterilising

Use jars that have lids that will seal well; jars that have rubber seals (e.g. Kilner jars) are best (remove the seals before placing in the oven). Preheat the oven to 140°C/Gas Mark 1. Wash the jars in hot soapy water and drain well. Place on a baking tray in the oven. They need at least 20 minutes, but can stay in the oven until needed, as they should be hot when the contents are added to prevent the glass cracking.

4. Cooking the ingredients

This method is ideal for fine or finely sliced ingredients such as courgettes, samphire and elderberries.

Bring the vinegar to the boil and add your chosen spice mix (see below). Lower the vegetables into the bubbling liquid. The boiling will likely stop. Maintain the high heat and watch for the liquid to return to a rapid boil. Scoop out the vegetables and add them to the hot sterilised jars. Continue until all the jars are filled, then pour the hot vinegar and spices into each jar, covering by 1cm depth. With tea towel in hand close the jars firmly (having replaced the rubber seals, if using) and turn the jars upside down.

Pickled rock samphire

PER LITRE OF CIDER OR PICKLING VINEGAR:

100g sea salt
1 tablespoon coriander seed
1 tbsp black peppercorns
8 star anise
16 allspice berries
8 fresh bay leaves
fresh rock samphire (see above)

Fry the spices (except the bay leaves) in a large frying pan over a medium heat until they start to release their aromas. Add to the boiling vinegar mix, followed by the samphire, and follow the instructions in step 4 above.

Water Buffalo Fillet with Clear Chicken Stock, Tarragon and Salt-baked Baby Beets

The chicken stock for this dish needs freezing and then defrosting through a layer of muslin to clarify it. It will have golden hues and be as brilliant and clear as brandy with this method. It is a somewhat lavish technique, given the reduction in volume that occurs, but for a special occasion such as a steak we think it is worth it. The chicken and tarragon pairing is truly a well-tested one and the tarragon makes a great bridge for the delicate, beef-like fillet of buffalo. For more on cooking steaks, see page 193.

SERVES 4

1 litre brown chicken stock (see page 295)

1kg baby beetroots, with their leafy tops still attached

100g rock salt

a bunch of tarragon

4 water buffalo fillet steaks, 2.5cm thick (see page 193)

rapeseed oil

sea salt

Freeze the stock, then turn it out of its container and wrap it in 2 layers of muslin. Place in a sieve set over a bowl, then put in the fridge. The gelatine, impurities and fat will stay solid in the muslin at fridge temperature, while the stock will run clear below. Resist the urge to squeeze the muslin; it will drain dry eventually. This technique yields about half the initial frozen weight of stock in finished clarified stock.

Heat the oven to 180°C/Gas Mark 4. Wash the baby beets and scrub them well. They will probably be pretty clean at this young age but be mindful of soil residue. Spread the salt on a baking tray and place the beets on top. Wrap the tray in foil, sealing it well, and bake for 1 hour or until the beets are tender. The salt will draw out moisture and season the beets perfectly.

About 15 minutes before the beets are cooked, heat the clarified chicken stock in a pan, then taste and season with salt if required. Now is a good time to get your steak pan smoking hot.

Brush the steaks very lightly with rapeseed oil. Season them with salt, but not pepper as it will burn. Put the steaks in the preheated pan and leave over a high heat, turning them with a long pair of tongs every 15–20 seconds. If you are cooking 4 fillets, this will require standing at the stove turning them in rotation during the few minutes needed to cook them. Periodically press each steak to gauge how well cooked they are, and when you feel you have them spot on, remove to a warm plate. Leave them to rest somewhere warm for 10 minutes, no less. This will allow them to relax and reabsorb some of the juice that comes from them. In this time, divide the chicken stock between 4 deep plates, finishing with fresh tarragon sprigs. Fill a side bowl with the beets, which are to be eaten unceremoniously with your fingers. Lay a steak on each plate. Job done.

WATER BUFFALO

We buy our water buffalo meat from Lower Oakley Farm, near Yeovil in Somerset. Tony and Jane Coupe keep a herd of 250 of these docile beasts, all descended from Asian water buffalo. The calves stay with their mothers for five to six months, then after weaning they eat nothing but grass and, in winter, silage from the farm. They are slaughtered at 22–30 months and the meat is hung for a minimum of 21 days. There is very little marbling in the meat, as most of the fat is on the outside of the animal and around the ribs. Water buffalo meat has high levels of omega-3 fatty acids and iron and is regarded as an all-round healthy alternative to beef.

COOKING STEAK

When cooking steak, there are a few rules to observe. Always bring the steak to room temperature for an hour before it hits the pan, as this will ensure it cooks evenly. Salt is the only seasoning to be added but not far in advance of cooking, otherwise it will draw moisture from the steak. The heavier and thicker the pan, the better the heat will be distributed; cast-iron pans are ideal. The temperature of the pan is the next thing to consider. It needs to be very hot, so put it on the heat and leave until it is so hot you cannot hold your hand an inch above the near-glowing surface.

To check whether a steak is done to your liking, press it with your thumb and gauge the pressure required to do so. Rare steak will feel as soft as the flesh of your cheek over your molars; medium will be more like the flesh at the top of your cheek on your eye socket, which is marginally firmer. Should you get asked to cook a steak 'well done' and you can't convince your guest that 'medium' will be perfect and tender with no hints of red blood normally associated with a four-day-aged cut, then here is how: press your forehead – pretty firm compared to your cheek and a good way to confirm that a steak is overcooked throughout. Painful to see that in the kitchen, we know.

Barbecued Horse Mackerel with Cobnut Salbitxada Sauce

Since we pride ourselves on having a direct relationship with the process of growing, we must admit that we are a little jealous of the Catalan winter celebration for calcots. Calcots are superb sweet onions that are forced to grow tall and pale by gradually building soil up around them. We know our onions and this one is a corker. Attentive gardening is rewarded with the *calcotada* festival in January, when tender stems are wrapped in newspaper and thrown on to hot coals till they are charred. The blackened skins are peeled away and dipped in salbitxada, a roasted pepper sauce that is a cachet of culinary brilliance. It is at its best when made with fresh almonds, which are delicately crisp and ever so slightly milky – qualities that our native fresh cobnuts and hazels share. Given the abundance of these nuts in August, we needed a recipe for them before they were snaffled by the squirrels. Salbitxada sauce proved perfect, using up gluts of peppers and tomatoes and any stale bread. In Spain, sherry vinegar is used but excellent vintage cider vinegar is what we have here and it has equal value in our eyes.

We decided to come up with our own event for the summer months, when heritage tomatoes are at their peak, four types of cobnut are dropping from the trees, and the baby leeks are nigh on impossible to prise out of the gardener's hands unless the word 'cider' is mentioned. This is a great celebration of all the hard work that has gone into the garden. You will need at least two good bags of charcoal, plus someone who used to be a scout who will know when the charcoal is just right to cook on. Oh, and ice in your cider. Dead posh.

We have used horse mackerel here but herring, sardines or pilchards, line-caught sea bass, sea bream and black bream, grey or red mullet and pollack are all ideal for cooking whole over coals and will love the salbitxada pairing.

PER PERSON:
1 corn cob
4–5 baby leeks
1 horse mackerel, weighing 400–
    500g, cleaned
a little rapeseed oil
a bunch of summer savory (or
    thyme or lemon thyme)
sea salt

FOR THE COBNUT SALBITXADA
SAUCE (ENOUGH FOR 8):
1 morita chilli (or chipotle chilli)
vintage cider vinegar
5 garlic cloves
500g heritage tomatoes
150g stale sourdough bread, cut
    into cubes
4 Romano peppers, flame-roasted
    (see page 178)

First make the sauce. To rehydrate the chilli, put it in a small cup of boiling water with a tablespoon of cider vinegar mixed in and leave for 10 minutes.

Heat the oven to 180°C/Gas Mark 4. Wrap the garlic cloves in foil and place them on a baking sheet alongside the tomatoes. Roast in the oven for 25 minutes, until both garlic and tomatoes are very soft. Put the cubes of bread on a baking sheet and toast in the oven for 4 minutes or until golden all over. Set the bread, tomatoes and garlic aside to cool, then peel the roasted tomatoes and garlic by squeezing them free of their skins. Reserve all the liquid and place it, along with the tomatoes and garlic pulp, in a blender with the peppers. Drain and chop the chilli and add that along with the salt and smoked paprika. Splash enough cider vinegar over the bread cubes to soften them. Don't be shy with the vinegar, as it is integral to the taste of the finished dish. Add the bread and cobnuts to the blender, turn it on and then add the rapeseed oil in a slow stream till the mixture is liquid enough to blend. Taste and check the seasoning. Although this can be made in advance, you will have to try to resist eating it all before the barbecue!

1 tsp salt

1 tsp smoked paprika

100g shelled cobnuts, finely
    chopped

about 4 tbsp rapeseed oil

Get your barbecue good and hot. The corn cobs need a
30-minute dunking in cold water, still in their husks, before
cooking. This will moisten the outer layers enough to protect
them from the direct heat of the coals while simultaneously
adding a little moisture internally to help the steaming process.
Place the cobs directly on the coals, still in their husks, and cook
for roughly 15 minutes, turning every 5 minutes, until tender.
Wrap each person's portion of leeks in 2 or 3 layers of dampened
newspaper, then set them directly on the white-hot coals. They
are cooked perfectly when the paper is entirely blackened and
almost burned away. The charred outers and steamed middles
are ever so moreish.

Brush the fish with a little oil, season with salt and stuff the
cavity with the herbs. Cook on the barbecue grill, turning once
(alternatively wrap in foil and place directly on the coals for 5
minutes per side). The fish on the grill can be considered cooked
when the skin is crisped all over and the flesh comes away from
the spine easily.

HORSE MACKEREL

We discovered horse mackerel when, one day, it was
all that was available from the boat that supplies us. It
turns out that horse mackerel are bright-eyed and great
served hot. These shiny 'scad' can be found natively
in the summer not far from Cornwall and are a great
alternative to common mackerel. Ever so slightly less oily
than mackerel and good for roasting over coals, we stuff
the belly with the peppery, marjoram-like herb summer
savoury. Mixed with vinegar, summer savoury can have
the same application as mint sauce. Suffice to say we make
a little of this to drizzle over the finished charcoaled fish.

CURING

Salting food, or 'curing', was a method developed to preserve food: bringing down a whole animal meant more meat than the hunter-gatherer could eat before it went bad. It is believed that drying meat was one of the first experiments with preservation, even pre-dating salting. People would leave meat in the hot sun to dry out, or build a small fire and place the meat over it. Along the way somebody found that salting meat offered a chemical means of achieving the same result. Salting was then combined with smoking to achieve a longer period when meat was safe from spoilage.

These days the need for preservation has been surpassed by people's taste for cured meat. Cured meats possess a unique texture and intense flavour; bacon is probably the most obvious example of this.

Curing is a similar concept to brining but has a different outcome. Brining, generally speaking, uses low percentages of salt in a liquid solution to break down filaments within the muscle, resulting in the muscle taking on and holding liquid during the cooking process. Curing, on the other hand, can be done either in liquid, using a much higher percentage of salt, or with a dry salt or spice rub.

Curing meat draws moisture out, causing the meat to undergo a permanent transformation in texture and flavour: the product becomes more concentrated, achieving a more intense flavour. And while the moisture is being drawn out of the meat, the meat can take on external flavours. This opens up a world of possibility for the cook to be creative. You can add spices and herbs to the salt, then blitz it in a food processor. This is what we do when we do when we cure our roe loin (see page 88), and the goat loin to make our 'goat bacon' (see page 172). Our goat bacon is often pilfered by the chef who's cooking on the stove. Needless to say we've almost always got goat loin curing in the fridge, in a fruitless battle against the constant snarfing of our fresh culinary creation.

There are many variables when it comes to curing, and you can be as creative and experimental as you like. Any recipes for which we use curing include the cure mix and time. However, do experiment with the time that the meat is in the cure, the types of spices and herbs used, as these will all result in different outcomes. Adopt a questioning attitude and seek out answers for yourself!

Fennel and Sumac Gravad Trout

This is our version of the traditional Scandinavian dish, *gravad lax*, which translates as 'buried salmon' – an indication of the way it used to be prepared. By burying fish in a hole in the ground in layers, it was preserved in an airtight space and left to ferment. The addition of salt came later on, when it became more readily available. Once the fish was dug out, it must have been pungent to say the least, but the beauty of this method was that it allowed people to eat fish even when the fresh supplies were long gone. Human ingenuity led to the addition of herbs to make it more palatable and the curing time was shortened. The cure injects some pungent flavours to balance out the subtlety inherent in fish. Here, the aniseed notes in the fennel pair well with the citrus tones of sumac.

SERVES 4–6
1–1.2kg fresh rainbow trout, filleted

FOR THE CURE:
40g fine sea salt
70g caster sugar
2 tsp fennel seeds
2 tsp sumac
1 tsp coriander seeds
½ tsp black peppercorns

Place all the ingredients for the cure in a blender or food processor and blitz until the spices are finely ground. Set aside.

Check that no pin bones remain in the trout fillets. Cut some aluminium foil roughly 4 times the width of a trout fillet and 1½ times the length. Use roughly a quarter of the cure mix to make a bed in the centre of the foil the same length and height as a trout fillet. Place one fillet skin-side down on top. Spread two-thirds of the remaining cure over the fish, then lay the second fillet on top of the first, flesh-to-flesh. Spread the remaining cure on top.

Bring the bottom half of the foil up and the top half of the foil over the trout so that they are edge to edge. Fold the bottom foil over the top to create a 1cm pleat. Keep folding this pleat over itself until the foil is flush with the trout. Repeat the same process on the left and right sides of the foil.

Place the trout on a tray and weight it down with a wooden board or a couple of good-sized plates. Leave in the fridge for 6 days. Liquid will be released from the fish but avoid the temptation to drain it off. This highly saline liquid will continue to cure the trout.

After 6 days, remove the fish from the foil parcel and rinse it under a cold tap. Pat the fish dry with kitchen paper and leave uncovered in the fridge for a couple of hours until completely dry. Place on a board and finely slice the flesh off the skin at an angle, using a very sharp knife.

The trout can be served with Pickled Pollack (see page 176) or Spelt Soda Bread (page 72) and Cobnut Salbitxada Sauce (page 194).

White Raspberry, Loganberry and Ewe's Yoghurt Terrine with Sweet Cicely Confit

This dessert uses some lesser-known berries, which grow easily in British soil. White raspberries are not thought to be native to Britain but the bushes at the Walled Garden seem to thrive and we obtain plenty of fruit. Children seem to like them, finding their colour, or lack of it, rather intriguing. They are very sweet, with little or no acidity, and are best used in dishes where their subtle flavour is not overpowered.

Loganberries are surprisingly difficult to find. A nineteenth-century hybrid between a blackberry and a raspberry, they look like elongated raspberries, acquiring a deep, purplish-red colour when ripe. They are on the tangy side and benefit from the addition of sugar when used in cooking.

You could also serve this terrine with two simple compotes of loganberries and raspberries, as shown in the photo.

SERVES 8–10

500g white raspberries (or ordinary raspberries, if unavailable)
500g loganberries
20g gelatine leaves
240g fructose (fruit sugar)
150g ewe's yoghurt
100g double cream
50g caster sugar
1 vanilla pod
mint leaves (optional), to garnish

FOR THE MACERATED
LOGANBERRIES:
100g loganberries
150ml cider vinegar
250g caster sugar

FOR THE SWEET CICELY CONFIT
(OPTIONAL):
100g caster sugar
100ml white wine
20g sweet cicely stalks, finely sliced

First prepare the macerated loganberries. Put the berries in a bowl, pour over just enough cider vinegar to cover, then leave in the fridge overnight. The following day, drain, reserving the vinegar. Add the caster sugar to the vinegar and stir to dissolve. Pour the liquid back over the berries and chill until needed.

Very lightly brush a 750ml terrine or loaf tin with oil, then line it with cling film. Fill it with water, then gently move the cling film so there are no bubbles remaining underneath. Discard the water and carefully dry the lined terrine.

Put 250g water in a steamer and bring to the boil. Put the white raspberries in the steamer basket, cover and steam over a low heat for 45 minutes. Discard the raspberries – they will have lost all their flavour – and reserve the raspberry-flavoured liquid that remains in the pan. You should have more than the original 250g because of the liquid from the raspberries. Weigh out 250g; you won't need the remaining liquid.

Steam the loganberries in exactly the same way, weighing out 250g of the liquid at the end.

Place 7g of the gelatine in a bowl of ice-cold water and leave for about 10 minutes, until soft. Meanwhile, add half the fructose to the white raspberry liquid and the other half to the loganberry liquid. Heat both the liquids separately, stirring to dissolve the fructose. Pour the loganberry liquid into a container, leave to cool and then refrigerate until needed.

† Berries form an integral part of our food heritage and are the quintessential fruits of the British summer. They were an important element in the Victorian family's fruit bowl; the prominent cookery writer Mrs Beeton stated adamantly in her *Book of Household Management* that there is 'no fruit so universally in favour'. The British population enjoyed a surprising peak of physical health during the mid-Victorian era (from around 1850 to 1880), when there was a tendency to eat more fresh fruit, vegetables, fish and meat.

Take the gelatine from the water, squeezing out the excess. Add the gelatine to the warm white raspberry liquid and stir until fully dissolved. Pour this into the lined terrine to create your first layer. Leave in the fridge for 2–4 hours, until set.

Soften another 7g of the gelatine in ice-cold water in the same way. Transfer the loganberry liquid to a saucepan and warm through over a medium heat. Add the squeezed-out gelatine and stir until fully dissolved. Leave to cool for a few minutes, then take the terrine out of the fridge and slowly pour the loganberry layer over the set white raspberry layer. Return to the fridge and leave to set again.

Meanwhile, soften the final 6g gelatine in a bowl of ice-cold water. Put the yoghurt, cream and sugar into a saucepan. Slit the vanilla pod open lengthways and scrape out the seeds. Put the seeds and pod into the saucepan and place on a low-medium heat. Using the back of a spoon, break up any clumps of vanilla seeds so they are evenly distributed. Stirring regularly, heat until the sugar has dissolved and the mixture is hot to the touch – no more. Anything above this and the yoghurt is likely to split, resulting in a grainy mouthfeel. Add the squeezed-out gelatine to the warm cream and yoghurt mixture and stir until fully dissolved. Take the terrine from the fridge and pour the yoghurt mixture over the loganberry jelly. Return to the fridge until set.

If preparing the sweet cicely confit, put the sugar and wine in an ovenproof pan with 100ml water and bring slowly to the boil, stirring to dissolve the sugar. Add the sliced sweet cicely stalks and place in an oven preheated to 80°C (or the lowest possible gas oven setting). Cook for 3–4 hours or until the sweet cicely is slightly woody. Drain, discarding the sugar syrup.

To serve, turn the terrine out on to a board, carefully peel off the cling film and slice it into 8–10 portions. Lay them on serving plates and dot around the macerated loganberries – and the sweet cicely confit, if you have made it – in a decorative fashion. Mint also works well as a garnish.

FRUCTOSE

Fructose is a type of sugar that is found naturally in both honey and fruit, and is different to sucrose, the sugar that we consume in tea and cakes on a daily basis. Sucrose is a bond between the components glucose and fructose and is a disaccharide. Fructose is a monosaccharide and one of the simplest forms of carbohydrates. It is worth noting that fructose is one and a half times sweeter than sucrose and is therefore often used in sweeteners, due to the fact that less is required. Bear this in mind when using fructose as you will need less to achieve the same sweetness as sucrose.

When it comes to fruity preparations, fructose is our 'go-to' ingredient. Matthew and Iain swear by it, especially around this time of year when the fruit arrives in gluts, and interesting creations need to be conjured up and attentively tested. Only then will they be added to the ever-changing menu. On the basis that using like with like is always preferable, we find that using fructose with fruit achieves a much greater impact than can be achieved with sucrose. It enhances the fruits' inherent flavours and noticeably boosts the 'fruitiness'.

GELATINE

Gelatine is a great means for setting liquids, and gives the 'classic jelly' mouthfeel that we are all so familiar with. Well-executed jellies should be delicate and soft, far from rubbery or chewy. The latter defect is usually down to an excess of gelatine. However, the age of a jelly will also largely affect its structure and consistency – desserts 'stiffen up' the older they are. Gelatine has a troublesome habit of networking and joining up with other networks of gelatine. The more this happens over time, the more water they trap and the stiffer the jelly becomes. We utilise this phenomenon to stick the separate layers together, creating one uniform terrine. Left for too long, the terrine will eventually lose its pleasant mouthfeel. It is worth attempting to devour the terrine within two days – an easy feat once you have tasted it.

Elderflower Sorbet with Fennel Sherbet and Wild Strawberries

Elder grows very quickly and will rapidly take up space needed by other hedgerow plants, such as hazel, chestnut and beech. Luckily for us, the neighbouring farmer has refrained from cutting back the elder and there are several trees that grow in the hedges opposite Mark's polytunnels, high up on a bank away from the field below. We collect as many of these delicate, perfumed flower heads in early summer as possible.

We make our own sherbet for this sorbet. Virtually any spice, within reason, can be added to icing sugar, citric acid and bicarbonate of soda to create this childhood confectionery. We use fennel with its anise flavour, sweet, sour and aromatic.

Wild strawberries add the finishing touch. These tiny morsels of sweet, musky acidity push their way up through the gaps in the red brick paths in the garden. They choose the shade of the low box hedges and shadows of the herb patch. They can be found growing on heathland and grassy verges and in many gardens. It's well worth trying to get hold of some, as they taste infinitely superior to the larger cultivated varieties.

SERVES 4–6

10 large elderflower heads

65ml elderflower cordial

50g glucose powder

195g caster sugar

TO SERVE:

4–6 ice-cream cones

20–30 wild strawberries (if unavailable, use small cultivated strawberries, cut into cubes)

Wild Fennel Sherbet (see page 167)

Remove all but the smallest stalks from the elderflower heads and put the flowers in a bowl. Put all the ingredients except the elderflowers in a saucepan, add 690ml water and bring to the boil, stirring to dissolve the sugar. Immediately remove from the heat and add the elderflowers. Leave to infuse for 15 minutes, then strain through a fine sieve. Discard the elderflowers and leave the syrup to cool. Transfer to the fridge and leave for at least 2 hours before churning. This allows the proteins present in the mixture to hydrate fully, which improves the whipping qualities, giving a smoother sorbet.

Freeze in an ice-cream machine according to the manufacturer's instructions. When the mixture is almost frozen, blitz with a stick blender for 15–30 seconds, then return to the machine and continue to churn. Decant into an airtight container and freeze for at least 2 hours before serving.

To serve, transfer the sorbet to the fridge for about 10 minutes to soften slightly, then scoop one or two balls of sorbet (or as many as you can fit!) into each ice-cream cone. Press the strawberries into the sorbet and then dust lavishly with the sherbet.

Pineapple Weed Jelly

Pineapple weed (*Matricaria discoidea*) can be found from May to September and looks just like chamomile but without the petals. Whether or not it has the same calming effect as chamomile is something to be explored – perhaps this is a calming and restorative jelly recipe. It grows on wasteland and in plenty of other places too. It is often resented by gardeners, as it will compete with other plants for valuable space and nutrients, and the tap roots will grip into any surface, however tough. This is all the more reason to find out whose garden you may be able to pick some from; we are sure they will thank you for it. The flavour is extraordinary, as it resembles pineapple almost perfectly. Both the flowers and leaves are edible.

We have given the measurements for the water for the jelly in grams rather than millilitres. This is because, although millilitres and grams are equal (i.e. 100ml weighs 100g), in recipes where precision is important you get a more accurate result if you weigh the liquid. This is easy to do with electronic scales, and in fact we now weigh liquids as a matter of course and rarely use a measuring jug.

SERVES 4

220g caster sugar

40g pineapple weed

13g gelatine leaves

Cherry Spoom (see page 277) or
　　Roasted White Chocolate Spoom
　　(see page 276), to serve

Put the sugar in a pan with 450g water and bring to the boil, stirring to dissolve the sugar. Remove from the heat and add the pineapple weed. Cover the pan and leave to infuse for 20 minutes. Strain through muslin or a fine sieve.

Soak the gelatine in ice-cold water for about 10 minutes, until softened. Remove from the water, squeezing out the excess. Add the gelatine to the pineapple weed water and stir until completely dissolved. If the gelatine does not dissolve, pour the mixture back in the pan and place over a low heat.

Pour the liquid into a jelly mould (a pineapple mould looks good, if you have one) and refrigerate overnight or until set.

Serve with the cherry spoom or roasted white chocolate spoom.

Elderflower and Lavender Marshmallows

The long country lane leading to Barley Wood is green and winding. By mid-summer, the trees and hedges around it form a dense, herbaceous tunnel in parts. At various spots along the lane are soft, almost furry-looking elderflower bushes, waiting to be picked.

It's the same when you stand at the top gates of the Walled Garden and look down the lane that runs alongside the main orchard. Here, it is impossible not to feel a sense of calm and serenity, induced by the delicately pungent smell of lavender growing along the left-hand wall. Like a group of playful children, heads bobbing in the sunshine, the soft purple flowers greet you every morning with their tranquil scent.

These two ingredients epitomise summer at the Walled Garden. They are traditionally celebrated at the summer solstice, an ancient Pagan festival that is intended to mark the start of more plentiful supplies in the garden. It is a festival of growth and life, where herbs gathered the night before, the point at which they were believed to be at their most powerful, are thrown into a big bonfire to ward off evil spirits, ensuring another year of fertility in the surrounding land. Summer solstice is therefore an opportunity for us to celebrate the garden at its most prosperous, and what better way to enjoy it than by gathering around a bonfire and roasting some marshmallows?

We sometimes toast these and sit them alongside our chocolate brownies (see page 127) instead of the cherry and elderflower sauce. Toasting marshmallows usually evokes nostalgic smiles from our customers.

They are fairly straightforward to make. You will need an electric whisk, preferably a freestanding one, for the amount of whisking needed to achieve the right consistency, but other than that, just some patience and they'll be ready before you know it.

3 tbsp icing sugar
3 tbsp cornflour
rapeseed oil, for brushing
40g gelatine leaves
750g granulated or caster sugar
3 large egg whites

FOR ELDERFLOWER
MARSHMALLOWS:
5–8 large heads of elderflower,
   stalks removed

FOR LAVENDER MARSHMALLOWS:
10 lavender spears, in flower
1 small red beetroot, finely grated
   (optional, but recommended, to
   make the marshmallows pink)

Sift the icing sugar and cornflour into a bowl. Very lightly brush a 35cm x 25cm baking tray with rapeseed oil, then dust with the icing sugar and cornflour. Shake any excess back into the bowl and set aside.

Put the gelatine leaves in a large bowl of very cold water and leave for about 10 minutes, until softened. Remove the gelatine from the water a couple of sheets at a time and squeeze out as much excess water as possible. Put all the drained sheets in a bowl and pour over 185ml hot, but not boiling, water. Stir until the gelatine has fully dissolved.

If you are making elderflower marshmallows, add the heads of elderflower to the liquid that the gelatine has been dissolved in and leave to infuse for 10–15 minutes. Strain the liquid through a fine sieve and continue with the next stage. If making lavender marshmallows, add the lavender and beetroot to the dissolved liquid and infuse for 10–15 minutes, then strain.

Put the sugar in a large, heavy-based pan, add 375ml cold water and place over a medium-high heat. Stir until the sugar has dissolved. Put a sugar thermometer in the syrup and cook the mixture, without stirring, until it registers 122°C. Remove from the heat and stir in the lavender or elderflower mixture.

Put the egg whites in the bowl of a freestanding electric mixer and whisk until they form stiff peaks. Turn the mixer down to a lower speed and pour in the sugar syrup in a slow, steady trickle, beating constantly. Leave the mixer to beat at a medium-high speed until the mallow mix cools and thickens. This usually takes about 30 minutes; it is ready when a thick ribbon is left on the surface when the whisking attachment is lifted out.

Using a spatula, scoop all the mix into the dusted tray. Be sure to scrape the sides of the bowl thoroughly, so as not to waste any of this fluffy decadence. Level the mixture and allow to cool to room temperature. Cover with baking parchment and leave overnight to set. Do not refrigerate.

Removing the marshmallow from the tray is arguably the hardest part. Start by peeling the mallow away from one of the narrow ends of the tray. When you get enough off the side, dust in some of the reserved cornflour and icing sugar mix, then keep gently peeling and dusting until you have a good couple of inches clear of the tray. At this point, flip the tray over on to a board and gently lift it off. Gravity should, in theory, do the rest of the job. If not, then continue peeling and dusting and turning it on to the board until it comes loose.

Have more cornflour/icing sugar mix ready and cut the marshmallows into 2.5–5cm cubes. Roll each marshmallow in the dusting mixture thoroughly to prevent sticking. They will keep, stored in an airtight container, for up to a week.

Spiced Ginger Beer

Ginger beer has been brewed in Britain since the 1700s. The taste for it spread across the world with the British Empire, becoming particularly popular in Africa and the Caribbean. Meanwhile, the 'Bristol glaze', which increased the strength of pottery, was developed locally in the 1830s and applied to earthenware containers. It allowed this very British tipple to be sent further and further afield. The mesmerising collection of photographs, observations and facts contained in John Thomson's *Victorian London Street Life* (Dover Publications Inc, 1994) estimates that in 1877, 300,000 gallons of ginger beer were sold in London. Quite often it was pulled through the streets by horses, in a contraption resembling an old piano, and dispensed with beer pump handles. By 1935 there were more than 3,000 producers in the UK but only a few remain. It really is the taste of British summer. Please serve in a jug in the garden, on a table covered with a linen tablecloth. We have also tried this recipe with raspberries and it was superb. We added a handful of raspberries with the spices at the heating stage and still put the ginger in muslin for the fermentation part. It was a luminous red.

MAKES ABOUT 2 LITRES
250g caster sugar
5–8cm piece of fresh ginger, diced
zest and juice of 1 lemon
2 cloves
3 juniper berries
½ cinnamon stick
3 black peppercorns
1 tbsp GBP (see page 137)

You will need a 2.25 litre container with a lid, plus a 25cm square of muslin and a piece of string for tying it into a Dick Whittingtonesque parcel. It is important to sterilise all the equipment, including the muslin and string. You can do this by pouring boiling water over everything.

Put the sugar in a pan with a third of the ginger, plus the lemon zest, spices and 250ml water. Bring this mixture to a light simmer, stirring to dissolve the sugar, then leave to cool.

Pour 1.75 litres of water and the juice of the lemon into your sterilised 2 litre container (a large, lidded plastic box is fine); the lemon will neutralise the chlorine in the water, which would otherwise affect the yeast's productivity. Strain in the sugar and water mixture, tie the rest of the ginger up in the muslin with a piece of string and drop it in. Add the GBP, then cover and leave at room temperature for 5 days. Be sure to open the lid briefly every day in order to let out any carbon dioxide that has built up, otherwise it will open of its own accord.

Strain the mixture through a fine sieve into a sterilised 2 litre plastic bottle and put on the top. Save the GBP and give it a rinse; it will have grown. (If you store it in the fridge in a small, sterile container, it will keep for up to 2 weeks.) After 2 days the ginger beer will be ready to drink, although if you desire a fizzier brew, leave it for longer. Refrigeration will halt any further fermentation.

Summer Elder

This initially sounds as though it might be a thoroughly sweet affair, but fear not. The botanicals in the gin revel in their meeting with the black pepper and raspberry tincture, creating an almost savoury flavour. The sorbet we use is from Mendip Moments whose pedigree herd of Holstein cows grazes just over the horizon on the Somerset levels. But this drink would work very well with any pre-made raspberry sorbet.

1 scoop of Mendip Moments
    raspberry and elderflower
    sorbet, at room temperature
50ml gin (we like Chase gin)
25ml elderflower cordial
dash of Angostura bitters
dash of black pepper tincture (see
    box, below)
dash of raspberry tincture (see box,
    below)
3 black peppercorns
freshly ground black pepper

First fill a tumbler with ice to chill it. In a mixing glass combine the sorbet, gin, elderflower cordial, bitters and tinctures. Give it a stir with a bar spoon to break up the sorbet before adding a handful of ice and place the tin part of the shaker over the glass, tapping with the palm of your hand to secure. A good hard shake will allow the ice to break up the sorbet and make a smooth textured drink. Discard the ice from the tumbler and strain the liquid through a strainer and sieve into the glass. Finish with a generous grind of black pepper and the three peppercorns on top.

MAKING TINCTURES

Fill a jam jar one third full with your chosen ingredient and cover with a high percentage proof vodka to twice the depth of the ingredients. Leave to infuse for 2 weeks and then strain into another clean jam jar. You will be left with an intense essence of your chosen ingredient.

Raw Rhubarb Smash

A smash is so named because the mint is smashed up during shaking. During the mid-nineteenth century, the smash became a symbol of intemperance in America and was a favourite summer drink. Compared to its older brother, the julep, this drink is, in the words of the cocktail historian, David Wondrich, 'a quick bracer, rather than a slow sipper'.

Before the drink is shaken, we also muddle the rhubarb. We build this cocktail in a jam jar and then add crushed ice. Raw rhubarb has good acidity and we use it instead of the citrus fruit of the original.

SERVES 1

25ml rhubarb syrup (see page 305)
7–8cm piece of rhubarb, finely
    sliced
a pinch of sugar
6 sprigs of mint
50ml bourbon whiskey
finely sliced rhubarb, dusted with
    sugar, to garnish

Place the syrup, rhubarb and sugar in a jam jar and 'muddle' it by pressing with a pestle to release the juice from the rhubarb and mix it with the sugar. Add a sprig of mint and muddle again, more gently this time. Add the bourbon, 2 more sprigs of mint and a few ice cubes. Screw the lid on and shake for 10 seconds. Pack in crushed ice and 2 more mint sprigs until the ice is piled just above the rim. Serve in the jam jar, garnished with a thin slice of raw rhubarb dusted with sugar, plus a good sprig of mint.

Double Sloe Gin and Tonic

We use a metal Victorian coffee pot to stir, chill and serve this tipple. After 10 good swirls clockwise, the outside gathers a divine frost. We pour the drink into a teacup and deliver it with a pot of ice cubes. In Victorian times, serving drinks in this manner was a way of consuming alcohol in the guise of afternoon tea. This was in order not to offend the beliefs of the locals in far-flung regions of the old British Empire. It is still a genius way of disguising those early-afternoon drinks.

SERVES 1

6 raspberries

200ml tonic water (we like the
    Fever Tree brand)

25ml gin (Chase gin is our choice)

25ml sloe gin

Put the raspberries in a glass, reserving one to drop in the teacup. Add a drop of tonic water and 'muddle' until as much juice has been extracted from the raspberries as possible. Strain into a small teapot and add the gin, sloe gin and the rest of the tonic water. Drop in 3 ice cubes and stir well. Pour into a cup to serve and drop in the remaining raspberry; the ice can be added with tongs, like sugar cubes.

AUTUMN

T HE vale below the garden gradually alters, at first a ripple of muted colour that transforms into a leaf sea of reds and browns, flecks of copper and orange and a faint shimmer of silver birch. The larches stand tall and green against this backdrop of colour.

We watch the orchards carefully as their fruit crops in tandem. Cheddar Cross and Ribston Pippin lead the way, while jack-of-all-trades Morgan Sweet follows. The cider barn smells just as it should, with the curative aromas of the sweet, spiced apples. Trugs, buckets and any containers available line the timber walls, windfalls set aside. The oak press, perfumed from seasons of work, is wound up as frames and cheesecloths are filled with scratted apples. There is a rhythm as frame after frame is stacked, levelled and secured, before the cogs are heaved and the apple tower is compressed. At first there is just a trickle, then the juice turns to a flow that quickly fills our containers. The colour is golden and the flavour sweet, acidic, caramel. Glasses are filled and clinked, smiles exchanged, varieties noted. Elena and Phil will debate and discuss the next blend.

Early autumn's blood-coloured damsons see off the last of the raspberries. Mark's tomatoes become a spiced soup along with fennel and are met in the bowl by turmeric-fried ling, horse mackerel and squid. Sourdough bread is toasted and drizzled with English truffle oil, with flavours of bosky woodland and four-star petrol. Found by a canine truffle hunter in Somerset, these irregular black objects transform a supper.

Foragers deliver boxes and baskets of fungi, with textures ranging from powder to those that slip from your fingers. Some deliquesce by the evening.

Roe deer find their thick winter coat, muted to a darker shade. We claim a buck or two and stew some cuts with cider and quince, to be served with plump butter dumplings. Vince Castellano collects the shoulders and soon they hang as bundles of red chorizo. Braces of pheasants are hung, and a couple of these red-eyed firebirds, escapees from a nearby shoot, peck around the garden. The cock is a flash of colour, while his partner, the hen, is much more subdued in her sombre brown feathers.

Wood pigeons are perched on the posts securing the raspberries, unwittingly awaiting a meeting with Persian spiced bulgar wheat. The vine house is full of early-season Muscat grapes. The 100-year-old vine's crop once filled silver bowls in the dining room of Barley Wood house. Simon Wills, who grew up at Barley Wood, tells us of the pleasure of eating this sweet fruit during wartime rationing, and of mornings shooting rabbits with his mother's gundog. Boy and Spaniel were a team; when he crawled, so would she.

As the hedges begin to crop hips and haws, sloe gin is debated in the restaurant and each customer promises a finer recipe than the last.

Goat Bacon with Ox Tongue, Nasturtiums and Clarified Ham Broth

'Goat bacon ... what's that?' we hear you ask. Matthew and Iain take the goat loins (two muscles that run parallel to the spine) and dry cure them, much in the same way that ordinary bacon is made. They mix the salt with spices, so the resulting bacon is fragrant with notes of cumin and fennel that sit perfectly with the flavour of the goat (see the recipe on page 172). The texture is identical to traditional bacon, yet the flavour is pleasingly different. This bacon works well alongside one of our favourite pieces of offal: tongue. Tongue used to be very popular but has since fallen out of fashion and is rarely seen on restaurant menus. We think this is a shame. It is cheap, easy to cook, very versatile and one of the most overlooked muscles. See page 100 for Ox Tongue with Cauliflower, Gilliflower and Hazelnuts, and page 108 for cooking tongue.

SERVES 4

800ml ham hock broth (see page 79)

a little vintage cider vinegar, such as Ostler's

rapeseed oil

12 slices of Goat Bacon (see page 172), cut 3–5mm thick

4 eggs, poached (see page 81)

12–16 small-medium nasturtium leaves, washed and dried (if unavailable, use baby rainbow chard leaves)

4 nasturtium flowers, gently washed

fine sea salt

flaky sea salt

black pepper

FOR THE TONGUE:

1 ox tongue, brined and cooked (see page 108)

1 egg, lightly beaten

50g dried breadcrumbs (see page 34 to achieve the best breadcrumbs)

Freeze the broth in 1–2 tubs overnight, then a day or so before you plan to make this dish, turn out the frozen blocks and wrap them in 2 layers of muslin. Place them in a sieve set over a bowl large enough to hold the thawed broth, then put them in the fridge. The gelatine, impurities and fat will stay solid in the muslin at fridge temperature while the broth will run clear below. Resist the urge to squeeze the muslin; it will drain dry eventually. This technique yields about half the initial frozen weight of broth in finished clarified broth.

Slice the cooked tongue into 4 portions, about 5mm–1cm thick. Lightly brush the slices on both sides with beaten egg, then dip them in the dried breadcrumbs to give an even covering. Set aside.

Put the clarified ham broth in a saucepan and place over a low heat. Bring to a simmer, then taste. If it is too concentrated, add cold water a tablespoon at a time until you get the desired dilution. Season with a pinch of fine salt and a small splash of cider vinegar. When you are happy with the seasoning, set the broth aside in a warm place.

Place a frying pan over a medium heat and when it is hot add a splash of rapeseed oil. The oil should begin to smoke lightly if the pan is hot enough. Add the tongue, followed by the bacon, and fry for 1–2 minutes per side, until lightly golden. Remove from the pan and place on a layer of kitchen paper.

To serve, place a poached egg in each bowl and then add the tongue and the bacon. Slowly pour in the broth. Garnish with the nasturtium leaves and flowers, then add flaky salt and cracked pepper to the eggs.

Wild Mushrooms with Sourdough Toast and Thyme Stichelton Crème Fraîche

This is supper for an autumnal day. The sum of all of its parts and a collection of flavours that have been enjoyed together for centuries. Autumn means that it is time for mushrooms. A number of foragers drop in with boxes of them throughout the season and we also try to get out as much as we can – especially into the woods and hills framed in the windows of our glasshouse.

Please try to get hold of a sourdough loaf for the toast. We pick ours up from Mark's Bread in Bedminster. They have their own *levain*, or starter, that they use to make their Bristol sourdough. The lactic acid in sourdough, produced by the *lactobacilli* bacteria, gives this bread its unique taste, which works so well in this simple meal. Our businesses have grown in tandem and Mark Newman and his fellow bakers have similar values to ours. For one, they make all their deliveries on their 'Breadmobile', a heavy iron bicycle with a big box on the back.

The warm, woody aroma of thyme is both bitter and sweet. It was always destined to be paired with an assortment of wild mushrooms. Jekka McVicar, our queen of herbs, points out that thyme aids digestion and will help to break down fat in foods – another good reason to be liberal when pairing it with cheese. We chose Stichelton for this recipe. It has toast and caramel flavours with an underlying butteriness, while its blue veins provide piquancy. The blue softens the cheese, altering its texture and flavour, changing the colour from white to soft cream. The whole truckles are a thing of beauty, a combination of white crust through to a bright rust that is almost pink.

SERVES 4

2 tbsp rapeseed oil

300g mixed wild mushrooms, such as slippery jack, penny bun, russula, horse mushroom, sheep's foot and puffballs, cleaned and sliced into 1cm strips

leaves from 4 sprigs of thyme

25g unsalted butter

8 very thin slices of sourdough bread

fine sea salt

flaky sea salt

FOR THE THYME STICHELTON CRÈME FRAÎCHE:

25g Stichelton cheese, roughly chopped

75ml crème fraîche

leaves from 5 sprigs of thyme

For the thyme Stichelton crème fraîche, put all the ingredients in a blender or food processor and pulse to a semi-coarse consistency. Season with flaky salt to taste and set aside.

Place a large frying pan over a high heat and leave until it is very hot. Add the rapeseed oil; it should begin to smoke. Immediately add the mushrooms and thyme leaves, plus a dusting of fine salt, and toss to coat them evenly with the oil. Leave undisturbed for a minute or so, until the mushrooms colour ever so slightly, then toss and colour on the other side. Remove from the heat and add the butter to the pan. Toss until it has melted and the mushrooms are evenly coated, then check the seasoning.

While the mushrooms are cooking, put the sourdough bread under a hot grill and toast, turning every minute, until both sides are golden brown. Thin slices of bread will curl under the grill, and the regular turning prevents this happening.

Remove the sourdough from the grill and add a couple of slices to each plate. Cover with the mushrooms, season with flaky sea salt and add a heaped tablespoon of the Stichelton crème fraîche.

† From the old English 'Stichl' (meaning 'style') and Tun ('village' or 'hamlet'), Stichelton is the result of a collaboration between cheesemaker Joe Scheider and cheesemonger Randolph Hodgson of Neal's Yard Dairy, on the Welbeck Estate in Nottinghamshire. This blue cheese is made using unpasteurised organic cow's milk and traditional animal rennet. The dairy is located on the farm and the cows graze just yards away. Joe and Randoph are focused on promoting a rediscovery in Britain of the raw milk tradition. They wanted to name their cheese Stilton but were not allowed to under the Protected Designated Origin (PDO) scheme, which does not allow an unpasteurised cheese to be added to its ranks. We think Stichelton is an even better name: it was an early form of the word 'Stilton', recorded in the twelfth century. We really appreciate their desire to make the best possible product, using the finest ingredients, with integrity and tradition. Bravo.

WILD MUSHROOMS

We are fascinated by these fruiting bodies that appear in a matter of hours – mycelium networks. Please use a mushroom guide that is fully illustrated and offers comprehensive instructions on identifying whether a mushroom is possibly poisonous; Roger Phillips' *Mushrooms* (Macmillan, 2006) is very useful.

A few times we have been lucky enough to cook this recipe with Penny bun, russula, horse mushrooms, slippery jacks, puffballs and sheep's foot mushrooms. However, some of these are difficult to find and easily confused with non-edible varieties. A good place to start is with some common varieties that are relatively easy to identify. Once you have built up a good knowledge of these, have a tentative look further afield.

Mushrooms love damp weather followed by sunshine, so try to pick on a dry day. Brush off any debris with a small mushroom brush – a toothbrush works a treat but make sure you use it exclusively for that activity! Check for maggots and parasites before cooking. These are some of our favourite varieties:

Chanterelle – *Cantharellus cibarius*
They have a superb flavour. They are associated with pine, beech and birch and smell of apricots. They can be found on mossy banks and damp woods between summer and late autumn.

Chicken of the woods – *Laetiporus sulphureus*
Along with the beefsteak mushroom this is the only other bracket fungus worth eating. It can potentially yield up to a kilo of flesh and can be found growing on old trees such as oak and yew, cherry, sweet chestnut and willlow, between April and autumn. The yellower the better.

Giant puffball – *Calvatia gigantea*
These must be a clean, milky white and predominately unblemished on their outside and within. They can be found in grassy fields, gardens, hedgerows and on wood edges between late summer and autumn.

Jew's ear – *Auricularia auricula-judae.*
These have a colour that will be anywhere between a pale reddish brown through to dark. This gelatinous-textured mushroom can only be found on dead or dying wood, usually elder. Find it at any time of the year.

Field mushroom – *Agaricus campestris*
This one resembles the mushroom that most of us will have had from the shops. It is easy to find and grows on pasture and grassland between late summer and autumn. Be wary of the yellow stainer

which can be confused with the field mushroom; its cap has yellow streaks and smells of carbolic acid when cut.

Morel – *Morchella esculenta*
A joy to discover and eat. It resembles an irregular honeycomb. Can be found on open scrub woodland, chalky soil, ash, elm or apple during late Spring, often around St Georges's day.

Oyster mushroom – *Pleurotus ostreatus*
These are coloured silver-grey to a fawny beige. Find them on trunks or branches of dead or dying deciduous trees, such as beech, all year around.

Parasol and shaggy parasol – *Lepiota procera* and *Lepiota rhacodes*
These look like an umbrella with a nipple on the top. The stem and cap are scaly and there will be a ring on the stem where the cap was attached. Find them in open woods and pastures between summer and autumn.

Penny bun – *Boletus edulis*
It's an absolute win if you discover this one. This mushroom has no gills but tubes like a sponge instead. Find it along edges of woods and in grassy clearings. Beware of Devil's Bolete – *Boletus satanas*, which has a white grey cap with orange spores and a flush of red on the stem, as it will cause an upset stomach.

St George's mushroom – *Calocybe gambosa*
A favourite eaten raw at The Ethicurean (see page 70), it can be found on grassy clearings, roadsides and on the edges of woods. A good one to identify since it is specific to early May, often appearing a week after the 23rd April.

Wild Mushroom and Spelt Pressed Terrine with Spinach and Rainbow Chard

The ridge opposite The Ethicurean is called Black Down. The highest hill in the Mendips, it is covered in a mixture of heather and bracken. In its shadows are patches of deciduous woodland, where we have found wood blewit mushrooms with the expert guidance of our friend and forager, Adrian Boots. Wood blewits grow in leaf litter and range in colour from lilac to a rich purple-pink, with an intensely perfumed aroma. They have been sold in English markets since the thirteenth century. We love using them in this terrine but it is important to have them expertly identified, as some harmful varieties can be mistaken for them. Always cook them thoroughly, as they should not be eaten raw.

Wild mushrooms vary dramatically in flavour depending on the variety. Any good edible wild mushrooms you can get your hands on will work perfectly well here. If you are interesting in picking your own, book yourself on to a good foraging course – they are run in most parts of the country. Otherwise, bought button mushrooms or brown mushrooms can be used in this recipe and you will still have a delectable terrine.

We wrap the terrine in a mixture of spinach and chard for a spectacular appearance and layer it with the colourful stalks of rainbow chard. Its earthiness is completely at home with the mushrooms and spelt. Pearled spelt has a firm texture and gentle, nutty flavour. Although it is a type of wheat, some people with wheat intolerances find it easier to digest. It has been eaten in Britain for thousands of years and was favoured by the Romans. Ours comes from Sharpham Park, close to Glastonbury in Somerset. They are a great outfit and true proponents of a more sustainable way of farming.

SERVES 6–8

300g pearled spelt

a sprig of rosemary

2 sprigs of thyme

400ml vegetable stock (see page 297)

200g mixed spinach and rainbow chard, preferably with large leaves

50g salted butter

300g wild mushrooms, such as blue foot, hedgehog fungus, sheep's foot, penny bun, russula or slippery jacks (or button or brown mushrooms), cut into slices 1cm thick

3 medium egg yolks

1½ tsp Dijon mustard

1½ tsp vintage cider vinegar, such as Ostler's

rapeseed oil, for brushing

fine sea salt

Put the spelt into a saucepan with the rosemary and thyme, add the vegetable stock and 550ml water and bring to the boil. Cover the pan, reduce the heat and cook for 1–1½ hours, until the spelt is tender but still retains a little bite. All the liquid should be absorbed.

Meanwhile, put a large pan of water on to boil, adding 3 tablespoons of salt. Fill a pan or bowl with cold water and ice and set aside. Separate the stalks from the leaves of the spinach and chard, keeping the leaves whole. Chop the stalks into 3cm pieces. Add the leaves to the boiling water and blanch for 30–45 seconds, then remove with a slotted spoon and transfer straight to the ice bath. This will help retain the vibrant colour. Stir the leaves to chill them quickly. Once they are thoroughly cold, remove them a couple at a time and squeeze as much moisture from them as possible. Next, blanch the stalks in the rapidly boiling water for 1–1½ minutes. Transfer them to the ice bath and stir to chill rapidly, then drain and pat dry with a tea towel or kitchen paper. Separate the large spinach and chard leaves from the small ones, then place all the leaves and stalks in the fridge until required.

† Spinach was only introduced into England around the 1500s; prior references to this leaf would have mentioned plants such as chicory, orache and Good King Henry (*Chenopodium bonus-henricus*). We have used the latter a lot in our kitchen. It can be found along roadsides and on cultivated land. With triangular or spear-shaped leaves, it grows year-round and makes a great substitute for spinach.

Melt the butter in a saucepan, add the mushrooms and a pinch of salt and cook over a medium heat for 5–10 minutes, until the mushrooms have softened. Set aside, retaining any liquid.

Once the spelt is done, pick out the herbs and discard. Put the spelt and mushrooms into a blender or food processor, add the egg yolks, mustard, vinegar and some salt and pulse until thoroughly mixed. Check the seasoning and add more salt if required. Continue to pulse until the mixture has a fairly coarse texture. Whole grains of spelt may still be present but the majority will have been broken down into a paste. Check the seasoning once more.

Lightly brush an 800g terrine or loaf tin with rapeseed oil and line it with a large piece of cling film. Gently coax the cling film into the corners of the terrine, making sure not to tear it, then fill the terrine with water. At this point, you will see any air bubbles beneath the cling film. Manipulate the cling film to remove them, then pour out the water and carefully dry the inside. Have the larger spinach and chard leaves at the ready. Drape them down one side of the terrine, making sure there are no gaps, so the tip of each leaf reaches the centre of the base of the dish. Any excess leaf should overhang the edge of the terrine. Repeat on the other side and the ends. If any terrine is visible through the leaves, then patch these areas using smaller leaves until it is completely covered.

Decant half the spelt and mushroom mixture into the terrine and press down until it is completely level and filling all 4 corners. Layer the spinach and chard stalks lengthways, end to end, on top of the spelt mix, so that they completely cover it. Add a second layer of stalks of different colours, if you wish. Cover the stalks with the remaining spelt mix, so it reaches the top of the terrine. Layer some smaller spinach or chard leaves over it, then fold over the overhanging leaves, so that the spelt mix is completely wrapped in the spinach and chard leaves.

Place in the fridge and leave for at least 2 hours. Turn the terrine out, peel off the cling film and then cut into slices and put them on serving plates. Cover with cling film and leave to come to room temperature for 30 minutes before serving. It's great with bread, chutney and a few salad leaves.

Swedish Knäckebröd with Cottage Cheese, Pickled Beetroot, Caraway, Beetroot Crisps and Tom Thumb Lettuce

Autumn signals the start of the game season and it is easy to eat nothing but meat at this time of wonderful gluts. This salad is our way of redressing the balance and offering a fresh starter to what might be a meaty autumnal feast.

We use Longley's cottage cheese, which we find far superior to all the others we have tried. Its clean, lactic freshness works particularly well with the sweetness of the beetroot.

The spices are heated in a dry pan to help release their essential oils. This makes them more pungent and with greater depth, as if something within them had come to life. As the aroma fills the air, it is a great time to think about what character a spice has. Some will show menthol tones, others will be resinous, citrus, grassy, bitter. When you break down the taste into separate components it is easy to decide where they might be useful in relation to other ingredients. Cumin has an earthy flavour similar to that of beetroot. Citrus will also come through, mimicking lemon peel, which is an ideal pairing with beets. Caraway is included here to offer a sweet spice edge, complementing the light sourness in the rye crispbreads. It also has anise tones, which we heighten with the addition of fennel seed.

SERVES 4

1 tsp cumin seeds

1 tsp caraway seeds

2 Tom Thumb lettuces, or other round, soft, butterhead lettuces

225g cottage cheese, preferably Longley Farm

4 tbsp Pickled Beetroot (see page 298)

sea salt

FOR THE BEETROOT CRISPS:

2 Chioggia beetroot (if you can't get them, use ordinary beetroot)

icing sugar, for dusting

To make the beetroot crisps, finely slice the pink and white candy-striped beets through their equator. Lay the slices on a wire rack that will fit on an oven shelf. Dust the finest possible layer of icing sugar over them, then turn them over and repeat. Place in an oven set at 50ºC (or the lowest possible gas setting) and leave for 4–6 hours, until crunchy and crisp.

Meanwhile, make the bread. Heat the milk and honey to 45ºC (just above body temperature). Sprinkle the yeast into it and stir a couple of times. Set aside for 10 minutes and it will froth as the yeast is activated .

Sift the flours into a bowl and add the fine sea salt and toasted crushed seeds. Pour in the yeast mixture and stir to make a dough. Turn it out on to a lightly floured surface and knead for 5 minutes, until smooth and elastic. Return it to the bowl, cover with a towel and leave in a warm place to rise for 1 hour.

Heat the oven to 230ºC/Gas Mark 8. Knock back the dough by giving it a smart, percussive slap that will knock the air free. Satisfaction for the pacifist. Fold the dough over a couple of times and roll it back into a ball, then divide it into 8 pieces. Roll these back into balls, cover with a tea towel and leave to rest for 10 minutes.

FOR THE KNÄCKEBRÖD:

240ml milk

45g honey

½ sachet (3.5g) of dried active yeast

270g wholemeal flour

80g rye flour

30g spelt flour

½ tsp fine sea salt

1 tsp caraway seeds, toasted in a dry
    frying pan and then crushed

1 tsp fennel seeds, toasted in a dry
    frying pan and then crushed

1 tsp flaky sea salt

Lightly dust the work surface with rye flour and roll each ball out until it is 2–3mm thick. Transfer to baking sheets lined with non-stick baking paper and use a pastry wheel or a large, sharp knife to cut them into long (ish) rectangles about 5cm wide. Some will be shorter than others, the ends might not necessarily be square but the flavour is set to be bang on. Prick them lightly all over with a fork and finish with a coating of flaky sea salt. Place in the oven and bake for 10 minutes, until lightly browned. Turn them over and cook for a few minutes more to colour the other side. Remove from the oven and leave to cool on a wire rack. They will keep for a week in an airtight tin but good luck trying not to eat them with the cottage cheese in the fridge.

Toast the cumin and caraway seeds in a medium-hot pan until the aroma is heavy, then tip them out on to a plate to cool. Crush them together with a little salt and set aside for use as a garnish. Separate the lettuce leaves and place them in iced water for 20 minutes to crisp up. Dry the leaves, then serve the crispbreads, cottage cheese, pickled beetroot cubes and beetroot crisps with a little pot of the fragrant seasoned cumin and caraway garnishing salt.

† From a historical perspective, it is likely that the first ever attempts to make cheese resulted in a foodstuff similar to what we now call cottage cheese. It is a simple cheese to make and one that can be attempted without the need for expensive or complicated kitchen equipment. The first references to cottage cheese-making in the UK date back to 1831. The milk would be brought into the home and placed somewhere warm where the natural bacteria in cheese would produce enough acid for the milk to form. In the days when farmers transported milk by non-motorised means, the milk would be very quickly affected. Inevitably, it would develop too much acidity, particularly in warm weather. Cheese was therefore a simple but brilliant solution, enabling the preservation of vast quantities of milk obtained during the milking season. Cottage cheese was not only easy to make but it was often made from leftover milk that had already started to turn.

Caraway is thought to have been among the first spice plants cultivated in Europe. Indeed, Harold McGee suggests that caraway helped to shape world history: 'ancient European hunger for Asian spices was an important driving force in the development of Italy, Portugal, Spain, Holland and England into major sea powers during the Renaissance' (*On Food and Cooking*, 2004). This gives resonance to the significance of caraway to our own local area, given the importance of Bristol as a main UK seaport.

† The history of squash is rather interesting. Most vegetable foods leave no archaeological traces; squash is a rare exception. Evidence suggests that it was first cultivated in Central America more than 8,000 years ago. It is believed that the English word for 'squash' derives from the native American word *askutasquash*, which means 'eaten raw or uncooked'. This is a somewhat surprising choice of name, given that squash is certainly not at its best when eaten raw.

It is evident why squash was a staple food back then: it is easy to grow, high in carbohydrates and dependably versatile. When it was later transported by the Spanish conquistadores to Europe, it was initially rejected for being too bland. The fruit (for it is a fruit rather than a vegetable) was later rediscovered as it became known for storing well and providing the energy required for a hard day's graft in the colder European climate.

Roast Crown Prince Soup with Tandoori Spice, Walnut Oil and Crisp Sage Leaves

The arrival of the Crown Prince squash signals the end of autumn. For us, it is the king of squashes. This sweetly flavoured regal friend is a staple ingredient that will remain with us for most of the winter months. Its vibrant orange flesh is delicately sweet and has an excellent texture for roasting. The violet-grey skin is hard to cut through, so our chefs arm themselves with their best knives to release the golden sumptuousness within. Perhaps due to its shape, the Crown Prince is sometimes referred to as a pumpkin rather than a squash. Both are members of the Cucurbitaceae family, close relatives of cucumbers, courgettes and melons. Their flesh is high in water, so they benefit from long cooking, which brings out their honeyed nuttiness. The addition of sage to this soup was a revelation. It adds an earthier, more meaty tone to the whole ensemble. Try it; you will see a side of squash that you might have never seen before.

SERVES 4–6

1.2–1.4kg Crown Prince squash, peeled, deseeded and cut into 2.5cm cubes
rapeseed oil
500g onions, finely sliced
250g carrots, finely sliced
250g celery (or celeriac), finely sliced
150g clarified butter (see below)
4–6 small sage leaves
vintage cider vinegar, such as Ostler's
2 tbsp tandoori spice mix
walnut oil, for drizzling
fine sea salt

Heat the oven to 180°C/Gas Mark 4. Spread the squash cubes out on a roasting tray in a single layer. Lightly coat with rapeseed oil and a fine scattering of sea salt. Roast for 30–45 minutes, stirring occasionally, until tender and beginning to blacken around the edges. Take out of the oven and set aside.

Heat a tablespoon of rapeseed oil in a saucepan, add the onions, carrots and celery and cook over a medium heat for 10–15 minutes, until the vegetables are softened but not coloured. Add the squash, 1½ teaspoons of salt and enough water to cover. Bring to a simmer and cook for 5 minutes. Transfer to a blender and blitz until smooth. Adjust the consistency of the soup by adding more water if necessary, season with salt and cider vinegar to taste and blitz once more.

Heat the clarified butter in a small saucepan until very hot, but not smoking. Add the sage leaves and cook for 1–2 minutes, until they go a dark shade of green and are crisp. Drain on kitchen paper and keep in a warm place. Pass the soup through a fine sieve into a clean pan and reheat gently. Decant into serving bowls, dust with the tandoori spice and garnish each portion with a crisp sage leaf and a generous drizzle of walnut oil.

Clarified Butter: Melt 250g unsalted butter in a pan over a low heat until the butter has separated. Gently pour into a tall, clear jug and leave to settle. When it has formed three layers (white frothy top, clear yellow middle and white solids), start skimming. The aim is to keep as much of the clear middle layer as possible, while removing all of the milk solids. Using a small ladle, skim off the top layer and discard. Slowly pour the butterfat into a clean saucepan, leaving all the white milk solids behind (discard these).

Salt-baked Celeriac, Portobello Mushroom and Apple Soup

Celeriac's close relationship to celery is the reason it is possible to detect hints of celery in what would otherwise be a nutty, earthy taste, common to root vegetables. This knobbly vegetable is not very common outside Europe. We like to regard it as a hidden gem. Its delicate aniseed notes, coupled with a touch of parsley, are intriguing and never disappointing.

    In this recipe, we pair it with Portobello mushrooms to enhance the earthiness inherent in the celeriac. Apple and celery are a classic combination and, being surrounded by over 70 different varieties of apples at the Walled Garden, we could not resist this addition. We find that the apple complements the soft citrus hints present in this ugly duckling of the root vegetable world remarkably well.

SERVES 8

1.25kg celeriac

100g coarse sea salt

500g onions, sliced

rapeseed oil

butter

125g carrots, sliced

250g Portobello mushrooms, sliced

500ml white chicken stock (see page 295)

125g Blenheim Orange (or Bramley) apple

flaky sea salt

white pepper

Heat the oven to 200°C/Gas Mark 6. Peel the celeriac and cut it into 4–6cm chunks. It can be determined to hold its form, so go easy with your hands around the knife. Scatter the coarse salt over a baking tray and place the celeriac chunks on top. Cover the tray with aluminium foil, sealing it well around the edges. Bake for 30–45 minutes, until the celeriac begins to soften. The salt will extract some of the moisture and the flavour will intensify.

In a large saucepan, sweat the onions in a little rapeseed oil and butter until softened. Remove the celeriac from the salt, brushing away any that has stuck to it (the salt can be used again for baking vegetables in the same manner). Add the celeriac, carrots, mushrooms, chicken stock and 500ml water to the onions and bring to a simmer. Cook for 30 minutes or until the vegetables are just soft to the point of a knife.

Peel and grate the apple. Ladle the soup into a blender, filling it only half full, and blitz until smooth. Pass the blended soup through a sieve into a clean pan, returning anything too coarse to the remaining unblended soup. Blend the remaining soup, adding the grated apple, then strain it into the pan and reheat gently. The apple will remain a fresh flavour if you add it at this point. Season with salt and cracked white pepper, then serve.

Deep-fried Aubergine with Rose Hip Syrup

With their tanned skin and Mediterranean looks, you would be forgiven for thinking that aubergines grow only in warmer climates. Whilst they do require a certain amount of warmth and water, they are perfectly able to thrive in British soil in the summer – or indoors when the temperature drops. They belong to the same nightshade family as potatoes and tomatoes, and are not vegetables in botanical terms but enormous berries. The gentlemen of the nightshade family, they are rarely assertive. Instead, they like to blend with their surroundings, offering a smooth, delicate flavour. Even if their presence sometimes borders on the side of fleshy, it is still wonderfully understated. Despite the occasional hint of bitterness, they are far too good mannered for this to become insulting – which is not to say that they are bland; simply that they seek to complement their companions rather than impose on them. Some would call this versatility.

We fry the aubergines in this dish to emphasise the creaminess of their flesh. The pairing with rose hip is intended to inject some intensity of flavour, the syrup magnificently counteracting the slight bitterness in the aubergine. We would recommend experimenting with the amount you add. We strongly suspect that adding an indecent amount of syrup on this occasion can only be good for the soul. There is still likely to be some left over. It will keep for a year in a sterilised jar and can be served with Duck Terrine (see page 18) or Rabbit Confit (page 34) and is also very good with the brownies on page 127.

SERVES 4–6

2 aubergines

1 litre rapeseed oil, for deep-frying

cornflour, for dusting

sea salt

sheep's sorrel or common sorrel
    leaves, to serve

FOR THE ROSE HIP SYRUP:

400g rose hips

375g caster sugar

Cut the aubergines into 8cm-long chips, roughly 5mm thick. Place them in a large bowl and salt lightly, ensuring an even coating. Cover and set aside for 1 hour.

Put the rose hips in a food processor and blitz on full speed until they are completely broken down. Transfer them to a saucepan, add 650ml water and bring to the boil. Remove from the heat and leave to infuse for 20 minutes. Transfer the mixture to a sieve lined with 2 layers of wet muslin, set over a bowl. Leave for about 30 minutes, until all the liquid has drained through. Pour the liquid into a pan, add the sugar and bring to the boil, stirring to dissolve the sugar. Boil for 5 minutes, or until reduced to a syrupy consistency, then set aside to cool a little.

Heat the rapeseed oil to 170°C in a large, deep saucepan or a deep-fat fryer. While the oil is heating, lightly coat the aubergine in cornflour. Fry in the hot oil in small batches for about 2 minutes, until crisp and lightly golden. Remove from the oil using a slotted spoon and drain on kitchen paper. Keep warm while you continue through the remaining batches, ensuring the oil stays close to 170°C.

Arrange the aubergine on serving plates, dress with the rose hip syrup and scatter over the sheep's sorrel leaves, if using.

† Aubergines are not in fact a Mediterranean vegetable: they originated in India and are known to have been part of the Chinese diet from as early as the fifth century. We have the Arabs to thank for the introduction of aubergines into Europe, having been brought to Sicily in the eleventh century. Food writers such as Elizabeth David played a large part in introducing them to the UK in the mid-1950s.

Pear, Native Nape, Hazelnut, Cardamom and Ewe's Cheese Salad

Autumn offers us a lot of pear varieties in the Walled Garden. Comice and Anjou can be seen from the west-facing windows of the glasshouse, while growing on the other side of the wall in the orchard, near our beloved quince tree, is a lesser-known variety, Beurre d'Avalon. It has firm, white, juicy flesh with an initial sweetness that ends slightly sour. It is specific to Somerset and its name is rooted in the mythology of Glastonbury and legends of King Arthur. First found in the area around Glastonbury Tor, it was finally recorded a few years later in 1842. During the thirteenth century the names of Avalon and Glastonbury began to overlap, and stories were told of King Arthur dying on the island of Avalon. This island has also been associated in Celtic history with apples. All of these threads of myth, history and naming of fruit have become woven into one another.

This pear has an equal flavour partner in Fosse Way Fleece cheese. A hard ewe's cheese with a close, smooth-bodied texture and a gentle nuttiness, it is made by Philip Rainbow and Anita Robinson of the Somerset Cheese Company. You can mature this cheese to intensify its flavour: wrap it in non-stick baking paper and store in the salad drawer of the fridge. The key is to keep it in a place where there is little air circulation so it doesn't dry out. Check it every few days and wipe away any mould that builds up.

Native Nape is an air-cured ham made by Native Breeds, which produces some of the finest charcuterie we have come across. It is run by Graham and Ruth Waddington, who source native and rare-breed animals from small farms in Gloucestershire to make their award-winning products.

We dress the salad with cardamom and truffled honey from a British company called Truffle Hunter.

SERVES 4

200g Native Nape cured ham (or other good air-cured ham)

200g aged Fosse Way Fleece cheese (or other aged ewe's cheese), cut into shavings

1 large pear, preferably Beurre d'Avalon, cored and sliced wafer thin on a mandoline

40g hazelnuts, roughly crushed

FOR THE DRESSING:

4 tbsp vintage cider vinegar, such as Ostler's

2 tsp Dijon mustard

1 tsp ground cardamom

1 tbsp truffled honey

¼ tsp xanthan gum (optional, but recommended)

½ tsp fine sea salt

100ml rapeseed oil

To make the dressing, put all the ingredients except the oil in a blender and blitz for 30 seconds. Slowly pour in the oil while the blender is running, as you would for mayonnaise. Once all the oil has been incorporated, blitz for 1 minute. If you are making this in advance, decant into a suitable bottle. Shake well before using.

Putting the salad together couldn't be easier. Decoratively arrange the ham slices on 4 serving plates and arrange the shaved ewe's cheese amongst them. Add the slices of pear, lightly dress with the dressing and scatter the crushed hazelnuts over the top.

Preserved Duck Leg, Chorizo, Butter Bean and Confit Tomato Pot Stew with Yin Yang Beans

Inspired by the French cassoulet, this pot stew is a mixture of all our favourite things. Instead of haricots we use butter beans for their fluffy texture and mild, mineral flavour. We also add chorizo, making this similar to the Spanish stews you would find in Asturias. Made by Vince Castellanos, our chorizo is sublime with the tomatoes and beans. We serve our pot stew with confit duck legs, also a component of the hallowed cassoulet. We treat the tomatoes in this recipe in a similar manner, roasting them slowly in a light coating of rapeseed oil with plenty of seasoning. We are very fond of this method of preserving and it may well become one of your favourites too.

The yin yang, orca or calypso bean is a Mexican heirloom variety, thought to be over 300 years old, that is passed around carefully by gardeners with a warning to take care of it and help prevent its demise. Its drought-resistant growing qualities show why it is highly valued, consistently cropping year on year.

Serve the stew with an authentic sourdough loaf – its dry texture will be perfect for mopping up the juices – and a bottle of Perry's Tremlett cider. You will understand why we recommend this cider the moment after the heady farm silage taste passes and, oddly, you want to drink the whole bottle in one. Contrary forces are interconnected and interdependent in the natural world, according to the concept of yin and yang, and this cider certainly embodies that.

SERVES 4

200g celeriac
200g onions
rapeseed oil
4 garlic cloves, finely chopped
4 cooking chorizo sausages
300g butter beans, soaked for 24
    hours in 2 changes of water,
    then drained
500ml ham hock broth (see page
    79) or white chicken stock (see
    page 295)
300ml cider
1 teaspoon par-cel (see page 164) or
    1 tbsp chopped celery leaf
4 Confit Duck Legs (see pages 36–7)
100g yin yang beans (if unavailable,
    use broad beans, fresh peas
    or sugar snaps, cooked in boiling
    water for 1 minute, then drained)
100g Confit Tomatoes (see page 37)
cider vinegar
sea salt

Heat the oven to 160°C/Gas Mark 3. Peel the celeriac and cut it into 2cm chunks. Chop the onions to roughly the same size. Heat a little rapeseed oil in a large casserole, add the celeriac, onions and garlic and cook gently until softened. Add the chorizo sausages, butter beans, ham hock broth, cider and par-cel. Bring to the boil, then place the duck legs on the surface. Cover the casserole, transfer to the oven and bake for 1¾ hours. Add the yin yang beans and the tomatoes and bake for 15 minutes longer or until the beans are tender. Season with salt and cider vinegar to taste.

† A casserole means 'a large pot' to us today, and for many of us that constitutes a cast-iron Le Creuset inherited from our parents, seasoned and cared for. Within this precious pot, meat, vegetables and liquid are slowly cooked with the lid on, until everything is tender and caramelised. Set upon the table it is served straight to the plate, everyone fighting over the crunchy, burnt edges. Eliza Acton and Mrs Beeton offered recipes for casseroles very unlike the kind we make today, including curious affairs of rice crushed to a paste and smoothed to the outside of the pan.

Wood Pigeon Breasts with Persian Spiced Bulgar Wheat, Cucumber, Aniseed and Black Cabbage

At Barley Wood, the pigeons are quite happy grazing the crops cultivated by the local farmer and Mark, the gardener, in the Wrington Vale. In autumn they also enjoy chestnuts and acorns, and whenever you disturb a pair they clatter upwards, taking off into the wind. From the glasshouse you see them rise into the southwesterly towards Crook Peak.

We love pigeon meat. Cooked rare, it is irresistible, with a rich, red hue that is the result of this bird's ability to travel vast distances without resting. We serve it with bulgar wheat seasoned with our own spice blend. In Iran the spice mix would be called *advieh*, a mixture of spices chosen for their use in a particular dish, with infinite combinations. The ancient Silk Route travelled though the north of Iran and left its culinary legacy. Cooks in the uplands and the northwestern areas often incorporate the delicate fragrance of dried rose petals into their *advieh*. We have combined allspice, turmeric, cinnamon, black pepper, saffron, raisins and pistachios to make a blend that complements pigeon perfectly.

We serve this dish with crisp black cabbage (cavolo nero) flash-fried in rapeseed oil and cider vinegar with a pinch of cumin. It is without doubt our favourite way of serving this brassica. Finally, we garnish the dish with cucumber and anise buttermilk. Traditionally, milk would have been left overnight to separate, so cream could be churned into butter. What remained was the buttermilk. Thicker than milk and thinner than cream, it has a sour tang that is just wonderful with the sweet cucumber and the rich spice of the rest of the dish. If you cannot find buttermilk, then soured cream will work very well too.

Jane Grigson wrote in *English Food* (Macmillan, 1974), 'No cookery belongs exclusively to its country, or its region. Cooks borrow – always have borrowed – and adapt through the centuries.' We certainly have.

SERVES 4

100ml buttermilk or Greek-style
   yoghurt
a little rapeseed oil
8 wood pigeon breasts, skinned
200g black cabbage (cavolo nero),
   stalks removed
a pinch of ground cumin
1 tbsp cider vinegar
flaky sea salt

FOR THE SWEET PICKLED
CUCUMBER:
1 small cucumber, cut into 1cm dice
fine sea salt
cider vinegar
caster sugar
1 tsp aniseed

For the pickled cucumber, weigh the cucumber cubes, then lightly salt them and leave to drain for 1 hour.

Measure out the same weight of vinegar as the cucumber, then do the same with the caster sugar. Put the vinegar and sugar in a saucepan, add the aniseed and bring to the boil, stirring to dissolve the sugar. Remove from the heat and leave to cool. Rinse any residual salt from the cucumber and mix it with the vinegar and sugar solution. Store in the fridge (you won't need it all for this recipe but the remainder will keep for 4 weeks and can be used as a salad garnish or as an accompaniment to a burger). Combine 50g of the pickled cucumber with the buttermilk, stir well and refrigerate till needed.

Put all the ingredients for the bulgar wheat in a saucepan, add 600ml water and stir until combined. Place over a medium heat, cover and bring to the boil. Reduce the heat to its lowest setting and cook for about 30 minutes or until the wheat has absorbed all the liquid. Stir to check it has not caught on

† Historically eaten by the aristocracy and not commoners, up until the seventeenth century only the lord of the manor was permitted to build a dovecote. These structures were often impressive and many resemble our cider barn, which is of round Norman design. The dove manure would have been used as fertiliser, not an approach that is commonly practised today!

FOR THE PERSIAN SPICED BULGAR
WHEAT:
300g bulgar wheat
2 tsp salt
1½ tbsp ground allspice
1½ tbsp ground cinnamon
1 tsp ground turmeric
1 tsp ground black pepper
6 saffron stamens
20g raisins
50g shelled roasted pistachio nuts

the bottom of the pan. Keep warm while you cook the pigeon. Heat the oven to 200°C/Gas Mark 6 and put a baking sheet in it to heat up. Place a heavy-based frying pan over a high heat until it is really hot. Splash a drop of rapeseed oil on to each pigeon breast and rub it over it. Dust lightly with flaky sea salt. Take the baking sheet out of the oven. Lay 4 of the pigeon breasts in the frying pan and cook for no longer than 30 seconds per side, until lightly browned. Place them on the baking sheet. Clean the pan briefly with a wad of kitchen paper and repeat with the 4 remaining breasts. Put them in the oven and cook for 2½ minutes for pink and perfectly cooked or 3 minutes for medium. Transfer them to a board to rest while you cook the black cabbage.

Heat a little rapeseed oil in a frying pan, add the cabbage, cumin and a little salt and fry until just heated through. Add the cider vinegar; the steam from the vinegar will cook the cabbage in a few seconds. Once the liquid has evaporated, tip the contents into a warm serving dish.

Slice the pigeon breasts and serve accompanied by the cabbage and bulgar wheat along with a spoonful of the buttermilk dressing. Warn your fellow diners to be mindful of any lead shot that may be hidden in the breasts.

Chicken Mole

The intricacies of mole (pronounced 'mo-lay') were not fully understood by us until Matthew and Paûla came back from a visit to Paûla's large, boisterous family in Mexico. It was a memorable experience, in which they had eaten some form of chilli at every single meal. Breakfast was not spared from this joyful and sometimes painful chilli marathon. It was, in fact, the most important meal of the day, the choice of chilli being paramount. For Mexicans, chilli is as important as salt and pepper. It is an essential means of seasoning and lack of chilli in a meal is frowned upon, unless you are a very young child, practically a baby. It was bliss.

Capsaicin is the chemical found in chillies that makes them spicy. It is believed to stimulate the production of endorphins in the brain, causing some people to feel a sense of euphoria when eating spicy foods, which can become mildly addictive. For Matthew and Paûla, it was certainly a lot of fun to push the endorphin boundaries through the consumption of endless chillies time and time again. Their withdrawal symptoms started becoming apparent the moment they stepped off the plane and were faced with an overly sweet breakfast cereal. So back in The Ethicurean kitchen, a plan was set in motion to attempt to crack the quintessential Mexican chilli chocolate dish with as many British ingredients as possible.

The word 'mole' comes from the pre-hispanic Nahuatl, meaning 'sauce'. It is unlikely that the Aztecs added any chocolate to their mole sauce originally – it was simply a combination of chillies. With time, each region in Mexico developed its own mole and there are now a multitude of colourful versions, ranging from red to green and even a pink one from the town of Taxco. The Mexican estate of Oaxaca alone has seven different versions of mole.

Paûla's grandmother took the laborious task of cooking mole very seriously. Her collection of spices stood in jars on the kitchen shelves, ready to be called into action. The aim was to make a thick, shimmery sauce and you knew it was ready the moment the spoon was able to stand up in it on its own.

Epazote is a highly popular herb in Mexican cooking. Many people consider it to be a weed, so it is very easy to grow, even in the UK. You should be able to buy seeds online but if you prefer not to grow it, it is possible to buy it as a dried herb too. Alternatively, you can substitute winter savory.

It is highly likely that you won't be able to get the chillies listed in this recipe at your local supermarket. Do not be put off by this. They are well worth tracking down and a simple search online will reveal several suppliers. Having them delivered to your door will save you a trip to the shops.

Mole is traditionally served with turkey or chicken. The brine for seasoning the chicken has to be made in advance, as it needs to be chilled. It will keep indefinitely in the fridge, so make it at your leisure.

SERVES 8

2 free-range chickens

½ garlic head

rapeseed oil

8 mulato chillies

8 guajillo chillies

4 ancho chillies

a dash of cider vinegar

1kg tomatoes

300g onions, chopped

4 slices of stale bread, cut into
    small cubes

150g dried cobnuts or hazelnuts,
    finely ground in a food processor

150g unsalted peanuts, finely
    ground in a food processor

150g raisins

1 tsp ground allspice

½ tsp ground cloves

½ tsp ground cumin

1 tbsp dried epazote (or 2 tbsp fresh
    epazote)

2 litres brown chicken stock (see
    page 296)

1 tbsp salt

150g dark chocolate, with 75–80
    per cent cocoa solids

50g muscovado sugar

FOR THE 8 PER CENT BRINE:

80g salt

80g dark muscovado sugar

1 tbsp dried epazote (or 2 tbsp fresh
    epazote)

1 bay leaf

TO FINISH:

16–24 corn tortillas

4 tbsp sesame seeds, fried in a dry
    frying pan until lightly coloured

4 tbsp coarsely chopped coriander

Put all the brine ingredients in a pan with 1 litre of water and bring to the boil. Leave to cool to room temperature, then chill.

Remove the skin from the chickens and set aside. Cut the breasts and legs from the chickens, then divide the legs into drumsticks and thighs (keep the carcasses for stock, see pages 295–6). Place the thighs, drumsticks and breasts in the brine and leave for 2 hours.

Meanwhile, make the sauce. Heat the oven to 180°C/Gas Mark 4. Wrap the garlic in foil with a splash of rapeseed oil and bake for 20 minutes. Leave to cool and then squeeze out the roasted pulp. Break open the dried chillies and remove the seeds. Rehydrate the chillies by placing them in a bowl of hot water with a dash of vinegar and leaving to cool. Drain and chop finely, trying not to stain your fingers as the capsaicin will remain.

Score each tomato with a cross on the base, put them in a pan of simmering water for 2 minutes, then drain and peel off the loosened skins. Chop the tomatoes roughly, keeping all the juice and seeds separately. Pour the seeds and juice through a fine sieve into a bowl, reserving the juice.

Divide the chicken skin between 2 hot frying pans and cook until it is brown and the fat has been released. Discard the skin but keep the fat in the pans. Add the onions, bread, nuts and raisins to one pan and the tomatoes and their juice, chillies, spices and epazote to the other. Once the onions are beginning to colour, transfer the mixture to a large saucepan and add the chicken stock. Let the tomatoes continue to cook until they are broken down, adding a splash of water if the mixture starts to look dry. Transfer the tomatoes to the saucepan along with the salt. Add the chocolate, roast garlic and sugar, stir, then simmer with the lid off for 45 minutes or until thickened, stirring regularly.

Meanwhile, poach the brined chicken in a large pan of barely simmering water for 35 minutes. The water should hardly be moving, resulting in succulent, pale and moist chicken. Warm the tortillas. Put them in a basket and cover with a damp, hot tea towel to retain the heat and keep them pliable. Strip the chicken meat off the bone and serve on the tortillas topped with lashings of mole, then scatter over the toasted sesame and coriander.

Venison, Cider and Quince Stew with Herbed Butter Dumplings

As the crops are harvested, the stubbled fields spell the end of field cover for the roe deer. Soon the leaves will begin to colour and drop, making it more difficult for them to hide from the stalker. The rut has finished and bucks, no longer fixated on mating, are a little the worse for wear and lacking in energy. Family groups begin to form as the territorial activity of late summer subsides. They have spent the previous months fattening themselves for the coming winter and, as the farmers move the cattle from the pastures around Barley Wood, it seems a good time to bring home a roe buck. For stewing, we use the neck or shoulder – don't combine them, as the cooking time will vary. The neck contains a fair amount of connective tissue, which will need slow cooking to tenderise it.

This is a recipe we make before a day's picking in the orchard – one for a weekend when you're tidying the garden before winter or just relaxing. Cooking the venison in cider is ideal, as the acidity does marvellous things. A stew needs a night to cool down slowly, so that the meat reabsorbs its juices, becoming more succulent.

No stew can possibly be served without dumplings. We've often caught Jack eating them all on their own when we've made too many. They are very welcome during autumn when we need a touch more stodge. Eliza Acton, Hannah Glasse and Constance Spry give numerous recipes for Suffolk and Norfolk dumplings and the main style seems to be for a 'hard dumpling' that contains neither suet nor butter. We make our fluffy dumplings with flour, butter and eggs and they resemble those eaten in central Europe. Chopped fresh herbs add fragrance.

SERVES 6–8

200g goose fat

1.2kg venison neck or shoulder, cut into 3–4cm chunks

900g red onions

450g carrots

225g celeriac

2 quinces

600ml beef stock (see page 294)

300ml cider

1 bay leaf

8 sprigs of thyme

1 tbsp juniper berries

1 tbsp dried pineapple weed (optional), to garnish

cider vinegar

sea salt and black pepper

Heat some of the goose fat in a large, heavy-based frying pan and fry the pieces of venison in small batches until coloured all over, transferring them to a large casserole as they are done. Cut the onions, carrots and celeriac into large chunks – they should be too big to eat in one mouthful, as they are going to spend a long time in the stew. Colour them in the pan in which the meat was browned, adding more goose fat as necessary (the generous amount of fat is needed for this recipe, as venison is a lean meat). Add the vegetables to the casserole.

Wash the soft down coating off the quinces and then core and chop them; their aroma will be pineapple rich. Add to the casserole with all the remaining ingredients except the pineapple weed, vinegar and seasoning The casserole needs to go in the oven but don't preheat it, as it benefits from a really slow rise in temperature, as Harold McGee advises in his seminal book, *On Food and Cooking* (see box opposite). Start the oven at 95°C (or the lowest possible setting in a gas oven), putting the casserole in with the lid off to the side slightly to allow some evaporation. This will slowly raise the internal

Harold McGee makes some interesting points on stewing meat in his book *On Food and Cooking* (Hodder & Stoughton, 2004, page 163). The more a muscle is used, the more collagen it will contain and the tougher it will be. But when you heat collagen to 70–80°C, it is converted into gelatine, which is soft, wobbly, easily dissolved and keeps meat beautifully tender. However, at this temperature, although the collagen is converted into gelatine, you also lose moisture, which makes the meat drier. McGee's method therefore advocates keeping the meat below 50°C for a long time, which weakens the collagen, then quickly raising the temperature when the meat is almost cooked to convert the collagen into gelatine. This will retain more of the moisture than if the meat had stayed at a constant 80°C throughout the entire cooking time. It sounds complicated but in reality it is just the scientific explanation of the slow-cooking technique we have used for hundreds of years.

FOR THE HERBED BUTTER
DUMPLINGS:

390g self-raising flour

3 eggs

105g salted butter, diced

1½ tsp salt

2 tbsp chopped mixed herbs, such
    as sage, thyme, parsley and mint

a few tbsp double cream

black pepper

temperature to 50°C. Leave for 2 hours, then increase the oven temperature to 120°C/Gas Mark ½, which should increase the temperature to 80°C. Cook for 1–2 hours, with the lid still askew, then test the meat for tenderness with a knife. Keep checking at half-hour intervals until you are satisfied it is tender enough. Taste the sauce and decide if you would like to reduce it to concentrate the flavour. To do this, remove the meat and vegetables from the casserole and set aside. Place the sauce over a high heat and let it simmer vigorously for about 5 minutes, until slightly reduced in volume. Taste and decide if this strength suits you. Repeat until the flavour is as you like it, then season with salt, pepper and a dash of cider vinegar. Return the meat and vegetables to the casserole and leave to cool overnight, then chill it in the fridge the next morning. It will be ready after a gentle reheat while the dumplings are being made.

To make the dumplings, sift the flour into a food processor and add the eggs, butter, salt, herbs and black pepper. Process until the mixture resembles breadcrumbs, then with the machine still running, slowly pour in enough cream to form a dough. Let the processor turn for a couple of minutes to stretch the dough. It should be fluffy, with a slightly tacky exterior, and break apart easily. If not, add a dash more cream and mix again. Take the dough out and shape into 2.5cm balls. Keep covered before cooking them.

Poach the dumplings in a large pan of fast-boiling water in batches of 8. It is essential that the water is boiling rapidly so they fluff up quickly. They will float to the surface as they begin to cook. Cook for a further 2 minutes from this point, then remove with a slotted spoon. Serve the dumplings dropped into that toothsome, tender stew, with a light dusting of the chamomile relative, pineapple weed, roughly chopped, if you have any.

QUINCE

Apples and quince grow side by side in our orchard; we only have one quince tree and its crop is prized by us. These bright yellow fruit resemble a plump pear and they have a downy fur that grows on their skin. Their perfume is fresh and flowery and is the result of lactones and violet-like ionones contained in the skin (see Harold McGee, *On Food and Cooking*, page 357). In the process of stewing the tannins are broken up and as a result the mellow flavour and apple-like texture of quince can be enjoyed.

Fish Soup with Spiced Heritage Tomatoes, Fennel Seed and English Truffle Oil Toast

This soup is a quest to combine two of our major obsessions: curry spices and truffles. At first, this might seem an unlikely marriage. Reason dictates that these strong flavours have the potential to overpower any soup. However, the finesse arising from the use of heirloom tomatoes makes the whole dish a harmonious, spice-infused affair. Heirloom varieties have desirable characteristics that have been passed down for generations, and they are far superior in taste to bland commercial varieties.

To add fresh truffles to this soup might be considered not only extravagant but downright cavalier. Instead, we use a dash of truffle oil for both the soup and the toast. Truffle Hunter, based in the Cotswolds, makes an oil from English rapeseed oil and English black summer truffles that is good enough to match its Italian counterparts. The result is a warming, terracotta-coloured, velvety soup that will inspire anyone to head out to the British countryside in search of that coveted English truffle. Training of Ocho, our resident dog, has commenced.

It's best to avoid oily fish such as mackerel, salmon or tuna here. Instead, stick to white fish such as ling, sole (lemon, Dover, witch or dab), pollock and cuttlefish. Squid also works well and, from a sustainability point of view, is regarded as one of best fish to eat – particularly if you can find squid from small, seasonal British fisheries.

SERVES 4

500g tomatoes (the best you can find)
rapeseed oil
450g onions, roughly chopped
250ml fish stock (see page 297)
4 garlic cloves, chopped
2 heaped tbsp Dijon mustard
400g white fish fillets, skin on, and cleaned squid, cut into 2.5cm pieces
1 tsp ground turmeric

FOR THE SPICE BLEND:

2 tsp fennel seeds
1 tsp aniseed
1 tsp coriander seeds
2 black cardamom pods
15g salt
1 tsp ground cinnamon
1 tsp ground cardamom
½ tbsp ground turmeric

To make the spice blend, heat the seeds and cardamom in a dry frying pan for 2–3 minutes to release their oils. Crush them finely in a pestle and mortar with the salt, then stir in the ground spices.

Score a cross on the base of each tomato, put them in a pan of boiling water for 2 minutes, then drain and peel off the skins. Quarter the tomatoes and scoop out the seeds and juice into a sieve set over a bowl. Press on the seeds with the back of a spoon to ensure you get as much juice as possible, then discard them.

Heat a little rapeseed oil in a large pan, add the onions and cook until softened but not coloured. Stir in the spice blend and cook for a few minutes, then add the tomatoes and their juice, fish stock, garlic, mustard and 250ml water. Bring to a simmer and cook, covered, for 40 minutes. Purée the soup in a blender or food processor and then pour into a clean pan through a fine sieve to catch any large spice pieces. Reheat gently.

Heat the oven to 200°C/Gas Mark 6. Cut the sourdough slices into squares and toss them in a bowl with a drizzle of rapeseed oil and an even smaller drizzle of the pungent truffle oil. Add some coarse salt, shake through once more, then

TO FINISH:

250g sourdough bread, cut into
    slices 2.5cm thick

rapeseed oil

truffle oil

1 tsp nigella (black onion) seeds

1 tsp fennel seeds, crushed

coarse sea salt

spread out on a baking sheet and bake for 7–8 minutes, until golden all over. Keep the toast somewhere warm while the fish is fried.

Place a large, non-stick frying pan over a medium heat. Add a splash of rapeseed oil to the hot pan, then fry the fish for about 3 minutes, until it has coloured slightly, then dust with the turmeric and fry for no longer than a minute more.

Ladle the soup into bowls, divide the fried fish and squid between them and drizzle a smidgen more truffle oil on top. Finish with a few nigella seeds and crushed fennel seeds.

TRUFFLES

Truffles are the endearingly shy members of the fungus family. Unlike their brash overground relatives who explode in a myriad of shapes and sizes, unfazed by the thought of being spotted by a keen mycophile, truffles' introverted demeanour finds them deep underground, having formed an amicable relationship with the roots of a suitable tree. France and Italy are popular areas for truffle hunters but they can certainly be found in Britain in limestone or chalk areas up and down the country. The Royal Botanical Records at Kew document truffles having been found in our local area. The traditional way to find the much-prized fungi is through the use of pigs, although dogs are now much more commonly used. English truffles can be found from July all through the winter.

Slow-braised Goat's Leg with Cider, Shallots, Lentils and Glazed Carrots

During autumn, much of the goat that we use comes from Stawley Farm in Wellington. On their 20 acres of land, Caroline Atkinson makes a fresh cheese using raw milk from the goats farmed by her husband, Will. Kidding – the goat equivalent of lambing – takes place around April. The billies, with their obvious lack of milking potential, are destined for our pot. At the beginning of autumn they are around 5 months old and weigh 10–12kg. The legs are just right for gentle braising. The principles of stewing discussed on page 251 are just as relevant to this recipe. Not only is liquid an effective means of transmitting heat but its flavour enhances the food that is cooked in it.

At the restaurant, Matthew and Iain pressure cook the leg rather than braising it in the oven. Both cooking methods will give immaculately tender meat that falls away from the bone. Pressure cooking has its own benefits, however (see page 260), and we find it the most reliable way to achieve perfection here.

Very few ingredients are cooked with the goat but the shallots and carrots play a crucial role. The shallots offer natural sugars as well as sharpness and a savoury flavour. The carrots are their sidekick, releasing sugars gradually during the slow cooking time.

We serve the goat with Puy lentils, which hold their texture and have a unique, peppery flavour. We use the same vegetables for both the lentils and the braise. We honestly think goat has never tasted as good as it does in this recipe. It is a meal of classic clean flavours, food for the soul.

SERVES 4–6

rapeseed oil

100g shallots (or spring onions), finely sliced

200g carrots, finely sliced

100g white mushrooms, finely sliced

300ml medium cider, such as Perry's Morgan Sweet

500ml brown chicken stock (see page 296)

2 tbsp cumin seeds

1 tbsp fine sea salt

1 goat's leg, shank removed so only the thigh remains

FOR THE LENTILS:

rapeseed oil

150g onions, very finely diced

100g carrots, cut into small cubes

50g brown mushrooms, cut into small cubes

350g Puy lentils

To braise the goat, pour a thin film of rapeseed oil into a large pressure cooker and place on a high heat. Add the shallots, carrots and mushrooms and cook for 10–15 minutes, until they begin to colour. Deglaze the pan by adding the cider and scraping any sticky bits away from the base with a wooden spoon. Add the chicken stock, cumin seeds, salt and the goat's leg. Place the lid on the pressure cooker and keep over a high heat. When the cooker reaches full pressure, turn the heat down to low and maintain at full pressure for 2 hours. Remove from the heat and allow to cool naturally, without venting the pressure cooker.

For the lentils, heat a thin film of rapeseed oil in a saucepan, add the vegetables and sweat for 5–10 minutes, until softened. Add the lentils and stir through. Pour in the chicken stock, add 550ml water and bring to the boil. Cover the pan, reduce the heat and cook for 25–30 minutes, until the lentils are tender and have absorbed all the liquid. Season to taste with fine sea salt and a small dash of cider vinegar. It is important not to salt the lentils before they are cooked or they will be tough and chewy.

200ml brown chicken stock (see
   page 296)
cider vinegar
fine sea salt

FOR THE GLAZED CARROTS:
8–12 small-medium carrots, peeled
   but left whole
125g unsalted butter, cut into 2.5cm
   cubes
1½ tsp fine sea salt
1 tbsp cumin seeds
1 tbsp coriander seeds

For the glazed carrots, put the carrots into a saucepan just large enough to hold them in a single layer. Add the butter, salt and spices and place over a medium heat until the butter has melted. Turn the heat down a little, cover and cook for 20–25 minutes, shaking the pan occasionally for even cooking. When the carrots are soft, take off the lid and turn the heat up high to caramelise them lightly. Remove from the pan and set aside somewhere warm.

After the pressure cooker has cooled for at least 40 minutes and the safety lock has released, remove the lid. Take out the leg and leave to rest on a board in a warm place. Strain the liquid from the pressure cooker through 4 layers of wet muslin into a clean pan. This may seem excessive, and it is optional, but the stock will form a sauce and straining helps remove impurities that would cloud the sauce, detracting from the final dish.

Skim off any excess fat from the liquid, then bring to the boil and simmer until reduced by about a third. Season with salt to taste.

To serve, carve the goat's leg and put it on serving plates with the lentils and carrots. Pour over a liberal amount of the reduced braising liquid and finish with a little sprinkling of sea salt.

If you braise the leg in the oven rather than a pressure cooker, colour the vegetables in a little rapeseed oil in a saucepan over a fairly high heat, then transfer to a roasting tray. Add the goat's leg and enough cider and chicken stock to come about a third of the way up it – you may need more liquid than the quantity stated above. Season with the sea salt and cover with 2 layers of foil. Place in an oven preheated to 120°C/Gas Mark ½ and roast for 4–5 hours, until the meat is impeccably tender. Check it every 30–45 minutes to ensure there is still enough liquid, topping up with a splash more chicken stock, cider or water if necessary. When you make the sauce, the liquid may require reducing more than a third to get the correct flavour, so keep tasting it and stop when you are happy with it.

PRESSURE COOKING

Our pressure cookers at The Ethicurean are constantly utilised for a wealth of tasks, ranging from vast quantities of stock to the slow braising of tougher cuts of meats, right through to the cooking of our beans and pulses. The pressure cooker is an unsung hero in the kitchen.

When it comes to stocks, pressure cooking achieves a depth of flavour that would otherwise be unobtainable. This comes down to two very simple concepts; first, when making stocks by the conventional method, the lid is uncovered. This results in what are called 'volatile aroma' molecules rising out of the stock. Although this may smell delightful, what you are smelling is lost flavour. Pressure cookers have lids that prevent these aromas from escaping, and when used correctly and allowed to cool, these aromas condense inside the pan and end up back in the stock. Less flavour is lost in comparison with traditional methods. And while the lid stops the aromas from escaping, pressure builds inside the pan.

At sea level, water boils at 100°C, give or take a few variations depending on weather. In order for water to boil, energy (in the form of heat) has to 'push' the water up harder than the atmospheric pressure 'pushes' the water down. When the force pushing up is greater than the force pushing down, water boils. At the top of Mount Everest, the atmospheric pressure is less than it is at sea level. So when climbers boil water at high altitudes, the water requires less energy (heat) to 'push' the water up. In fact, the boiling point of water at the top of Mount Everest is dramatically reduced, and is somewhere closer to 70°C. In relation to pressure cooking, the opposite is also true. If you increase the atmospheric pressure, there is more pressure pushing down on the water and what you are left with is a boiling point that is above 100°C. This is because to boil water under pressure, it takes more energy (heat) to push the water up against the atmospheric pressure pushing the water down. Your average pressure cooker is designed to take the temperature of water to 120°C. Iain and Matthew are fascinated by the idea of super-heated water, because flavours are diffused into the stock at a greater rate at higher temperatures – and we strive to create greater depth of flavour with every pressure cooking attempt.

There are further advantages to using a pressure cooker at home. Pressure cookers require less water for cooking; the food does not have to be immersed in liquid as the cooker contains steam as well as liquid. This means that less energy is required to heat the liquid to the desired temperature – something that is very much in line with our strong belief in reducing energy consumption. Vitamins are also said to be preserved more efficiently when cooked under pressure, due to the smaller quantities of liquid needed, combined with the faster cooking time: nutrients have less opportunity to leach out into the water.

When a pressure cooker is used correctly, liquid will not come to the boil. With stocks that are highly valued for clarity, this is a huge positive. Take your traditional stock method for a simple stock: bones are roasted, put in water with vegetables and herbs and cooked for 4 hours. Usually a stock will bubble away relatively unattended for most of this time, with the cook occasionally skimming off impurities. In the process of a stock bubbling, the bubbles create movement through the water which in turn breaks down vegetable matter into tiny pieces. Not only that, but motion created by water boiling emulsifies any fats into the stock. All of that vegetable matter and fat result in a cloudy stock. In a pressure cooker, water sits motionless at 120°C. What you are left with is a clear stock, which can in turn be used to produce crystal-clear sauces, or provide the hidden punch of flavour that makes your dish a hit.

Pheasant Kiev with Winter Tarragon and Strawberry Myrtle

The epitome of autumn comfort food, this was on the menu during The Ethicurean's first month. We opened in October, about a month into the pheasant season, and this was our play on chicken Kiev – a superior version, in our opinion, due to the complex nature of pheasant. The history of the Kiev begins in Russia and ends mostly in the supermarket chiller cabinet. As a concept it is flawless: crisp, breadcrumbed meat oozing with garlic, herbs and butter.

For the filling, we add two very underused ingredients. The first is strawberry myrtle, an evergreen shrub that has bright red berries, about the size of cranberries, in autumn. They are reminiscent of spiced strawberry and take first-time tasters completely by surprise. Jekka McVicar tells us that they were Queen Victoria's favourite fruit and she would often have them sent up from Cornwall. Their fruity spice is a complete hit with pheasant but, should you not be able to find them, juniper will do a good job too. The second special ingredient is winter tarragon (*Tagetes lucida*), a perennial with distinctly aniseed-flavoured leaves. It can be picked when French tarragon is no longer available, and half the amount is needed. For Paûla, it has a particular relevance, as the flower of winter tarragon forms part of the decorations during the *día de los muertos*, or the Day of the Dead. It has roots in South American culture that go right back to the Aztecs and is still used by many Mexican Indians as an ingredient in incense.

SERVES 4

4 large pheasant breasts, skinned

100g softened salted butter

2 tbsp finely chopped winter tarragon

3 tbsp strawberry myrtle (or juniper)

2 large eggs, beaten

250g stale bread, made into fine breadcrumbs

30g plain flour

fine sea salt and freshly ground black pepper

Valor Potato Mash (see page 38), to serve

FOR THE BRINE:

40g fine sea salt

2 tsp fennel seeds

1 tsp freshly ground black pepper

Begin by making the brine – this can be done well in advance and kept in the fridge until needed. Put the salt and spices in a saucepan with 500ml water and bring to the boil. Immediately remove from the heat and leave to cool, then transfer to a plastic box and chill thoroughly.

Put the pheasant breasts in the brine and leave for 2 hours. Drain off the brine, pour cold water over the pheasant and leave for 2 minutes. Drain again and pat dry on kitchen paper. Keep in the fridge until needed.

Meanwhile, mash together the butter and tarragon, using the back of a fork. Divide it into 4 portions and flatten each one out into a square shape that will fit inside a pheasant breast. Place the butter on some greaseproof paper and freeze for 1 hour.

Butterfly the pheasant breasts. To do this, lay each one on a board and, using a very sharp knife, cut into the breast, parallel to the chopping board, until you reach 1cm from the other edge. Essentially you are enabling the breast to open up completely, while the 2 sides stay connected by a 'hinge'. Once each breast has been opened up, place a portion of the butter in the centre along with a quarter of the strawberry myrtle. Brush around the edges of both sides of the breast with a little of the beaten egg, then close it, encasing the butter and herbs.

HANGING PHEASANTS

When buying pheasants try to ensure that you take home young birds; you can do this by
checking the beak and claws. Older means thicker and harder. A brace of pheasants is a cock
(male) and a hen (female). Old stalwarts of game would advise that cocks must be hung
longer than hens due to their more active lifestyle and larger size. In practice it all depends
on the temperature at which they are hung and on the age of the bird. We would advise
buying a brace that has already been hung by your butcher. The basic science behind hanging
is that enzymes in the meat attack other cell molecules and this in turn reduces these large
molecules into tastier, smaller, more tender pieces
(see McGee, *On Food and Cooking*, page 144).

Heat the oven to 200°C/Gas Mark 6. Spread out the breadcrumbs in a roasting tray and bake for 5 minutes. Stir well, then return them to the oven and continue to bake, stirring at 2-minute intervals, until the crumbs are completely dry and crisp. Set aside to cool.

Place the flour, breadcrumbs and remaining beaten egg in 3 separate bowls. Coat each breast in flour, then dip it in the egg and coat with the breadcrumbs. Finally, dip each breast back into the egg and then coat with a final layer of breadcrumbs. This 'double-dip' method ensures more crunch on the exterior, and also helps prevent the butter escaping.

Put the Kievs on a roasting tray, place in the oven and bake for 14 minutes. Serve with the mash and seasonal greens.

Winter tarragon

Strawberry myrtle

† The story goes that Jason and the Argonauts brought the pheasant back to Greece (along with the Golden Fleece) from the place now thought to be Georgia – the Latin name for pheasant is *cochicus*, a derivative of that area. It was then brought to Britain by the Romans and appeared in fossilised form at Corbridge around the site of Hadrian's wall. Eleventh-century remains of feasts that include pheasant bones abound. It was not until the eighteenth and nineteenth centuries that new varieties of pheasant were introduced from the Far East and China. The males really are splendid: their colours are autumnal and seem to mirror the trees' seasonal transformation to golds, reds and browns. These birds are not particularly clever and Dorothy Hartley had a cunning technique for poaching them from her garden in summer: 'Pheasant is fairly common in England in Summer, when the cock invades the cottage gardens to sneak the peas. You catch him quietly, with a paper bag and raisins. Smear the paper cone inside with treacle or gum, put a few raisins at the bottom, and prop the bag up against the peas. When he sticks his head in he cannot see where to go, so he stand still till you fetch him' (*Food in England*, page 202).

Rare Roast Sirloin of Beef with Bordelaise Sauce, Black Cabbage and Truffle Cauliflower

One of our favourite features at the Walled Garden is the main seating area of the restaurant, which we call the glasshouse. With its near-perfect 180-degree view of the Somerset hills, it gives us a real sense of the changing countryside throughout the seasons. From here, we have often observed the different weather patterns approaching and noted the effect they have on the landscape around us. Most importantly, however, the view of the vast, velvety hills serves as a daily reminder of our fantastic beef-farming heritage in the UK.

Britain's fertile pastures produce some of the best beef in the world and have led to the development of some superb cattle breeds. At the restaurant we use Hereford Cross or Charolais beef that has been aged for 28–35 days. The advantages of ageing are twofold: as the meat hangs, moisture evaporates from it, which means a greater intensity of flavour is achieved; at the same time, the tough connective tissue gradually breaks down, resulting in more tender meat. We would recommend seeking out beef that has been hung for at least 28 days.

This kind of meat is a magnificent testament to British beef farming. Yet its recent history has been troubled. Its reputation suffered greatly as a consequence of the BSE crisis in the late twentieth century and it was some time before its credibility was restored. Ironically, it was often small, family-run farms that suffered financially as a result, despite the fact that such farmers' closed herds of traditional grass-fed beef breeds were the ones that were most likely to be free of the disease. Once this fact became widely known, it led to the promotion of small-scale beef farming, which produced beef of high quality.

Our search for a butcher who shared our commitment to sustainable food production led us to Thornbury farmers' market and Scott Powell, from Powells of Olveston – a butcher who stood before a banner proudly proclaiming ethically sourced meats. Scott had clearly gone to great lengths to find his suppliers for beef, lamb, pork, chicken and duck, all of whom have high standards of animal husbandry and exceptionally well cared-for livestock.

To cook the sirloin accurately, it helps to have a digital probe – a modest investment that will have a great impact on your cooking. Familiarise yourself with the guide to roasting beef on page 267 before you start this recipe. The beef will take about 4 hours from leaving the fridge to serving. Don't worry if it is ready before the side dishes – better that it is well rested than rushed to the table. It can be held in a very low oven alongside warming plates after basting for as long as required. This relaxed approach marks out Sunday as an ideal time to catch up and mull over the week with family and friends.

SERVES 8

2kg beef sirloin, preferably aged for
    28–35 days
3 tbsp mustard powder
plain flour, for dusting
3 tbsp rapeseed oil
400g black cabbage (cavolo nero),
    kale or scarlet borecole, stalks
    removed, cut into 2cm strips
1 tbsp cider vinegar
a double quantity of Bordelaise
    Sauce (see page 41)
Valor Potato Mash (see page 38), to
    serve
flaky sea salt

FOR THE TRUFFLE CAULIFLOWER:
1 cauliflower
1 tsp smoked salt
4 tbsp double cream
truffle oil, preferably English (see
    page 254), to taste

Take the sirloin out of the fridge 2 hours before cooking to bring
it to room temperature. Remove any string and cover it with a
tea towel.

Divide the cauliflower into 2.5cm florets and slice the stem. Place
in a steamer basket and steam over a low heat for 35 minutes,
until very soft. Transfer the cauliflower to a blender or food
processor with the smoked salt and blitz a couple of times. Then,
with the machine running, pour in a slow drizzle of double cream
until it begins to combine. Once it starts to move around the
blender, add a light splash of truffle oil – somewhere in the region
of 1–2 teaspoons. Taste the mixture and decide if you want more
salt or truffle oil. Scrape down the sides to catch any remaining
unblended pieces and blend once more. If you want a very
smooth finish, pass the mixture through a fine sieve. Set aside.

Heat the oven to 200°C/Gas Mark 6. Get a large, heavy-based
frying pan very hot. It's important that the beef browns quickly,
so make sure the pan is practically humming. Dust the sirloin
on all sides with the mustard powder, then with flour, rubbing
it in to make the outside dry (don't add any salt at this stage).
Lift the joint up and give it a few percussive slaps to knock off
any excess flour. Carefully add 2 tablespoons of the rapeseed oil
to the hot pan and, using a carving fork, gently lower the beef
into it. It will colour quickly over this heat, so turn it regularly
until browned on all sides. Transfer to a roasting tray and
place in the oven. Decide to what degree you would like the
meat cooked (see the box on page 267, remembering that the
temperatures shown are the ones the meat should reach after
resting). Roast for 25 minutes, then take the joint out for its first
temperature test. Insert a digital probe into the side you would
carve from, at whichever end is thickest, as close to the centre
of the cross section as possible, and check the temperature.
Probe at a couple more points, the aim being to find the lowest
temperature reading in the joint. The temperature is likely to
measure in the mid twenties, in which case it can go back in
the oven for 10 minutes before testing again. As it nears your
chosen temperature, return it to the oven, probing at 5-minute
intervals, until the correct temperature is
reached. We cook our beef to an inner core
temperature of 37°C and when it is out of
the oven we watch the carry-over effect on

the thermometer as it climbs to 50°C. Perfectly rare.

Resting for 30 minutes is essential to finishing the beef properly. Straight after it comes out of the oven, the fibres will contract and juices will leave the meat. Then, as they stop contracting, it will reabsorb the juices. This window provides a great opportunity to season. Apply up to a tablespoon of flaky sea salt liberally to the joint. Over the next 10–30 minutes, regularly baste the meat by spooning the juices back over it. The salt will dissolve from the surface and the pan juices will be rendered too salty for use elsewhere, but as the beef absorbs some of this salt it will be seasoned to perfection. After the sirloin has been basted and rested, it can be returned to an oven set at 50°C, where it will 'hold' perfectly till you are ready to carve it – a technique used in many professional kitchens.

Heat the remaining rapeseed oil in a pan, add the cabbage and cook over a medium heat for 30–45 seconds. Add the cider vinegar, let it steam off in the heat of the pan, then season with salt and transfer to a warm serving dish.

Reheat the cauliflower purée, carve the beef and serve with the bordelaise sauce, mash and cabbage.

AGEING BEEF

When a beef or buffalo carcass is aged, the meat, as whole joints, is held between 1 and 3°C. Enzymes in muscle break proteins into savoury amino acids and this is where flavour develops from (see Harold McGee, *On Food and Cooking*). This process won't be noticeable until after 20 days and continues for a further 15 days. Further action of fungal microbes on the exterior complements this process. They don't cause spoilage in the true sense and in any case, the meat is trimmed of its crust as a matter of course by the butcher at the end of the maturing. A supermarket would most likely cut and package meat after only four days of storing in oxygen-less conditions. The supermarket benefits from having no loss in weight that a dry-ageing process would effect.

Search out an independent producer of British grass-fed beef at a farmers' market; talk to him or her and ask about this process. Upon knowing a little more about their artisan skills and pride in their product, you are much more likely to come away with a meltingly tender and flavoursome cut of meat. As Britain is the only country in the world to ban animal derivatives in feed, the beef is now the safest the world over; something to support and truly get behind. Once you have bought the best possible piece of meat, the kitchen process is simple to say the least.

ROASTING BEEF

Roasting beef to perfection requires an accurate thermometer. There are many other ways of judging when the beef is at the correct stage of 'doneness' but a thermometer is undoubtedly the most effective way to achieve the same result every time. Ovens operate at different temperatures, with their own unique cold spots and hot spots. Having a correctly calibrated thermometer to measure the internal temperature of the meat negates all the guesswork.

For our rare roast sirloin, which we serve most Sundays in the restaurant, the cut is roasted to an internal temperature matching that of our bodies. The meat is then taken out of the oven and allowed to rest for a minimum of 30 minutes before it is served. Meat is subject to a phenomenon known as 'carry-over cooking'. Essentially this means that even after the meat has been removed from the oven, the internal temperature will continue to rise a good few degrees. The thicker the piece of meat, the more heat it will retain and the higher it will climb. Sirloin and other large cuts usually climb around 10–13°C. The chart below shows the temperature the meat should reach after resting:

45°C	*bleu*, or very rare
50°C	rare
55°C	medium-rare
60°C	medium

When cooking steaks, remove them from the heat when they are roughly 5°C below the temperature you want to reach; for ribs of beef, 5–10°C. We would never recommend taking beef above 60°C, as it becomes almost as much of a task to eat as cold Midget Gems. And a lot less enjoyable too.

Almond, Pear, Cardamom and Chocolate Cake

We have used many fruits in the development of this dessert and although it works well all year round, we can safely say that it is best with pears, especially if you can get them when they are perfectly ripe. Pears tend to be less acidic than apples and we find their elegant, honeyed fragrance hard to resist.

It was inspired by the classic combination of pear and almond, exemplified in the traditional frangipane – a sumptuous paste made from ground almonds. It evolved into a cosmopolitan West Country affair when we were asked to design cakes to suit the menu of the Thali Café, an independent Indian chain based in Bristol. The addition of floral-scented cardamom seemed inevitable. The cake was the perfect match for all those wonderful spices used in Indian cooking. It has now become one of the most popular items at The Ethicurean, whether sold from the cake counter or served as a warm dessert. Above all, this cake has won a devoted following because we keep it gluten free. Gluten-free cakes are sometimes maligned for being dry and crumbly but this offering trounces that preconception. We encourage you to try it warm with a decent amount of cream. The chocolate will melt within and the frangipane will be transformed into a devastatingly moist ensemble.

315g salted butter, at room temperature

315g caster sugar, plus a little extra for dusting

5 eggs, lightly beaten

315g ground almonds

50g gluten-free plain flour (or ordinary plain flour)

1 tbsp ground cardamom

1 ripe pear

70g dark chocolate (we use Original Beans Cru Virunga chocolate but any good 70 per cent cocoa solid chocolate will work)

Heat the oven to 160°C/Gas Mark 3. Line the base and sides of a 23cm springform cake tin with non-stick baking paper.

Using a freestanding electric mixer fitted with the paddle attachment, beat the butter and sugar together for 10–15 minutes, until pale and increased in volume. Gradually pour in the beaten eggs while the mixer continues to turn. Add all the dry ingredients and mix on slow until just combined. Remove the bowl from the machine and fold the mixture a few times with a spatula to ensure it is well mixed. Turn it into the tin, level the top slightly, then place in the centre of the oven and bake for 20 minutes. In the meantime, thinly slice the pear, removing the core, and break the chocolate into pieces. Remove the cake carefully from the oven. It will be liquid, with only a touch of colour. Press the chocolate pieces vertically into the mix across the entire cake. Lay the pear slices in a pattern of your choosing on top. Dust them with a little caster sugar to aid caramelisation and then gently return the cake to the oven. Cook for 40 minutes longer, turning the cake around half way through to ensure it bakes evenly. If you have a digital probe, a good way to ensure that the cake is done to perfection is to check the temperature in the centre; it should be 94°C. Otherwise, insert a skewer and check that it comes out clean. Leave the cake to cool for at least 20 minutes before serving.

† The name frangipane (as the enlightening *Larousse Gastronomique* tells us) originates from a sixteenth century perfumer and nobleman, the Marquis Muzio Frangipani. In his vast repertoire of perfumes, he had a particularly memorable one based on bitter almonds, which was specifically used for scenting gloves. The scent was so pleasant that it led prominent Parisian chefs to design an almond-based paste in the Marquis's name.

---

† It seems that our love for pears was shared by Romans and Greeks alike. Pears were eaten in diverse ways and even made into an alcoholic drink. During medieval times, pears would only be eaten after dinner and they were generally roasted or eaten with sugar, fennel seeds or aniseed. They tended to be eaten in enormous quantities at times of gluts which inevitably led to upset stomachs and the incorrect assumption that they were a risky fruit to eat raw. The saying 'raw pears a poison, baked a medicine be' encapsulates this sentiment perfectly. The practice of cooking pears with sugar and spices continued well until the seventeenth century.

Sea Buckthorn Sorbet with Apple and Vanilla Purée, Toffee Apple and Caramel, Lemon Balm

Sea buckthorn has been used for centuries in Europe and Asia, both as food and for medicinal purposes. As its name suggests, it is a hardy, thorny bush, which might be why it has been forgotten about in recent times: harvesting it is not the easiest of tasks. This did not deter the Ancient Greeks, who used to feed it to their horses to promote weight gain and glossy coats – hence its Latin name, *Hippophae*, meaning 'shiny horse'. It's definitely worth looking out for the berries on seaside foraging trips. The dense bushes are easy to spot, as the berries are a cheerful, bright yellow-orange. In line with good foraging etiquette, try to resist the urge to cut the whole spiky branch in order to gain easier access to the fruit. It will damage the plant and minimise the chance of a future harvest. Instead, think of the intrepid Greeks on their shiny horses and arm yourself with a thick pair of gloves and tough clothing, so you can harvest in peace.

The berries often stay on the hedge well into the winter. Beware of their high acidity; it certainly makes for an interesting game of who can pull the funniest face as you eat them. We temper this tartness by making the berries into a syrupy sorbet. The apple and vanilla purée softens their astringency even further and provides a sweet, velvety base to dip your mini toffee apples into.

We could not resist including toffee apples. They are the epitome of autumn, conjuring up thoughts of woodland floors carpeted in golden leaves and amber sparks around a bonfire. These miniature versions are a more refined treat than the traditional childhood ones.

SERVES 6

FOR THE SEA BUCKTHORN SORBET:
700–800g sea buckthorn berries
250g fructose (fruit sugar)
50g glucose powder

FOR THE APPLE AND VANILLA PURÉE:
¼ vanilla pod
250g dessert apples, peeled, cored
   and cut into cubes
5 tbsp caster sugar

FOR THE TOFFEE APPLES:
175ml apple juice
100g caster sugar
2 Blenheim Orange apples (or
   Bramley apples)
4–6 lemon balm leaves (or mint
   leaves), finely sliced, to decorate
a few shards of salt caramel (see
   page 303), to garnish (optional)

First make the sorbet: pass the sea buckthorn berries through a juice extractor and measure the juice; you will need 400ml. Put the fructose and glucose in a saucepan, add 330ml water and bring to a gentle simmer. Leave to cool and then stir in the sea buckthorn juice. Pass through a fine sieve and leave in the fridge for at least 2 hours. This allows the proteins in the mixture to hydrate fully, which improves the whipping qualities of the sorbet and makes it smoother. Freeze in an ice-cream machine according to the manufacturer's instructions. When the mixture is almost frozen, blitz with a stick blender for 15–30 seconds, then return to the machine and continue to churn. Decant into an airtight container and freeze for at least 2 hours before serving.

For the apple and vanilla purée, slit open the vanilla pod and scrape out the seeds. Put the seeds and pod in a saucepan with the apples, sugar and 50ml water and place over a medium heat. Bring to a simmer and cook for 30 minutes, stirring often. Transfer to a blender, removing the vanilla pod, and blitz to a purée. Pass through a fine sieve and set aside. Allow to cool and then chill.

To make the toffee apples, pour the apple juice into a saucepan and bring to a gentle simmer. Remove from the heat and keep warm. Use the sugar to make a caramel, following the instructions for Salt Caramel on page 303 but omitting the salt. Let it reach a deep, even, gold colour, then instead of tipping it on to a silicone mat, remove from the heat and slowly add the apple juice. Be careful, as the caramel will bubble rapidly when the juice is poured in. Once all the juice has been added, the caramel will probably solidify. Place over a low heat and cook, stirring, until it has melted into the apple juice. Simmer until it has reduced to a loose, syrupy consistency. Remove from the heat and leave to cool.

Using a melon baller, scoop out 18–24 balls of apple, keeping the skin on. Put the balls in a saucepan just large enough to hold them in a single layer, then add enough of the caramel apple syrup to reach half way up them. Place on a high heat and cook, turning the apple balls regularly, until the syrup has thickened enough to coat them. Remove from the heat and set aside in a warm place until needed.

To serve, spoon some apple purée on to each plate, then add the toffee apple balls, dressed with a little extra syrup. Decorate with the lemon balm and salt caramel shards (if using), and place a scoop of sorbet on each plate.

Beetroot, Apple and Cobnut Crumble with Roasted White Chocolate Spoom

Given that we have so many apple varieties in the Walled Garden, we could not resist creating a version of the ubiquitous crumble. It is, after all, the quintessential British pudding, and one that can be enhanced greatly by the choice of ingredients used. Its beauty lies not only in its simplicity but also in its versatility. Surprisingly, crumbles didn't become popular until the Second World War, when they were a way of eking out sugar, flour and butter rations to make a pudding. Using beetroot might seem slightly risky but we have opted for the sweet, white-fleshed Albina Ice beetroot, which gives a subtle colour palette. If you can get Ribston Pippin apples, they offer the perfect combination of pear, malt and peach flavours, and also have a subtle, chestnut-like flavour that complements the cobnuts. We opt to turn the apple and beetroot out on to a crisp, separately baked crumble, and have borrowed the tarte Tatin idea of making a caramel to top the dish. So in essence, this is an upside-down crumble. The addition of a nutty element is optional but you will find that it improves the texture of the topping by making it crunchier – the hallmark of a good crumble, in our view. It is, of course, possible to substitute hazelnuts for the cobnuts but we would urge you to head outdoors and find your nearest cobnut tree. This is such a great native nut, with an amazing history (see page 157).

SERVES 6–8

350g Albina Ice beetroot (or substitute golden beetroot, Chioggia or red varieties for a very different colour finish)

500g Ribston Pippin apples (or Cox's Orange Pippins)

Roasted White Chocolate Spoom (see page 276), to serve

FOR THE CRUMBLE:

100g cobnuts

260g plain flour

165g demerara sugar

165g unsalted butter, at room temperature, cut into cubes

½ tsp ground cinnamon

FOR THE VANILLA AND CIDER BRANDY CARAMEL:

125g caster sugar

100ml aged cider brandy

1 vanilla pod

50g unsalted butter, at room temperature, cut into small cubes

First make the crumble. Heat the oven to 180°C/Gas Mark 4. Put the nuts in a food processor and blitz for a second or two, until they are coarsely chopped. Sift in the flour, add the sugar and turn on the processor again. Slowly add pieces of butter through the food tube until the mixture resembles breadcrumbs. (You can do this all by hand, if you prefer, rubbing the butter into the dry ingredients with your fingertips.) Scatter the mixture into a 24cm non-stick ovenproof frying pan without pressing it down. Bake for 25 minutes or until golden brown and crisp. Cooking the crumble separately like this means it retains its crunch against the moist apple. Remove from the oven and cool slightly, then turn it out on to a serving plate by placing the plate over the pan and carefully flipping them both over. Hopefully it will come out clean and unbroken. Set aside for later. Clean out the pan now, ready for making the caramel top.

Wash the beetroot well, trimming away the stems, then slice them finely from top to bottom. This will be easier with a mandoline, though entirely possible with a calm, steady hand and a sharp knife. Core the apples and slice finely into discs.

Put the sugar and cider brandy into the non-stick frying pan. Slit the vanilla pod down its length, scrape the seeds into the pan and add the pod halves as well. Set the pan over a medium heat and bring to the boil, stirring occasionally to

† The apples we have chosen for this dish are Ribston Pippin. The mid-season apple variety gained its name from Ribston Hall in Yorkshire where it is believed to have grown in the 18th century. This was another popular variety in theVictorian era and was believed to be one of the parents of Cox's Orange Pippin.

† Beetroot was a favourite sweetener and colouring agent of the Victorians; it was often used in salads and soups. Victorian food, particularly in noble houses, was all about creating the most stunning theatrical effect and it seems that the dramatic colour provided by this root vegetable was a favourite at the dinner table.

dissolve the sugar. The liquid may ignite as the alcohol cooks off. Continue to cook, without stirring but keeping a close eye on it, until it turns a light caramel colour, similar to that of demerara sugar. As soon as this occurs, remove the pan from the heat. Lay the slices of beetroot in the caramel to cover the base of the pan, then add alternate layers of apple and beetroot. Dot the butter over the top and place in the oven. Check it after 35 minutes; it is ready when the moisture has been cooked out and there is a clear layer of deep caramel colour around the edges. This could take up to an hour, depending on the moisture content of the apples and beetroot, so keep checking at 10-minute intervals. When it is ready, remove from the oven and leave for 15–20 minutes, until the pan handle is cool enough to hold. Slide the crumble off its plate on to the apple. Put the plate face down on to this, then flop the whole thing over, taking care to hold the plate steady too. The apple mixture should come free from the pan with a gentle shake; go slowly and gravity should suffice. Serve with the roasted white chocolate spoom.

Simple syrups for sorbets and spooms

Sugar syrups are an essential part of making sorbets, spooms and ice creams. For all sorbet and spoom recipes we use in this book, we use a 50 per cent sugar syrup, also known as 50:50 syrup.

Depending on its use, we either use sucrose (common table sugar) or fructose (fruit sugar) (for more on fructose see page 203). For fruity preparations, we will generally always use the 50:50 fructose syrup. If you are ever unsure, refer to the recipe that you are making.

50:50 COMMON SYRUP
500g caster sugar
500g water

50:50 FRUCTOSE SYRUP
500g fructose sugar
500g water

This method applies to both syrups.

Combine the sugar and water in a medium saucepan. Place on a medium-high heat and bring to a simmer. Stir to ensure all the sugar has dissolved, before pouring into a bowl placed in an ice bath. Allow to chill to fridge temperature before decanting into a tupperware container and storing in the fridge until needed.

You may also cool the syrup by pouring it into a roasting tray with a large surface area. Liquids with large surface areas cool down much more quickly.

Spoom

The name 'spoom' comes from the Italian word *spume*, meaning foam. Spoom resembles a smooth, airy sorbet. It is a forgotten dessert nowadays but it used to be very popular in England. It was made with a lighter syrup than a normal sorbet, and one would mix in Italian meringue for good measure. It was commonly sold in a tall glass so that you could see the layers and textures within. Spoom is such a versatile dessert that it is astonishing that we ever let it go off our culinary radar. In order to revive the spoom, we have come up with an autumnal and a summery option. Read on and spoom away.

Roasted White Chocolate Spoom

SERVES 4–6
350g white chocolate
180g glucose syrup
80g Italian Meringue (see page 278)

Preheat the oven to 110°C/Gas Mark ¼. Break up the chocolate into an ovenproof dish and place in the oven. Leave for 10 minutes before stirring with a spatula. Return to the oven, stirring every 5 minutes, until the chocolate has taken on a light–medium brown colour (like Caramac!). This usually takes 40–60 minutes. During this process, the chocolate will go through several stages: hard, melted, chalky and grainy, before becoming completely smooth. Don't panic! This is normal. Take care when removing it from the oven as it's incredibly hot. Decant into a plastic container and leave to cool. Once cold and solidified, chop roughly into small pieces and place in a mixing bowl.

In a saucepan, combine the glucose syrup with 850g of cold water. Place over a medium heat and bring to a very gentle simmer. Pour the simmering liquid over the chopped chocolate. Stir for a couple of minutes before blending with a stick blender (or pouring into a blender). Fold in the Italian meringue.

Spoon the chocolate mixture into a plastic container and refrigerate for at least 2 hours. (The refrigeration process allows the proteins present in the spoom to hydrate fully. This will in turn improve its whipping qualities, allowing more air to be incorporated and result in a smoother product.) Remove from the fridge and strain through a fine-mesh sieve.

Twenty minutes before you are ready to churn, switch on your ice-cream machine. Add the spoom to the ice-cream machine. When the machine begins to labour, remove the bowl and blitz the mixture with a stick blender (or spoon into a blender) for 15–30 seconds. Return the mixture to the ice-cream machine and churn for a further 2–3 minutes. Decant into an airtight, lidded plastic container and freeze for at least 2 hours before serving.

Cherry Spoom

SERVES 4–6

500g pitted cherries, stones reserved (see Note, below)

150g 50:50 Fructose Syrup (see page 275)

35g Italian Meringue (see page 278)

Place the cherries in a blender and blitz on full speed for 12 minutes. Pass through a chinois or fine-mesh sieve into a mixing bowl to remove any excess solids.

Add the syrup to the cherries, mixing well. Whisk in the Italian meringue until fully incorporated.

Spoon the cherry mixture into a plastic container and refrigerate for a minimum of 2 hours. (The refrigeration process allows the proteins present in the spoom to hydrate fully. This will in turn improve its whipping qualities, allowing more air to be incorporated and result in a smoother product.) Remove from the fridge and strain through a fine-mesh sieve.

Twenty minutes before you are ready to churn, switch on your ice-cream machine (it needs to be very cold before use, so as to form ice crystals as quickly as possible, making for a smoother finish). Add the spoom to the ice-cream machine. When the machine begins to labour, remove the bowl and blitz the mixture with a stick blender (or spoon into a blender) for about 15–30 seconds. Return the mixture to the ice-cream machine and churn for a further 2–3 minutes. Decant into an airtight, lidded plastic container and freeze for at least 2 hours before serving.

NOTE: as an optional step for this recipe, wrap the reserved cherry stones in a tea towel and bash them with a rolling pin to crush them. Place the crushed stones in a saucepan, along with the fructose syrup. Bring the syrup to the boil and then take off the heat. Allow to cool to room temperature and then place in the fridge until thoroughly cold. Strain through a chinois or fine-mesh sieve to extract the stones, before continuing with the same method as above. This will add an extra complexity to the spoon, contributing an ever-so-slightly bitter almond taste. Delightful.

Italian Meringue

Italian meringues are a thing of beauty. Their thick, unctuous texture is enough to make a grown man regress to a childlike state, scraping every last tiny morsel out of the bowl and hungrily licking the spoon.

A meringue is a type of foam made from whisking egg whites and then adding sugar. It is the egg whites that create the foam: as the white is whisked, the proteins, which are in a tangled form in their natural state, begin to unravel into strands. These strands then interact with one another, and as air is incorporated, through whisking, they wrap around the air bubbles and trap it, and thus a foam is created. The meringue most of us make at home is an uncooked meringue. These are not considered safe to eat in their raw state, simply because temperature has not been applied to kill any bacteria present. Usually these meringues are put into the oven to crisp up and form pavlovas or give the rise to soufflés. If left uncooked, a raw meringue will eventually deflate, as the raw or 'soft' proteins in the egg are no longer able to retain the air bubbles.

Italian meringues differ from the common meringue because, as the eggs are whisked to the correct consistency, boiling sugar is poured in. This boiling sugar cooks the egg white, rendering it safe to eat, but interestingly, as the hot sugar cooks the egg whites, the 'soft' proteins coagulate, trapping air almost instantly. Coagulated proteins are set, and are able to hold on to trapped air much more effectively than raw proteins. These are two good reasons we use Italian meringue: it is pasteurised, and far more stable than any other meringue. Italian meringue can be used to make crisp meringues and a whole host of other desserts. We use it for creating our spooms (see pages 276–7).

Italian meringues are the more complicated to make, but don't let this put you off. With a little practice you will hone a method that works for you and your equipment and you will be able to make a perfect meringue every time.

320g caster sugar
150g egg whites

Place the sugar and 100g of cold water in a small saucepan. Place on a medium heat and bring to the boil. As the syrup begins to boil, increase the heat to medium-high. If you have a jam thermometer then place it in the syrup. If you have an insta-read thermometer then periodically check the temperature – you need it to reach 110°C (see below) before you tackle the next step. Have a small bowl of water and a silicone pastry brush at the ready. As the sugar begins to boil, areas will most likely crystallise around the edge of the pan. Brush these away with the wet pastry brush to prevent the entire syrup from crystallising. Do not stir the syrup.

Add the egg whites to a meticulously clean mixing bowl. Make sure the sugar has reached 110°C before you start to whisk the egg whites (see box, opposite). Whisk the egg whites until they form stiff peaks. When the sugar reaches 121°C and the whites are at the stiff peak stage, slowly pour in the sugar syrup in a thin, steady stream, down the edge of the mixing bowl, while whisking at full speed. Once all the syrup is added, continue to whisk until the meringue returns to room temperature. This should take about 15–20 minutes. Time spent on this is most definitely worth it, so be patient. (A great way of entertaining yourself through tasks that require continuous attention is to take note of the characteristics of the contents of the pan or mixing bowl. Observing how they flow, their shine, texture or smell. How they slowly change vicosity, colour and aroma. Noticing little things like that may sound a little odd, but when you look closely you'll see how fascinating it can be!)

If you want to make individual meringues, preheat the oven to 60ºC (or the lowest possible gas setting). Line a baking sheet with greaseproof paper. Place generous tablespoons of the meringue mixture, about 5cm apart, on the baking sheet. Cook in the oven for 3–5 hours, until the outside of the meringue forms a fairly thick, soft skin. At this point switch off the oven and leave to cool for a couple of hours.

If making the meringue for the spoom recipes on pages 276–7, then we would recommend either making a half batch, or ensuring that you try both recipes then freeze them.

DIFFICULTY OF TIMING

This is the difficult stage of making Italian meringue, getting the timing right. You want the eggs to be at the stiff peak stage as the sugar hits 121ºC. If you have an electric hand whisk then starting to whisk the egg whites at 105ºC will probably be about right. If you have a Kitchenaid, it will whisk the whites far quicker than a hand whisk, so start it a few degrees later (try 108–110ºC). There are a few things you can do to control the mixture; having an ice bath ready is a useful tip. If the sugar reaches 121ºC before the egg whites are at stiff peak stage, then drop the base of the sugar pan into the ice bath. This will stop the sugar from continuing to cook, and the sugar will remain liquid for you to pour into the egg whites at the correct stage. With all things in the kitchen, nothing beats a bit of repetition and practice. From repeating the same recipes, you learn the subtle nuances of each ingredient and how it responds to what you do to it. It will quickly become second nature.

THE CHEESEBOARD

There is no doubt that British artisan cheesemaking is undergoing a revival. As part of a desire to reconnect with the physical process of making food, we want to trace our cheeses from source to table. The rich history of British cheese, along with the intricate specifics of our regional recipes, is something to be rediscovered and developed. The techniques employed by artisan cheesemakers today are, for the large part, the same as those used since time immemorial. Having distinctive styles of cheeses throughout the country is brilliant; tasteless uniformity is not.

A cheesemaker should have a direct link with his or her milk supply. In the past, the herd and the dairy would have been on the same farm – and in some cases they still are. The quality of the product is due in part to the communication between the cheesemaker and the person who looks after the herd. Regional, or territorial, cheeses are specific to the landscape in which they are made, and the geographical position will determine the character of the pasture on which the animals feed.

We have been lucky enough to host Cheese School at The Ethicurean. Organised by Jess Trethowan and Fiona Beckett, it takes place in a tent with wonky tables, hurricane lanterns and enough experts to sink a battleship. There are talks by cheesemakers, brewers, bakers and drinks experts, and we found it an invaluable way of learning how and why certain cheeses work with particular flavours and drinks. It also helped us understand how the cheesemaking process is affected by the seasons and the diet of the herd. A celebration of the distinctive character of British cheesemaking, it is a chance to share anecdotes and knowledge.

The word artisan sometimes comes under fire for its association with premium or higher-end, but the cost of artisan foods is indicative of the time, effort, research and passion that go into creating the best possible product. Ensuring that not one person in the chain of financial exchanges loses out is the responsibility of any business owner. A business that can grow, make or brew a good product and turn a profit without exploiting another person contributes to our local economy in the best possible way. The more we interact with the people who produce our food, and with the land from which it comes, the more we can enjoy the cultural history of our local area.

At The Ethicurean, we enjoy choosing the right pairing for cheese in the form of preserves and other accompaniments. Our staples are Hawthorn Jelly (see page 299), quince cheese (known to the Spanish as membrillo), celery salt, pickles and Dark Plum Chutney (page 298). When the fig tree decides to fruit, we will often serve the figs alongside fresh curd cheeses. During the autumn, our favourite apple to eat with cheese is Ashmead's Kernel, acidic and sweet like a pear drop.

Opposite are three of our favourite pairings. The key is to make sure the cheese is not overpowered by its accompaniment, and vice versa. We find picking out single flavours in the food and drink that are similar can lead to a harmonious match. Finally, bear in mind that salty foods can benefit from being paired with an accompaniment that is sweet in some way.

† In *Food in England*, Dorothy Hartley emotionally recalls the reasons for the decline of British cheese before the revival of the late twentieth century. It appears that motorised transport heralded the end of localised cheesemaking as milk was then delivered to large-scale factories. Following food rationing in both the First and Second World Wars, the government only allowed hard cheese to be made in order to conserve resources – cheese rationing continued until 1954. This had a profound effect on British cheese and accounts for the ubiquity of flavourless vacuum-packed blocks of varying colour. In 1989 the Ministry of Agriculture were on the verge of banning the use of raw milk in cheesemaking; luckily they were not successful. It is little wonder that it has taken until now for our artisan cheesemakers to build momentum and they are certainly gaining pace.

MARMALADE VODKA WITH DORSET BLUE VINNY AND CELERY SALT

Chase Distillery makes a marmalade vodka. This orange-hued tipple is made by marinating their own single-estate vodka, distilled in Hereford, with Seville orange marmalade. The vodka is sweet with the unmistakable aroma of oranges, contrasting well with the saltiness of the cheese. Dorset Blue Vinny copes with the high alcohol in this drink in much the same way as the traditional port and Stilton combination. Celery and blue cheese are destined to be together; a little more salt never did any harm.

OLD DEMDIKE WITH MEMBRILLO AND POT HOLER GOLDEN ALE

This is a Somerset version of Manchego and membrillo, and a compromise it certainly is not. A thin sliver of quince cheese with some of Homewood Cheeses' Old Demdike is an epiphany. A delightful drink match is an ale called Pot Holer, brewed by Cheddar Ales. It is a lively brew, a golden ale that, like Old Demdike, has a citrus fruit flavour. Cheddar Ales have hopped this beer with a blend of English whole hops. This is a very pleasant match indeed.

KEEN'S CHEDDAR WITH SMOKED CARDAMOM, PICKLED CARROT AND JJJ CIDER (JANET'S JUNGLE JUICE)

We pickle diced raw carrot in cider vinegar, coriander and black cardamom (see page 299). The acidity cuts right through this strong cheese. Choose a medium-dry cider, such as Janet's Jungle Juice, made by West Croft Cider, so it will balance the inherent salty-sweet nature of this unpasteurised Cheddar. The apple aroma in both the drink and the cider vinegar in the pickle make for a classic pairing.

We would love to list all of the great cheesemakers of the UK. Here are just a few of our favourites:

Keen's Cheddar
Unpasteurised cow's milk with traditional animal rennet. Made by the Keen family on Moorhayes Farm near Wincanton using a traditional pint starter with yoghurt-like cultures. The cheese is bound in cloth and matured for a minimum of 10 months, sometimes up to 18 months. Smooth, with a firm texture, it has a long-lasting flavour that is a combination of nuts, acidity and earth.

Ogle Shield
Unpasteurised Jersey cow's milk with traditional animal rennet. Made in North Cadbury, Somerset, by Jamie Montgomery and Wayne Mitchell. After being rind washed, the cheese forms a sticky, orange-coloured rind. The taste is similar to a raclette and it cooks very well.

Dorset Blue Vinny
Unpasteurised cow's milk with vegetarian rennet. Made on Woodbridge Farm in Dorset by Mike Davies. He uses 'leftover' milk after the cream has been skimmed off for butter-making. The cheeses are matured for 3–5 months and have a subtle flavour with a crumbly, creamy texture.

Gorwydd Caerphilly
Unpasteurised cow's milk with traditional animal rennet. Made on Gorwydd Farm at Llanddewi Brefi, Ceredigion, by Todd, Maugan and Kim Trethowan. The curd is worked by hand and a natural mould rind encouraged to develop. The cheese is kept true to the origins of traditional Caerphilly, a simple farmhouse cheese eaten young or after a little maturation. It has a springy, citric, lactic centre, oozy, mushroomy cream under the rind and a musty earthiness in the rind itself.

Single Gloucester
Unpasteurised cow's milk with vegetarian rennet. Made on Standish Park Farm in Oxlynch, Gloucestershire, by Jonathan Crump. In the days when all farmhouses made cheese, the cream would be skimmed off the evening's milk to make butter and the skimmed milk that was left was put with the following morning's full milk to make Single Gloucester cheese. Our Single Gloucester is traditionally matured and clothbound.

Kirkham's Lancashire
Unpasteurised cow's milk with traditional animal rennet. Made on Lower Beesley Farm near Goosnargh, Lancashire, by Graham Kirkham. Curd is combined from three days of cheesemaking – a technique that harks back to the tradition of not having a large herd, meaning the cheesemaker would need to consolidate a few days' milking. Very little starter is used, allowing the acidity to rise slowly. Graham's father milks the cows and they can discuss the herd's diet in the farmhouse kitchen. The entire cheese is smothered in butter rather than wax, allowing some air to penetrate. The flavour is lemony, with a mild acidity. Graham describes it as having a 'buttery crumble'.

OLD DEMDIKE

Unpasteurised organic ewe's milk with vegetarian rennet. Made by Tim Homewood and Angela Morris in Mells, Somerset, with milk from Shaftesbury. Similar to a young Manchego, the taste is clean and lemony.

WIGMORE

Unpasteurised ewe's milk with vegetable rennet. Made in Riseley, Berkshire, by Anne and Andy Wigmore at the end of their garden. This is a washed curd cheese, meaning a quantity of whey is removed during the make and replaced with water – a technique that reduces the acidity. It has a gentle flavour with a touch of caramel, the texture is smooth and liable to form a wonderful goo at room temperature.

LITTLE RYDING

Unpasteurised ewe's milk with vegetarian rennet. Made by James and David Bartlett on their family farm in North Wootton, Somerset. Mould ripened, it has a rich, creamy taste with a good saltiness.

PERROCHE

Unpasteurised goat's milk with traditional animal rennet. Made at Neal's Yard Creamery near Dorstone, Herefordshire, by Charlie Westhead (known affectionately to us Charlie Cheese) and Hadyn Roberts. A fresh cheese, it still has a little lactic taste. It has a lemon-like flavour with a good helping of goat.

STAWLEY

Unpasteurised goat's milk with traditional animal rennet. Made in Stawley near Wellington, Somerset, by Caroline Atkinson from hand-ladled curds. Caroline's husband, Will, looks after their herd of goats. A mix of morning and evening milks, this beautiful cheese has a soft texture and slightly honeyed flavour. We regularly have billy goats on our menu that they cannot use on the farm.

TYMSBORO

Unpasteurised goat's milk with traditional animal rennet. Made on Sleight Farm near Timsbury, Somerset, by Mary Holbrook. Hand ladled and made in flat-topped, pyramid-shaped Valencay moulds. A seriously smooth-textured cheese, the taste is lemon, nuts and the inevitable goatiness.

Lord's Lovage

Jason Mitchell makes Ashridge Sparkling Cider on Barkingdon Farm, near Totnes in Devon, with apples from his unsprayed orchards. He uses the méthode champénoise, which consists of a two-stage ferment. First the cider is fermented using wild yeasts, then after six months it is mixed with champagne yeast and cane sugar and transferred to champagne bottles, where it undergoes a secondary fermentation. The bottles are stored at a consistently low temperature for a year. This results in cider with very fine bubbles, much like champagne.

Mixing Jason's cider with our lovage syrup was an extremely good idea. Harvesting these precious seeds is a pleasure, and finding more and more recipes for them is even better. The lovage syrup, despite its sweetness, adds a savoury background note.

SERVES 1

125ml Ashridge Sparkling Cider

FOR THE LOVAGE SYRUP:

1 tbsp lovage seeds (or 1 tbsp
    chopped lovage leaves)
150ml caster sugar

To make the lovage syrup, place the lovage and sugar in a pan with 150ml water and heat gently, stirring to dissolve the sugar. Bring to a simmer, then remove from the heat and leave to cool. The syrup will keep in the fridge for up to 2 weeks.

To made the drink, simply pour 25ml of the lovage syrup into a champagne flute and top up with the cider.

---

† Leaving the cider on the yeast sediment (lees) gives the drink its characteristic toast-like flavour. This sediment is removed by inverting the bottles using a pupitre, over a month. Finally the top inch of the botttle containing the sediment is frozen and removed and a mixture of cider and sugar is added to replace it. There is evidence to suggest that this method of secondary fermentation so precious to champagne producers began with cider during the seventeenth century in England. It has been associated with two individuals, Lord Scudamore and James Merret, and very fine gentleman they were too.

Apple Flip

Jack drank something similar to this at the Hinds Head restaurant in Bray, and when he arrived back at Barley Wood he put together this version. The flip is a refined descendent of the egg drinks that were a staple in America up until the middle of the nineteenth century. Early flips were a mixture of beer, rum, egg and sugar, poured from container to container to aerate them. A red-hot poker would then be plunged into the flip, causing it to froth and adding a burnt caramel flavour. We have not tried this yet but it becomes increasingly tempting after a few flips. In England this style of drink never achieved the popularity that it had in colonial America, although the egg-based drinks of Christmas are a reminder of these old styles.

We particularly like the apple juice and brandy blends made by Julian Temperley of The Somerset Cider Brandy Company. As well as some excellent vintages of brandy and cider, he has created two drinks, Kingston Black and Pomona. Kingston Black is slightly sweeter and is similar in many ways to a Pineau des Charentes or white port.

SERVES 1

45ml Kingston Black

25ml 3-year-old Somerset Cider
    Brandy

20g caster sugar

1 free-range egg

a small grating of nutmeg

a large chunk of ice, or enough ice
    cubes to fill a cocktail shaker by
    two thirds

Combine all the ingredients except the nutmeg and ice in the glass part of a Boston shaker. Place the tin on top and tap to secure it, then shake vigorously. Break apart the shaker and then pour the contents from as high up as you dare back into the metal half of the shaker. This adds even more air to the drink. Drop in the ice – if you have a large chunk, this will chill the drink without diluting it too much and will also give a smoother-textured flip. Shake until the sides of the shaker condense, then pour the flip into a glass using a Hawthorne strainer. Finish with a fine grating of nutmeg.

The Orchard at Barley Wood

Barley Wood's main orchard was the first part of the Walled Garden we saw when we came to look at a prospective restaurant we were thinking of taking over. At first sight, the orchard did not stand out as being particularly different from others in the area but after we had walked around we became captivated by the history behind it. It had a mesmerising sense of a living past that had survived the test of time – and could continue well into the future. Our business was founded on the belief that cooking with local, seasonal produce was a principle worth striving for, and here it was – a place that perfectly epitomised this ideal, with the orchard at the centre of it all.

Having access to the orchard and the barn where the juice would be pressed became one of the most exciting facets of the new project we had embarked upon. We would have the opportunity to play a part in reigniting the passion for the British apple – and what better produce to showcase our belief in local, seasonal produce than the apple itself? Apples are most certainly seasonal but also extremely versatile, as they keep well for many months if you store them properly. They grow well without the use of pesticides or fertilisers, as the unsprayed orchard at Barley Wood demonstrates. There are over 70 types of apple growing there, making it an excellent living museum that features some of the best varieties around.

Apples are fascinating fruits. Their genetic make-up is so complex that if you were to eat an apple from a specific tree and plant a pip from it hoping to reproduce that tree, it is highly unlikely that you would end up with the same variety. This genetic characteristic is what led to the proliferation of varieties, although not necessarily the ones people most wanted to eat. The ancient process called grafting allowed people to replicate the most sought-after varieties. This simple yet effective technique consists of making an incision in the tree (known as the stock) and inserting a segment of the desired tree (called the scion). The graft is then secured with tape and covered with tar to prevent any water penetration. What seems to be a fairly rudimentary operation has worked remarkably well for centuries. The technique was first used by the Chinese before 2000BC and subsequently in Ancient Greece.

In the UK, we have the Victorians to thank for the many varieties of apples that grow here. The keen competitive spirit of gardeners on Victorian estates such as Barley Wood led them to produce a wide range of fruit and vegetables, some of which are still very popular today. There were so many apple varieties around at that time that it would have been possible to eat a different apple each day for six years.

Currently, there are over 2,300 varieties of apples preserved in the National Fruit Collection at Brogdale in Kent – although, sadly, 70 per cent of apples sold in the UK today are imported. Apple varieties that keep well and do not bruise when transported have pushed many other types off the market. One of our aims at the Walled Garden is to showcase the different varieties in our cooking, in the hope that this will promote diversity and encourage people to plant their favourite variety in their garden. The same applies to our juice, which is carefully blended from the apple varieties that complement each other best. No two batches are the same, since we press the apples as they become ripe, so the earlier batches will taste different from the ones made predominantly from late-season apples. The juice is truly an artisan product, made in a manual wooden press situated in a barn at the bottom of the Walled Garden.

Here is a brief list of some of our favourite
varieties, which deserve greater recognition:

Ashmead's Kernel
Blenheim Orange
Cheddar Cross
Morgan Sweet
Old Somerset Russet
James Grieve
Ribston Pippin
Laxton's Epicure
Tydeman's Late Orange
Summer Golden Pippin

MAKING APPLE JUICE

The apples are collected in separate trugs according to their variety, then placed on a metal table and
cleaned thoroughly with a powerful jet wash. They are subsequently moved to an electric scratter, which
is like a giant grater in the shape of a funnel. The grated apple is placed in a wooden frame on top of a
'cheesecloth' – effectively a sieve that prevents any grated apple passing through – then put on top of the
wooden press. The process is repeated until we have stacked up seven or eight frames of roughly one
variety of apple. This means it is time to wind down the press – an exhausting but highly rewarding stage
of the process as the blended apple juice starts flowing and you can see the result of all of your hard work.
More importantly, it is now time to do some tasting to ensure that the juice is palatable. This is also when
bets are placed about how many bottles we will make on this occasion.

   With the help of a bottle filler, we decant the juice into glass bottles. We like to use clear glass, as it shows
the wonderful amber colour of the juice. Most producers add ascorbic acid to prevent oxidation. This
results in a green colour, which we are told is the shade of apple juice the public is used to. We defiantly
believe that the natural amber colour of the juice is beautiful and should be celebrated, so we omit the
ascorbic acid.

   The bottles are placed in a pasteurising unit set at over 70°C for 20 minutes to ensure that we can keep
the juice for up to a year.

MAKING APPLE JUICE AT HOME

On a very small scale at home, you can make apple juice. Use a juice extractor, if you have one, or a blender and a sieve. This is the simplest method and is convenient if you have a tree in your back garden, so you can pick just the apples that you need for that day. The juice will keep for a day if stored in the fridge but without pasteurisation you won't be able to keep it for much longer.

If you are interested in larger-scale production at home, you can buy a table press with a capacity of anything from 5 to 40 litres. Depending on its size, you might need to cut the apples up before pressing them. To pasteurise the juice, simply place it in a saucepan and heat until it reaches a temperature of just over 70°C, then keep it at this temperature for 20 minutes. You will need to invest in a good thermometer to ensure not only that the correct temperature is reached but that it is maintained for the required time. Transfer to sterilised bottles.

Alternatively, you can pasteurise the juice in sterilised bottles that are specifically designed to withstand the heat of pasteurisation. Fill them with the juice (but leave the lids off). Take a large, deep pan that will hold the bottles standing upright and fill it with water. Heat until the temperature reaches 70°C, then add the bottles and check the temperature of the water again. Once it has returned to 70°C, leave the bottles for 20 minutes, then remove and screw the lids on. This process will allow you to keep the juice for up to a year.

With over 70 apple varieties in the orchards at the Walled Garden, it took some time until we could triumphantly say that we had sampled each and every one of them. Sadly, Morgan Sweet was not a variety that we chose to sample first. It is dreary-looking, and we became too smitten with Ashmead Kernels to spare any time for other types. We got suspicious about these hidden gems when an elderly couple came into the gardens looking specifically for Morgan Sweets. That year, we had a copious crop and gladly let them have a bucketful. After the couple's third visit, we thought we had better try them. Because they were labelled as cider apples, we expected them to be too sharp to eat. A single mouthful was enough to put their name into context.

Morgan Sweets were popular in Somerset in the first half of the twentieth century. Our older customers tell us they were cherished treats during the War, when food was scarce. We also hear of Morgan Sweets being great scrumping prizes, so valuable at wartime that tree locations were kept secret to ensure a steady supply for those in the know.

These apples are extremely juicy when ripe and we initially added them to our apple juice to balance the sourness of early crops. We would love to see a revival of Morgan Sweet apples in the UK, if only as a poignant reminder of how certain varieties become unfairly pigeonholed as dessert/cider/cooking types.

Salsify and Ogle Shield Gratin

The salsify at Barley Wood grows opposite the main entrance to the restaurant. It is stunning to look at, especially when its delicate flowers turn into an enormously soft dandelion as they go to seed. Seeing it daily for a whole season encourages us to include it in every form of recipe.

We came up with this dish when a gardening magazine asked us to produce a set of lunchtime recipes for gardeners to eat while at work – something that could be prepared in advance but enjoyed outdoors. It was originally intended to be eaten cold. However, as soon as we added the cheese, it took on a whole new dimension and we became convinced that our concoction had to eaten while still hot.

Ogle Shield is a worthy Somerset equivalent to French raclette. It melts very well and in our opinion is one of the best cheeses for gratins. We dare anyone who does not like cheese to try a melting slice of Ogle Shield. It has the ability to turn any cheese sceptic into a true turophile.

SERVES 4–6

1 tbsp cider vinegar

600g salsify

200ml white wine

800ml vegetable stock (see page 297)

200g Ogle Shield cheese (or raclette)

50g butter

65g plain flour

2 tbsp double cream

½ nutmeg, finely grated

sea salt and freshly ground white pepper

Heat the oven to 180°C/Gas Mark 4. Fill a large bowl with water and add the vinegar to it. Working quickly, peel the salsify and wash thoroughly under cold water. Cut it into 10cm lengths and then slice them thinly lengthways, preferably on a mandoline, to achieve 10cm batons. As soon as each length has been sliced, place it the acidulated water. This will prevent the salsify oxidising and turning brown.

Put the white wine and vegetable stock in a pan and bring to the boil. Strain the salsify, add to the pan and cook for 6–8 minutes, until it is tender but retains a slight bite. Strain the salsify, retaining the cooking liquor. Return the liquor to the pan and boil until reduced by two thirds.

Meanwhile, thinly slice 150g of the cheese and grate the rest. Arrange a layer of salsify in a gratin dish approximately 23cm x 13cm, completely covering the base. Add another layer of salsify, followed by a thin layer of Ogle Shield slices, and repeat until all the salsify and sliced cheese have been added.

Melt the butter in a saucepan, add the flour and stir to make a thick paste. Gradually pour in the reduced cooking liquor, stirring constantly. You may not need all the liquid – stop when the consistency is like single cream. Stir in the double cream, then add the nutmeg and some salt and pepper to taste.

Slowly pour the sauce over the layered gratin. Cover the dish with foil, place in the oven and bake for 25 minutes. Remove the foil, sprinkle the grated cheese over the top and place under a hot grill until the cheese has melted and begun to brown.

Vincent Castellano's Venison Chorizo

Our friend, Vincent Castellano, put together this recipe for when we have a healthy-sized roebuck in the kitchen. He began his career as a pot-washer at a charcuterie in Grenoble in the early 1970s. Seeing whole pigs arriving on a Monday and leaving as terrines, pâtés, salami and hams just a few days later inspired him to turn a summer job into a two-year apprenticeship. He moved to the UK in 1983 and worked as a chef, since there were few opportunities for charcutiers then. It is only in the last decade that he has taken up his original profession full time once again, firmly declaring, 'It is what I know best.'

The UK has never developed a tradition of cured sausages for the simple reason it has a damp climate. Instead we have become experts at making fresh sausages. The countries with a culture of dry-cured meats are largely confined to mountainous regions with a prevailing dry wind from the north. The Spanish have developed a particular skill in curing that has evolved, in part, due to their ideal weather conditions.

The recipe we have developed with Vincent is based on a traditional cured Spanish chorizo containing paprika, smoked paprika and garlic. Our version also includes turmeric, cloves, juniper, coriander and smoked chilli, plus our own sloe gin. Alternatively our house vermouth (see page 132) works beautifully. Both offer a gentle background flavour. During autumn we make the chorizo with neck and shoulder cuts from a roebuck. Due to its low fat content, additional fat is needed, so we add pork belly and back fat taken from Gloucester Old Spot pigs. The sausage is hung for 6–7 weeks, during which time it is fermented by lactic-producing bacteria. The increase in acid and the parallel dehydration, coupled with the high salt content, preserve the chorizo while intensifying its flavour. For the casing, Vincent uses ox runners, a natural, porous casing, distinguished by its gentle curve.

The ingredients below are given in relation to 1kg of total meat. A manageable amount to make is 3kg, which will fill a 3-metre length of hog casing (32mm diameter) or a 1.5-metre length of ox runners (50–55mm diameter). The quantity of curing salt is critical but all the other spices can be adjusted according to taste. The curing salt contains salt petre, which preserves the colour of the meat and inhibits unwelcome bacterial growth.

You will need a sausage maker or a mixer with a sausage-making attachment. These can be bought online from www.weschenfelder.co.uk, which also sells curing salt and casings. All the equipment used for making the sausages should be sterilised first.

hog casings (for smaller chorizo) or
    ox runners (for larger ones)
a little vinegar

EACH KILO OF MEAT SHOULD
CONSIST OF THE FOLLOWING:
800g boneless venison shoulder,
    belly flap and neck meat
100g pork belly
100g pork back fat

Thoroughly wash the salt off the casings, then soak them in a large plastic tub of cold water for at least an hour. Change the water, adding 1 part vinegar to 40 parts water, and soak for 30 minutes before use.

Cut all the meat into 3–5cm pieces, place in a bowl and add the curing salt. Mix thoroughly and then store in the fridge for 24 hours. Mix in the alcohol and return to the fridge for a further 24 hours.

Mince the meat on the fine setting of a mincer (an 8mm mincing plate), ensuring that the temperature remains below 8°C. Add the remaining seasonings and mix until all the ingredients

FOR THE SEASONINGS (ALL CALCULATED PER KILO OF MEAT):

25g curing salt

20ml sloe gin or vermouth

20g paprika

5g smoked paprika

3g smoked chilli powder

1g cayenne pepper

1g turmeric

2g garlic powder

¼ tsp ground cumin

1g ground coriander

¼ tsp ground cloves

⅛ tsp ground juniper

⅛ tsp ground star anise

adhere together, then press the mix down firmly with your hands in order to push out as much air as possible. Place in a sausage filler.

If using ox runners, cut them into 30cm lengths before filling. Hog casings can be filled continuously and tied into 15cm-long sausages.

Make a knot at one end of your chosen casing, slide the other end over the nozzle of the sausage filler and fill gradually, ensuring enough tension is kept. Remove from the filler and tie the end as tightly as possible with string, making a loop in it with which to hang the sausage. Prick the skin with a needle to let out any air pockets.

Hang the chorizo at room temperature (ideally 25°C) for 24 hours. After this stage, the chorizo can be used for cooking. If you want a cured sausage, move the chorizo to hang in a cool place (preferably 12–14°C) with a humidity level of 80 per cent – you can buy hygrometers in garden centres with which to check the humidity. Over the next few days a white 'mould' should develop on the skin. Maturation can take from 3 weeks (for hog casings) to 7 weeks (for ox runners). It's worth checking your chorizo on a daily basis. Because it is dependent on temperature, humidity levels and the length and diameter of the sausage, the maturation time will vary. When the chorizo is ready, it will feel firm when squeezed. If you slice it with a sharp knife, the meat should hold together well. The skin can be eaten or removed, as you prefer. The flavour of the chorizo should be intense, with a good acidity and sweetness, and spice flavours coming through in the aftertaste. It will keep well in the bottom of the fridge, wrapped in foil or a clean cloth, for up to a month.

BASIC RECIPES

Stocks

A good stock is a vital component of your repertoire. Stock forms the base of countless dishes, and having a stock that packs a massive punch of flavour means that you are halfway to creating a delicious meal. Investing a little bit of time and money in stock is a worthy cause, and we guarantee you it will improve your cooking no end.

Many people – chefs included – only use bones for stock-making. We like to use the slightly tougher, more flavourful cuts of meat – they can boost a stock's complexity and they're also quite cheap; they may cost a little more than bones, but the extra flavour more than makes up for it. Combine that with a good ratio of vegetables and herbs, tweaking the sweetness or freshness according to taste. Iain likes to use more carrots, onions and garlic to achieve a sweeter result. Herbs can be added at the very end, adding freshness to the base flavour. You can even add them as a warm infusion right at the last second. This gives you great control over the flavour of the stock.

You can make the recipes in this book for immediate use, or double or triple the quantities and freeze most in small batches for up to 3 months. If you devote half a day or so every month to making stocks, you should have a constant supply in the freezer. As always, use these recipes as a guide and once you understand the basic principles, experiment. Some of our dishes have undergone countless reinventions to get them to where they are now. We make all our stocks in the pressure cooker (for more on pressure cooking and why we do this, see page 260).

Beef Stock

YIELDS ABOUT 2KG

1kg beef bones, chopped into 2.5–5cm pieces (ask your butcher to do this)
600g oxtail, sectioned
rapeseed oil
360g onions, finely sliced
1kg beef shin or chuck, chopped into 2.5cm cubes
220g carrots, finely sliced
130g button mushrooms, finely sliced
220g tomatoes, sliced
½ small head of garlic, separated into cloves and smashed with the flat side of a knife

Heat the oven to 180°C/Gas Mark 4. Lightly and thoroughly rub the bones and the oxtail with rapeseed or vegetable oil. Place in a roasting tray (or separate roasting trays if necessary) and roast for 45–60 minutes, turning the pieces every 15 minutes until dark golden brown. If any parts of the oxtail become brown before everything else, remove from the oven and set aside.

Meanwhile, coat the bottom of a pressure cooker with rapeseed oil and place over a medium heat. Add the onions and cook over a medium-low heat until dark and caramelised – this will take about 30–45 minutes, stirring regularly and scraping any sticky bits from the bottom of the pan. Do not allow to burn. Take off the heat and allow to cool.

Heat a frying pan until extremely hot. Add a film of rapeseed oil; the oil should begin to smoke. If it does not, then keep on the heat until smoking hot. Add the beef shin or chuck and cook, turning, until dark brown on all sides, avoiding burning. Take the meat out of the pan and set aside. Drain any fat out of the pan, before placing the pan back on a high heat. Add enough water to cover the base of the pan and bring to the boil. Scrape away any leftovers that are stuck to the bottom of the pan. Add this deglazing liquid to the pressure cooker.

Wipe out your frying pan, add a film of rapeseed oil and place over a medium heat. Add the carrots and fry until soft and lightly golden (about 20–30 minutes). Add the carrots to the cooked onions along with the mushrooms, and set aside until ready to use. Deglaze the pan, using the same method as above, and add the liquid to the pressure cooker.

Repeating the process, fry the tomatoes in oil until they take on some colour, scraping off any sticky bits from the bottom of the pan. Add the garlic and fry for a further couple of minutes, ensuring nothing burns. Add the tomatoes and garlic to the pressure cooker, and deglaze the frying pan with water, as before. Add the deglazing liquid to the pressure cooker.

Remove the bones from the oven when they are a deep golden colour. Pour off any excess fat from the roasting tray. Place the bones and oxtail in the pressure cooker. Put the roasting tray(s) over a high heat. Deglaze with water, as before, and add the liquid to the pressure cooker.

Add enough water to the pressure cooker so that the ingredients are only just covered. Place over a medium-high heat and bring to a gentle simmer, skimming away any fat and impurities that rise to the surface. Once at a gentle simmer, place the lid on the pressure cooker and turn the heat up to full. Allow the pressure cooker to come to full pressure before reducing the heat. Cook at full pressure for 2 hours. Remove from the heat and allow the pressure cooker to cool to room temperature before removing the lid. Strain the stock through two layers of wet muslin. Immediately chill in a bowl set over another bowl filled with ice. Remove the layer of fat that forms before using. Use within 4 days or freeze for up to 3 months.

White chicken stock

We use white chicken stock when we want a great base flavour that doesn't overpower the taste or colour of other, more delicate ingredients. It is more subtle than our brown chicken stock (see page 296). The vegetables are gently softened and the bones briefly blanched to remove any impurities, then pressure cooked for 90 minutes. It is great for risottos, soups and sauces.

YIELDS ABOUT 2KG
1.5kg chicken wings, chopped into 3 at each joint
rapeseed oil
300g onions, finely sliced
150g carrots, finely sliced
120g button mushrooms, finely sliced
4 garlic cloves, smashed with the flat side of a knife

Put the chicken wings in a saucepan and cover with cold water. Place on a medium heat and bring to the boil, skimming off any scum that rises to the surface. Once boiling, drain immediately, discarding the water. Rinse the wings thoroughly under cold water.

Coat the bottom of a pressure cooker with a film of rapeseed oil and place over a medium-low heat. Add all the vegetables and cook until softened, without colouring this will take about 10–15 minutes. Add the chicken wings and enough cold water just to cover. Place on a medium-high heat and bring to a gentle simmer, skimming away any fat and impurities that rise to the surface. Once at a gentle simmer, place the lid on the pressure cooker and turn the heat up to full. Allow the pressure cooker to come to full pressure before reducing the heat. Cook at full pressure for 90 minutes.

Remove from the heat and allow to cool to room temperature before removing the lid. Strain through two or more layers of wet muslin, or a very fine chinois or sieve. Immediately chill in a bowl set over another bowl filled with ice (or put straight into the fridge). Use within 4 days or freeze for up to 3 months.

Brown Chicken Stock

YIELDS ABOUT 2KG

2kg chicken wings, chopped into 3 at each joint
a few tablespoons of skimmed milk powder
  (see box, below)
rapeseed or groundnut oil
300g onions, finely sliced
150g carrots, finely sliced
150g button mushrooms, finely sliced
4 garlic cloves, smashed with the flat side
of knife (or 2 wet garlic cloves if available
and in season)

Heat the oven to 200°C/Gas Mark 6. Place the wings in a roasting tray, evenly spread in a single layer, and sprinkle over enough milk powder to lightly coat them. Roast for 45–60 minutes, turning every 15 minutes, until the wings are a beautiful dark brown colour. The first time you turn the wings, give the pale underside a light sprinkling of milk powder too. This will ensure the wings are an even colour and impart more flavour into the stock.

Place the pressure cooker over a medium heat to get it warm before adding enough rapeseed oil to cover the bottom. Add the onions. Reduce to a medium-low heat and cook the onions until sticky and caramelised this will take about 30–45 minutes. Stir them regularly, taking care not to let them burn and adjusting the heat as needed. Scrape any sticky bits off the bottom of the pan. When the onions are caramelised, add the carrots and cook until soft. Remove from the heat and add the mushrooms and garlic. Set aside.

When the wings are evenly coloured, remove from the oven and drain the fat from the tray. Place all the wings into the pressure cooker..

Place the roasting tray over a high heat, and add a covering of water and bring to the boil. Scrape off the sticky bits of meat with a spatula or wooden spoon. Pour the deglazing liquid and crispy bits of meat into the pressure cooker.

Add enough cold water to the pressure cooker to just cover the bones. Place on a medium-high heat and bring to a gentle simmer, skimming away any fat and impurities that rise to the surface. Once at a gentle simmer, place the lid on the pressure cooker and turn the heat up to full. Allow the pressure cooker to come to full pressure before reducing the heat. Cook at full pressure for 2 hours.

Remove from the heat and allow to cool naturally to room temperature, before releasing the lid. Remove the lid before straining the stock through several layers of wet muslin, or through a very fine chinois or sieve. Refrigerate immediately, removing the layer of fat from the top before use. Use within 4 days or freeze for up to 3 months.

Using milk powder to dust the wings may seem a little odd but the milk powder is extra protein that boosts the Maillard Reaction (the browning on meat that gives it its characteristic flavour). It is a revelation. It gives the liquid an extra hit of meatiness and results in a stock that is a rich, deep brown. It's an excellent and simple way of boosting your stock's flavour profile.

Fish stock

YIELDS ABOUT 1KG

rapeseed oil

100g onion, finely sliced

80g carrots, finely sliced

80g button mushroom, finely sliced

1 tsp fennel seed

1 tsp coriander seed

1kg fish bones (avoid oily fish like mackerel, trout or salmon)

Place a pressure cooker over a medium heat and add a thin film of rapeseed oil. Add all the ingredients except the fish bones, and cook until softened – this will take about 5–10 minutes. Add the fish bones to the pressure cooker and add enough cold water just to cover.

Place over a medium-high heat and bring to a gentle simmer, skimming off any impurities that rise to the surface. Once at a gentle simmer, place the lid on the pressure cooker and turn the heat up to full. Allow the pressure cooker to come to full pressure before reducing the heat. Cook at full pressure for 20 minutes. Remove from the heat and allow to cool to room temperature. Strain through two layers of wet muslin into a bowl set over another bowl filled with ice. Refrigerate for up to 3 days, or freeze for up to 1 month.

Vegetable Stock

This vegetable stock is delicate, sweet and lightly aromatic. It's great in risottos, soups, stews and for making vegetarian sauces. For convenience, make at least double this recipe and freeze smaller quantities for use at a later date.

YIELDS ABOUT 1KG

rapeseed or vegetable oil

550g onions, finely sliced

500g carrot, finely sliced

500g mushrooms, finely sliced (button or brown)

200g celery, finely sliced

10 garlic cloves (or 1 small garlic bulb), smashed with the flat side of a knife

2 tbsp coriander seed

1 tbsp fennel seeds

4 whole star anises

2 tsp black peppercorns

2 bay leaves

Place a pressure cooker over a medium heat and add a thin film of rapeseed oil. Add all the vegetables to the pan and sweat for 5–10 minutes, until the vegetables have softened. Add all the spices and bay leaves and cover with water. Add the lid and turn the heat up to full. Bring to full pressure and then reduce the heat. Cook at full pressure for 15 minutes. Remove from the heat and allow to cool to room temperature.

Remove the lid and pass the stock through two layers of wet muslin. Refrigerate immediately and use within 5 days or freeze for up to 3 months.

Mushroom Stock

This mushroom stock is one of the more simple stocks that you will come across, utilising only two ingredients. Its simplicity does not detract from its ability to impart a rich umami flavour into the dish (see page 123), or to help boost this taste in dishes already rich in umami.

YIELDS ABOUT 500G

500g button or portobello mushrooms, finely sliced

500g cold water

Put the mushrooms and water in a pressure cooker and place over a high heat. Bring to full pressure, before turning the heat down to low. Cook at full pressure for 15 minutes before turning the heat off. Allow to cool to room temperature. Remove the lid and strain the stock through two layers of wet muslin. Refrigerate immediately.

Use within 5 days or freeze for up to 3 months.

To make this stock without a pressure cooker, place the ingredients in a saucepan and bring to a simmer. Keep at a steady simmer for 20 minutes, before removing from the heat. Allow to cool before straining and refrigerating, as above.

The Ethicurean Salad Dressing

> 100g rapeseed oil
> 60g vintage cider vinegar, such as Ostler's
> 8g Dijon mustard
> ¼ tsp xanthan gum (optional, but
>   recommended)

Add all the ingredients, except the oil, to a blender or stick blender jug. Blitz on full speed for 30 seconds before slowly pouring in the oil, as you would to make a mayonnaise. Continue adding in a thin, steady stream until all the oil is incorporated. Blitz for a further 30 seconds on full speed. Refrigerate for up to a week.

To make by hand, combine all the ingredients, excluding the oil, in a bowl. Whisk vigorously until airy. Gradually add the oil while whisking hard.

Dark Plum Chutney

> MAKES ABOUT 1KG
> 550g plums, halved and stoned
> 450ml malt vinegar
> 550g dark brown sugar
> 300g sultanas
> 150g onions, finely diced
> 10g garlic, finely diced
> 35g salt
> 10g mustard seeds
> 15g ground ginger
> ½ tsp onion (nigella) seeds
> ½ tsp ground star anise
> ½ tsp ground cinnamon

> 1 black cardamom pod

Put the plums in a large, heavy-based saucepan or a preserving pan along with the vinegar and sugar. Simmer until the fruit breaks down, then add all the remaining ingredients. Return to a simmer and cook for around 40 minutes, until thickened. Stir often, while being mindful of splashes. It has a tendency to spit when it is close to the correct consistency. When it is ready, all the thin liquid will have evaporated and the chutney will smell deeply rich, like liquorice.

Pour carefully into hot sterilised jars (see page 190) and seal. Invert the jars for a moment to ensure the lids are sterilised, then turn the right way up and leave to cool, while you write a label for each jar.

Pickled Beetroot

Preserving vegetables with salt and vinegar is invaluable to a seasonal kitchen. This method also suits carrot, cauliflower and any other firm vegetables. The method of calculating the salt and vinegar content in this method is adaptable to varying weights of produce and therefore great for seasonal gluts. Change the spices to suit the veg.

> 450g peeled beetroot, cubed into 1cm cubes
> cider vinegar
> fine sea salt
> 4 star anise
> 1 tsp peppercorns
> 1 tsp cumin seeds

Sprinkle the beetroot generously with salt and leave for 1 hour. Drain and rinse under cold water.

Place the beetroot into a 500ml Kilner jar or lidded tupperware container. Place the container on a set of scales and set them to zero (or 'tare'). Cover the contents in water and make a note of the weight. Discard the water. Weigh out the same amount of cider vinegar as it took water to cover the beetroot. Calculate 10 per cent of this weight and add that weight in salt (e.g. 200g of cider vinegar would require 20g salt). Place the vinegar, salt and spices in a saucepan over a medium heat and bring to the boil. Immediately pour the hot liquid over the beetroot in the jar or container. Ensure the beetroot is completely covered before sealing the lid and allowing to cool to room temperature. Refrigerate once opened. It will keep for up to 2 months.

Pickled Nasturtium Seeds.

At the start of November, as the first frosts descend, the nasturtiums that have been so useful for their leaves and flowers will begin to go to seed. A self-seeding plant such as this won't miss a few seed pods so we harvest as many as we can and pickle them as a 'poor man's caper'.

as many nasturtium seed pods as you can find
fine sea salt

PER LITRE OF PICKLING OR CIDER VINEGAR:
pickling or cider vinegar
10g sea salt or 10 per cent by weight of vinegar
2 cloves
4 fresh bay leaves
5 allspice berries
5 black peppercorns

Sprinkle the nasturtium seed pods generously with salt and leave for 1 hour. Drain and rinse under cold water.

Place the nasturtium seed pods into a 500ml Kilner jar or lidded tupperware container. Place the container on a set of scales and set them to zero (or 'tare'). Cover the contents in water and make a note of the weight. Discard the water. Weigh out the same amount of cider vinegar as it took water to cover the seed pods. Calculate 10 per cent of this weight and add that weight

in salt (e.g. 100g of cider vinegar would require 10g salt). Place the vinegar, salt and spices in a saucepan over a medium heat and bring to the boil. Immediately pour the hot liquid over the seed pods in the jar or container. Ensure the seed pods are completely covered, before sealing the lid. Invert the jars for a moment to ensure the lids are sterilised before allowing to cool to room temperature. Refrigerate once opened and keep for up to 1 month.

Pickled Carrots

250g carrots, cut into 1cm cubes
cider vinegar
4 black cardamom pods
2 tbsp coriander seeds
sea salt

Start by generously sprinkling the cubed carrots with salt. Set aside for 1 hour for the moisture to be drawn out.

Drain the carrots, and rinse off any excess salt. Place in a tupperware container, large enough just to hold them. Place the container on a set of scales and set them to zero (or 'tare'). Cover the contents in water and make a note of the weight. Discard the water. Weigh out the same amount of cider vinegar as it took water to cover the carrots. Calculate 10 per cent of this weight and add that weight in salt (e.g. 200g of cider vinegar would require 20g salt). Place the vinegar and salt in a saucepan with the cardamom and coriander, and bring to the boil. Once boiling, remove from the heat and pour over the carrots. Allow to cool to room temperature before refrigerating. The pickled carrots will keep for up to 4 weeks.

Winter Fruit Jelly

We have a hedgerow that reads like a book of autumn and winter fruits – blackberry, bullace, damson, hawthorn, loganberry, rose hip, rowan and sloe. Preserving them as jellies gives us fresh bursts of vitamin C through the winter and adds depth to dishes cooked over the colder months.

Use whatever fruits you have in whatever combination, following this basic method. We have found that freezing the berries first and then steaming, for juice extraction, produces a satisfying clear jelly. The second benefit to freezing the fruit is that you will have a little more time to forage before making your jelly.

We developed this method after we learnt that rowan berries require freezing before use as they contain parasorbic acid, an acid that is indigestible to humans. This acid degrades to a safe sorbic acid when frozen. Our steam basket method for extracting juice from fruit proved to be more effective when the fruit had spent time in the freezer, presumably because the cell walls are broken down by freezing, thereby releasing more liquid at the steaming stage.

MAKES ABOUT 5 JARS PER KG OF FRUIT
500g hedgerow fruit
500g Bramley or crab apples, peeled and
    roughly chopped (pips and cores left in)
750g caster sugar per litre/kg of juice
    (see below)
30ml organic preservative-free lemon juice
    (bottled juice has a set acidity) per litre/kg
    of juice (see below)

YOU WILL ALSO NEED:
a jam thermometer or digital kitchen probe
a sheet of muslin
sterilised jam jars and lids or Kilner jars
    (see page 190 for instructions on sterilising)

Line a steaming basket with a folded piece of muslin: this is not essential though it will allow only juice to fall into the pan below, aiding the clarity of the finished jelly. Place the hedgerow fruit and Bramley or crab apples in the steaming basket and steam over a pan of boiling water, set over a medium to low heat, for 1½ hours. Remove both the steamer and water from the heat, and leave to cool and drain overnight.

The next day check that the fruit is well drained. You can squeeze any last moisture from the muslin but this will make the jelly cloudy. Compost or discard the now flavourless fruit.

Measure the volume of the liquid in the pan – or better still, weigh it for accuracy – and pour into a large clean, stainless steel pan. Add 750g of sugar and 30ml of lemon juice per kilo of liquid. Cook over a high heat, stirring until the sugar is dissolved. Leave to boil vigorously, without stirring, for 10–20 minutes and then check the temperature: it should be around 102°C. You are aiming for a setting point temperature of about 103–105°C. If you don't have a thermometer, put a spoonful of the jam syrup on to a chilled plate and place in the fridge for 1 minute. Slide your finger across the plate into the dot of syrup and see whether it crinkles up and holds form for a moment. If it does then it has reached setting point. If not, continue to cook the jelly over the same high heat, testing every 5 minutes. A perfectly set jelly once chilled will only give slight resistance to a spoon and hold shape. (It is worth noting that a jelly that is over-firm is more useful than one that has not set at all so until you are confident with your thermometer, aim for the higher end of the temperature setting zone.)

Skim the jelly (or add a little knob of butter and stir) to remove any scum, then carefully pour into warm sterilised jars, leaving a centimetre of space at the top. Close the lids tightly then invert them for no more than a minute to ensure the lid is heated well and sterilised. Return to an upright position and leave to cool before storing in a dark cool place for immediate consumption or up to one year.

VARIATIONS:

Crab apple, medlar and quince will work perfectly well without additional pectin from Bramley apples but be sure to include their cores and pips during steaming and the citrus during cooking to set them. You can include extra apple to increase the volume if you like. Quince need their fine, downy hairs washing off prior to cooking. Quince jelly has pineapple overtones and an unbelievable amber glow when finished in the jar. The medlars need to be 'bletted' before using. They fall from the tree still hard and need to be left somewhere cool to go soft, squishy and blackened. Crab apple jelly is a great vehicle for other herbs which you can add during the steaming process. Star anise, lavender, tarragon, rosemary, mint and sage are all great and geranium leaf worked a treat when we tried it on a whim.

Flaky pastry

Making flaky pastry is a lengthy but relatively simple process. It requires resting for an hour between each 'turn' (a turn refers to each time it has been rolled out, butter and lard added, then folded and returned to the fridge).

Always resist any urge to knead, as this will make the pastry elastic. Perfect flaky pastry should be crisp and very light. What you want is a pastry that incorporates the multilayered fat, and pockets of air that create the flaky texture.

  150g salted butter, at room temperature
      but not oily
  150g lard, at room temperature but not oily
  350g strong white flour
  1 tsp fine sea salt
  1½ tsp lemon juice

Measure out 200ml cold water, add a handful of ice cubes and set aside.

Put the butter and lard in a small mixing bowl and mix together with a wooden spoon. This will take some work, but the aim is to get the two fairly homogenous. Weigh out three 70g portions and place each in its own dish. Cover two of them with cling film and place in the fridge. You will be left with 90g of butter/lard in the mixing bowl and one dish of butter/lard at your side.

Sift the flour and salt into a bowl and add the lemon juice. Add the 90g fat left in the mixing bowl, thoroughly scraping the sides of the bowl with a spatula to get all of it out. Rub the fat into the flour with your fingertips until the mixture resembles rough breadcrumbs. If there are still lumps of fat, don't worry – this will help create air pockets in the pastry. Make a well in the centre of the mixture and place the bowl on to weighing scales. Keeping back the ice cubes, pour the iced water into the centre of the well, making sure you don't add more than 200g. Mix the water into the flour with a round-bladed knife, until a pliable, slightly sticky dough has formed. Turn out on to a lightly floured work surface. Shape the dough roughly into a cube and, using a rolling pin, roll it out away from you to create a rectangle approximately 30cm x 15cm.

Take the 70g fat that did not go in the fridge, break it roughly apart into chunks and dot evenly around the bottom two thirds of the rectangle. Fold the top third of pastry over the middle third, then fold up the bottom third of pastry – like folding a letter. Seal the left and right edges and then seal the horizontal fold by pressing with your thumb and fingers. Using your thumb, mark an indent in the centre of the pastry 'envelope'. This dot signifies that it is the pastry's first 'turn'. It's well worth doing, as remembering where you're up to after a long afternoon can be challenging. Wrap the pastry in cling film and place in the fridge for at least 1 hour.

Remove the pastry from the fridge and give it a quarter turn anticlockwise so that one of the shorter sides is nearest to you. Roll the pastry out

away from you to produce another 30cm x 15cm rectangle. Repeat the process with one of the dishes of chilled lard and butter, filling the bottom two-thirds of the pastry with dots of the mixture, then folding, sealing and marking 2 indents in the pastry (to signify its second 'turn'). Wrap in cling film and return to the fridge for at least 1 hour.

Repeat the entire process using the final ramekin of fat, remembering to give the pastry a quarter turn anticlockwise. Mark 3 indents to signify its third and final turn. It is not unusual for flaky or puff pastry to have 6 turns. This is time consuming, but if you want to try it you will have an even lighter, flakier pastry. If opting for the extra turns, you will have run out of fat at the end of your third turn. Continue rolling and folding as you have been, but without the addition of fat. We strongly recommend these 3 extra turns as the extra layers will result in a crispier, less dense pastry that is far superior.

Puff pastry

Puff pastry is made in the same way as the Flaky Pastry above but using all unsalted butter instead of salted butter and lard.

Candied Peel

1 lemon, peeled, with all the white pith still attached to the peel
1 blood orange, peeled with pith still attached
1 thumb-sized piece of fresh ginger, peeled
500g caster sugar

Place the citrus peel and ginger in a pan, cover with cold water and bring to the boil over a medium heat. Drain, discarding the water. Return to the pan, cover with fresh water and bring slowly to the boil again, then drain. Repeat this process once more (it helps to extract the bitterness), then place the peel and ginger in ice-cold water for 10 minutes.

Meanwhile, put the sugar in a pan with 750ml cold water and heat, stirring occasionally, until the sugar has dissolved. Remove from the heat and set aside.

Cut the ginger and fruits into 5mm cubes and add them to the sugar syrup. Cook on the lowest possible heat for 6 hours; a thermometer will be useful here, as you need to keep the syrup at 70–80°C. You may need to have the pan half-on, half-off the heat, depending how hot the burner is. When the peel is done, it will be sweet and soft, in a thick syrup. Strain and leave to cool, then store in an airtight container. It will keep for about a month.

Ethicurean Mixed Spice

10g allspice berries
2 nutmegs, grated
10g whole mace
4g fennel seeds
10g cloves
4g cassia
4g cardamom seeds
2 tsp ground cinnamon
15g granulated sugar

Warm all the ingredients except the cinnamon and sugar in a heavy-based frying pan until a very light smoke is created and the aromas and oils of the spices are released. Place in a spice grinder and blitz to a fine powder. Mix with the cinnamon and sugar and then store in an airtight container. It will keep for about 3 months.

Salt Caramel

200g caster sugar
2 tsp flaky sea salt

Heat the oven to 120°C/Gas Mark ½. Place a silicone baking mat on a baking sheet and put it in the oven (if you don't have a silicone baking mat, put a layer of baking parchment on the tray once it has been heated). Have a small bowl of cold water and a silicone pastry brush at the ready.

Put the sugar into a meticulously clean frying pan, add 4 tablespoons of water and stir until there are no dry patches of sugar. Place on a medium-high heat and cook, without stirring. The mixture will start to bubble. As the temperature rises, the sugar will begin to caramelise in certain areas of the pan. You may also notice it beginning to crystallise around the edges of the pan. If left unchecked, these areas can cause the syrup to crystallise, resulting in a pan full of grainy sugar crystals – not the desired result. To prevent this, brush cold water over these crystallised patches on the edges of the pan, using a silicone pastry brush. When the sugar begins to caramelise, gently scrape these darkening patches into the centre of the pan using a heatproof spatula. Keep gently moving any patches of caramelising sugar into areas that are not caramelising. This

will ensure an even colour. When the caramel has turned a good, deep golden colour (if you use a sugar thermometer, it will register 178–180°C – however, you can keep checking the true colour by dripping a few drops on to a white plate), pour it immediately on to one side of the silicone mat. Preheating the mat means that the caramel doesn't cool down so quickly when you pour it on, and this allows you to tilt the baking sheet in order to achieve a very thin layer of caramel. You need to work quickly, however. As soon as the sugar begins to cool, it will start to set. Sprinkle the sea salt over the caramel while it is still hot.

Let the caramel cool to room temperature, then snap it into 2.5–5cm shards. It should be brittle. When you eat it, it should be crunchy and not stick to your teeth. Keep in an airtight container in a cool dry place for up to 2 weeks (caramel is susceptible to moisture content and will go very sticky if exposed to it).

Rhubarb syrup

MAKES ENOUGH TO FILL A 700ML BOTTLE

500g rhubarb, washed, trimmed and cut into 5cm
    pieces
350g sugar

Place the rhubarb in a saucepan with 200ml cold water. Bring to the boil, then reduce to a simmer and cook until all of the juice from the rhubarb has been extracted and the rhubarb is almost completely broken down; this will take around 30 minutes (please do not waste the cooked rhubarb, try it with porridge or a bowl of yoghurt).

Strain the cooked rhubarb through a piece of muslin; it can be left for a few hours. Place the strained liquid in a clean saucepan, add the sugar and bring to a simmer to dissolve the sugar for around 5 minutes. Pour the hot liquid into a sterilised bottle. Once opened refrigerate and consume within 2 weeks.

FRUIT VINEGARS

Anyone with an interest in food history and the effect certain ingredients have had on our cooking, would agree that the invention of vinegar changed the culinary map beyond recognition.

The origins of vinegar date back to the Middle Ages, when its importance centred on it being a tool for food preservation. Preserving food was crucial for survival, particularly in countries prone to more extreme weather. Vinegar also had the highly desirable quality of being a substitute for wine when diluted with water, which is perhaps why Roman soldiers insisted on it being part of their rations (Brothwell, 1969, pages 160–2). At that time, vinegar was manufactured from wine that had gone flat. Ancient Roman cookery records, such as Apicius, a famous Roman collection compiled in the 4th or 5th Century AD, mention plenty of uses for vinegar. And so it was that the imaginatively gluttonous Romans started using vinegar as much more than a preserve, creating the now common salad dressing. Such was the Romans' love of vinegar that they made sure that nothing was eaten without a sauce or dressing. The obsession with vinegar seemed to have carried through to Elizabethan times when there were plenty of reports of the overly enthusiastic use of vinegar in British cooking. A famous Italian named Castelvetro made a point of complaining about the state of the salads in this country which, he found, were served swimming in vinegar, without either salt or oil (Wilson, 1973, pages 363–4). The British, indeed, came up with Salamagundy, a 17th-century salad in which vegetables were dressed with vinegar, oil and sugar (Wilson, 1973, page 360).

Bibliography

Beeton, Isabella. *Mrs Beeton's Book of Household Management* (Cassell and Co, 2000 edn).

Bode, Willi. *European Gastronomy* (Grub Street, 2000).

Brothwell, Don and Patricia. *Food in Antiquity* (Thames and Hudson, 1969).

Brown, Jared and Miller, Anistatia. *The Mixellany Guide to Vermouth & Other Aperitifs* (Mixellany, 2011).

Clifford, Sue and King, Angela. *England in Particular* (Hodder and Stoughton, 2006).

Conigliaro, Tony. *Drinks* (Ebury Press, 2012).

The Culinary Institute of America and Migoya, Francisco. *Frozen Desserts* (Wiley & Sons, 2008).

David, Elizabeth. *Summer Cooking* (Penguin 1955).

Davidson, Alan. *The Oxford Companion to Food* (Oxford University Press, 1999).

Downing, Graham. *The Deer Stalking Handbook* (Quiller, 2008).

Fearnley-Whittingstall, Hugh. *The River Cottage Cookbook* (Collins, 2011).

Fearnley-Whittingstall, Hugh. *The River Cottage Meat Book*, (Hodder and Stoughton, 2004).

Grigson, Jane. *English Food* (Penguin, 1974).

Hartley, Dorothy. *Food in England* (Macdonald, 1954).

Hicks, Susan. *The Fish Course*, London (Guild Publishing 1987).

Larousse Gastronomique (Hamlyn 2009).

Leith, Prue and Waldergrave, Caroline. *Leith's Cookery Bible* (Bloomsbury publishing PLC, 1991).

Mabey, Richard. *Food for Free* (Collins, 1972).

McGee, Harold. *On Food and Cooking* (Hodder & Stoughton, 2004).

McVicar, Jekka. *Jekka's Complete Herb Book* (Kyle Cathie, 2009).

Parsons, Brad Thomas. *A Spirited History of a Classic Cure-All with Cocktails, Recipes and Formulas, Bitters* (Ten Speed Press, 2011).

Phillips, Roger. *Mushrooms* (Macmillan, 2006).

Regan, Gary. *The Joy of Mixology* (Clarkson Potter, 2003).

Segnit, Nikki. *The Flavour Thesaurus* (Bloomsbury 2010).

Spry, Constance and Hume, Rosemary. *The Constance Spry Cookery Book* (Aldine Press, 1956).

Wilson, C. Anne. *Food and Drink in Britain, From the Stone Age to the 19th Century* (Academy Chicago Publishers, 2003).

Wondrich, David. *Imbibe* (Pedigree, 2007).

Friends and Suppliers

This section is dedicated to people we have had the pleasure of working with over the last few years, many of whom share our beliefs in sustainability and preserving the things we enjoy for future generations.

Ashridge Cider
www.ashridgecider.co.uk

Adrian Boots
www.walkthemendips.com

Albam Clothing
www.albamclothing.com

Aspall Cider Vinegar
www.aspall.co.uk

Barbour
www.barbour.com

Box Steam Brewery
www.boxsteambrewery.co.uk

Bristol Beer Factory
www.bristolbeerfactory.co.uk

British Saffron
www.britishsaffron.co.uk

Cabrito Goat Meat
www.cabritogoatmeat.co.uk

Vincent Castellano's Charcuterie
www.castellanos.co.uk

William Catcheside
www.catchesidecutlery.com

Chandos Deli
www.chandosdeli.com

Chase Distillery
www.chasedistillery.co.uk

Cheddar Ales
www.cheddarales.co.uk

The Community Farm
www.thecommunityfarm.co.uk

Corks of Cotham
www.corksof.com

Mark Cox at Barley Wood Kitchen Garden
www.walledgarden.co.uk/garden1.html

Creedy Carver
www.creedycarver.co.uk

Crook and Churn Dairy (John and Kate Howell)
Applins Farm, Blandford Forum, Dorset DT11 8RA

Jonathan Crump's Cheese
Orchard House, Standish Park Farm, Oxlynch, Stonehouse, Gloucestershire GL10 3DG

Otter Farm (Mark Diacono)
www.otterfarm.co.uk

Discovery Tortillas
www.discoveryfoods.co.uk

Dorset Blue Vinny
www.dorsetblue.moonfruit.com

The Watercress Company
www.thewatercresscompany.co.uk

Essential Trading
www.essential-trading.co.uk/home.aspx

The Ethical Shellfish Company
www.ethicalshellfishcompany.co.uk

The Exmouth Mussel Company
www.exmouthmussels.com

Extract Coffee Roasters
www.extractcoffee.co.uk

Fentimans
www.fentimans.com

Finisterre (Ethical Cold Water Surf Company)
www.finisterreuk.com
Finisterre is a cold-water surf company that thinks differently, raises questions about the supply chain and the way products are manufactured,

and believes that great products can be born of responsible practices. Their suits keep Iain toasty-warm on the occasional chance he goes for a surf.

Forager
www.forager.org.uk

Forest Produce
www.forestproduce.com

Fussels
www.fusselsfinefoods.co.uk

The Ginger Beer Plant
www.gingerbeerplant.net

G&G Goodfellow's
www.goodfshop.net
Goodfellow & Goodfellow Ltd are suppliers of exclusive tableware, chefs' clothing, kitchen equipment and specialist tools for molecular gastronomy. They can design and produce unique tableware products.. We thank them for their support in providing some of the plates for our photography.

Gransfors Bruks
www.gransfors.com

Harkila of Scandanavia
www.harkilauk.co.uk
Swedish clothing company, for gear that has kept Jack and Matthew warm and dry on countless hunting trips.

Hill Farm Dairy (for Stawley goats' cheese)
www.hillfarmdairy.co.uk

Hobbs House Bakery
www.hobbshousebakery.co.uk

Homewood Cheeses
www.homewoodcheeses.co.uk

Hurstwood Farm
www.cobnutoil.co.uk

Keen's Cheddar Ltd
www.keenscheddar.co.uk

Kernowsashimi
www.kernowsashimi.co.uk

Mrs Kirkham's
www.mrskirkhams.com

Laverstoke Park Farm
www.laverstokepark.co.uk

Le Creuset
www.lecreuset.co.uk

Longley Farm
www.longleyfarm.com

Jekka's Herb Farm
www.jekkasherbfarm.com

Madgett's Farm
www.madgettsfarm.co.uk

Mark's Bread
www.marksbread.co.uk

Mendip Moments
www.mendipmoments.co.uk

Montezuma's
www.montezumas.co.uk

Moor Beer
www.moorbeer.co.uk

Native Breeds Curers and Charcutiers
www.nativebreeds.co.uk

The Cornish Shellfish Company Ltd
www.cornishshellfish.co.uk
Cornish-assured oysters; they specialise in the supply of oysters specially purified to remove the threat of norovirus food poisoning.

Neal's Yard Creamery
www.nealsyardcreamery.co.uk

Norfolk Saffron
www.norfolksaffron.co.uk

Manor Farm (for Ogleshield cheese)
www.montgomerycheese.co.uk

Old Town
www.old-town.co.uk

Oliver Harvey British Chef's Whites
www.oliverharvey.co.uk

Original Beans
www.originalbeans.com

Ostlers Cloudy Cider Vinegar
www.ostlerscidermill.co.uk

Perry's Cider
www.perryscider.co.uk

Powells of Olveston
www.powellsofolveston.com

Prestige Event Equipment Hire
www.prestigehire.biz

Rational Self-Cooking Centre
www.rationalcombiovens.com

Sharpham Park
www.sharphampark.com

Sipsmith Gin
www.sipsmith.com

Somerset Cheese Company
www.somersetcheese.co.uk

Somerset Cider Brandy
www.ciderbrandy.co.uk

Somerset Farmers' Markets
www.somersetfarmersmarkets.co.uk

Stichelton
www.stichelton.co.uk

The Story
www.thestorygroup.co.uk

Thali Cafe
www.thethalicafe.co.uk

Toast
www.toast.co.uk
Thanks Toast and special thanks to Lara Smrtnik

Trethowan's Dairy
www.trethowansdairy.co.uk

Truffle Hunter
www.trufflehunter.co.uk

Ultracomida
www.ultracomida.co.uk

Village Maid
www.villagemaidcheese.co.uk

West Country Water Buffalo
www.westcountrywaterbuffalo.com

West Croft Cider
www.burnham-on-sea.co.uk/west_croft_cider

Westcombe Dairy
www.westcombedairy.com

The Wild Beer Co
www.wildbeerco.com

Wild Stoves
www.wildstoves.co.uk

Wings of St Mawes
www.wingofstmawes.co.uk

Wootton Organic Dairy
www.wootton-dairy.com

Paul A. Young
www.paulayoung.co.uk

Acknowledgements

FRIENDS AND FAMILY

The Ethicurean would like to thank first and foremost Elena, Wendy and Phil for believing in us even when this was just a distant dream, and for their help with running The Ethicurean (very often requested at short notice). Additionally, we would like to thank Phil and Elena for their outstanding management of the apple juice production. We would also like to thank Mark and Linda Cox, Lilly, Tessa Tricks for her enthusiasm, hard work and great research skills, Charlie Tricks, Andrew Elder for being lovely, committed and hard-working, Sam Lacey and Big Mike Cannings, Ian and Monique Hillman and Joseph, Sarah Lavelle, Jason Ingram, Jaine Bevan, Jane Middleton, David Eldridge, Tim Bates, Ivor the Bee Keeper, Adrian Boots, Cleave Nursery-Alan Down, Emma Dibben, Katie Chard and Paul Farrel for lending us their prints, Bill at Clayability, Helen Downing, Fiona Beckett, Paul Winch-Furness, Brett Ellis and last but not least Ocho the dog (best dog).

Paûla would like to thank:

Elena – this book would not have seen the light of day without you. Your support with admin, Ocho's walks, apple pressing, proofreading and generation of ideas has been invaluable to this project. Thanks for always believing in me and supporting everything I do. I would not be where I am if it wasn't for you. Pablo – some of my happiest moments and the best childhood food memories are shared with you. You have kept me sane throughout the writing of this book, you are my best friend and favourite brother. Poppy – your smiling presence and relentless optimism make me feel lucky to be in your life. Mario – for taking me to all those restaurants, for teaching me about regionality of food in Mexico, for showing me the value of good food and ensuring at all times that we ate the best meals that we possibly could, for showing me that food is worth feeling passionate about. Mike – I have no doubt that you would have done anything in your power to support this project and I know you would have been proud. Abue Tomasita – there is no better cook than you. The meals you prepared for us as children are cherished memories that I hold very close to my heart. Thank you for taking me to the mercado as a child despite my winging. Many valuable lessons about food were learnt in those trips. Abue Natalia – for cooking those delicious feasts on Sundays. I will be eternally grateful to you for filling my life with all those special memories of family meals. Todos los Zarates – Su apoyo siempre me ha inspirado a convertir en realidad todos mis suenos. The Penningtons, especially Matthew and Iain, whose natural ability to produce outstanding food continues to drive us to places we only dreamt of before. Thanks for your dedication, hard work, sense of humour (which has kept our spirits up during difficult times) and admirable creativity. The Bevans – for their unequivocal support and especially to Jack for his relentless energy and passion for our business. I think of you all as part of my family. Neil, Si, Lo and Amy – for being the best friends that anyone could ever wish for. Thank you for making me feel happy and safe when I am around you. I have enjoyed some of the best meals in my life with you. Corinne, Henry, Rosie, Tom, Liam, Emily, Amy H., Katie and Jackie – we could not have done it without you.

Jack would like to thank:

Thank you Wendy and Phil Bevan for being the greatest pillars any man could ask for. Kevin and Abigail, for all the limitless adventures and conversations that ultimately revolved around beer and food. Elena Zarate for being the fifth member of The Ethicurean. Jane 'Baggage' Billyard for being the beautiful inspiration to join the trade. Chloe Blackman for being talented, supportive and downright awesome. Huw Ruddal for being a gentleman and a scoundrel. All the Arley Villains that became Gwynn Street, thank you of all your help, music, food and toasted seeds. Mark, Jemma and the Calver family for those first formative food and booze experiences. Alex Cue, Daniel Snow and their families for being wonderful. Jamie Pike for your friendship. Richard Tring and Justyn Bell for all those incredible boozy, nerdy cocktail conversations. To all my friends that live in our wonderful home, what an absolute dream. Tim Hayward and *Fire and*

Knives for always replying to my emails, however obscure. Thank you Jackie Rabaioitti, you taught this man how to tell a story. Finally, cheers Matthew Pennington for poaching me, wet behind the ears, from a life of 9-5 crime and Paûla and Iain for being such marvellous friends and colleagues.

Iain would like to thank:

Michelle, your tireless support this last year has meant more to me than I could ever say, and I thank you immensely. The writing of this book would not have been possible without you. Peter, I would not be where I am, had we not met. What you do is phenomenal and I am eternally grateful to have the two of you in my life. To my sisters, Tara and Ellie. Both of you have been nothing but supportive and loving since the day I was born. The word 'privileged' doesn't even come close when talking about you. To all of the bossaii's; Andy, Arran, Burger, Frith, Guy, Imogen, Lauren, Lois, Matty, Nikki, Peeeete, Rob, Swain and Zola. Some of the fondest memories I have in my life are of being with all of you. I am as happy as I can be when we're together and I love you all. Thanks for your support and I delight in the moment we're next together. To Clare: your friendship has been one of the most meaningful things I have experienced. Sorry that communication can be distant, but know that you are always in my heart, however many miles separate us. Thanks for over a decade of support and smiles. To Rachel, and all of the Perrys, your welcoming of me into your family was one of the most significant events in my life. Your humble way of life, how close you all are and how delicious your food was is something I will always strive to achieve throughout my life. 'Thank you' could never come close to what I want to say, but thank you nonetheless. It was a truly happy time for me. Matthew, for inviting me to start this business with you, I am eternally grateful. You, like my other siblings, are a legend and I love you; and to Paûla and Jack, I love you both. There are no three people I would rather work this hard with. It's been more than a mammoth undertaking, but it's the best thing we've done to date. Here's to a successful and happy business. Dad, your support and ability to make your children smile is praiseworthy. I am grateful to have had you as a role model and I hope to see more of you in the future. To Mum, thank you for bringing the best family into existence. I love both of you. To Toby, Dan and all the Pump House crew, to Josh, Holly and all at the Pony & Trap; thanks for welcoming us newcomers on to the Bristol scene. We look forward to working with you in the future. To the great chefs before me that were willing to share their knowledge: you never cease to inspire me, teach me and help me grow. And finally to the Ocean. The most beautiful thing on this Earth and the place where I feel most at home.

Matthew would like to thank:

I am eternally grateful to the following friends who are the most amazing people in the world. The Zarate Family, Elena, Mike, Paûla, Pablo & Poppy. I owe everything to your support and embracing me as family, home from home. The Pennington Family: John, Janey, Angela, David, Tara, Jonty, Ellie, Dan, Macy, Lisa, Iain and Michelle. The Bevans are one stunning family: Wendy, Phil and Jack and Kevin. Simon Wilkinson, Neil Wilkinson, Lois Woodward, Amy Martin, Liam Knapp, Emily Wallis, Amy Howerska and Emily Wright. The Armistead Family. Iain Keith Smith, Jackie Chard, Andrew Griffin and Terry Roberts for helping me embark on my journey into seriously great food. Julia and Paul Pilcher, the friendliest foragers and their superb mushroom hauls. My Kitchen Family. Iain, Rich Bowman, Justyna Szumlewska, Thomas Parslow, Sophie, Lucy and Andy Elder. Chefs Josh Eggleton and Toby Gritten for welcoming us so readily into the Bristol restaurant scene. Thanks to chefs who have inspired me, Elena Arzak, Niki Segnit, Heston Blumenthal, Simon Rogan, Fergus Henderson, Magnus Nilsson and Jonny Mills. Benjamin Hoff for 'The Tao of Pooh & Te of Piglet'. Paûla, Iain and Jack: a monumental achievement of work and dedication that has tested us all. You are my greatest friends. I love you.